The EUROPEAN DRIVER'S HANDBOOK

Published by AA Publishing, a trading name of AA Media Ltd, whose registered office is Fanum House, Basing View, Basingstoke, Hampshire RG21 4EA. Registered number 06112600.

First edition 2008
Second edition 2010
Third edition 2012
Fourth edition 2013

Designed by Tracey Butler Design

Motoring regulations supplied by AA International Motoring Services

Turkish Republic of Northern Cyprus regulations verified by the Office of the London Representative of the Turkish Republic of Northern Cyprus

ISBN: 978-07495-7519-9

Maps made with Natural Earth and data from openstreetmap.org © OpenStreetMap contributors

Visit **theAA.com/motoring_advice/overseas** for the latest information on driving in Europe.

A CIP catalogue record for this book is available from the British Library.

Printed in Dubai by Oriental Press

Visit AA Publishing at **theAA.com/shop**

A05143

The Automobile Association would like to thank the following photographers, companies and libraries for their assistance in the preparation of this book.

Abbreviations for the picture credits are as follows: (t) top; (b) bottom; (l) left; (r) right; (c) centre; (AA) AA World Travel Library.

1 AA/P Kenward; 6 AA; 8/9 AA/A Baker; 11 AA; 12 South West News Service; 13 AA; 14l AA; 14tr AA; 14cr AA; 15 AA; 16 AA/J Smith; 18 AA PR; 19 Digitalvision; 20 AA; 21 AA/M Birkitt; 25 AA/P Baker; 32 E.J. Baumeister Jr./ Alamy; 39 Graham Lawrence; 42 AA/T Souter; 45 AA/J Smith; 48 AA/A Kouprianoff; 56 AA/J W Jorgensen; 59 Pictures Colour Library; 62 AA; 76 AA/P Wilson; 79 AA/D Tarn; 80 AA/T Souter; 85 AA/C Sawyer; 93 AA/L Blake; 97 AA/K Paterson; 103 Pictures Colour Library; 106 Pictures Colour Library; 109 Pictures Colour Library; 112 isifa Image Service s.r.o./Alamy; 117 DIOMEDIA/Alamy; 120 AA/A Kouprianoff; 123 AA/K Naylor; 127 AA/J Smith; 130 AA/A Mockford & N Bonetti; 131 AA/A Kouprianoff; 134 Pictures Colour Library; 137 AA/K Paterson; 143 AA/J Smith; 146 Pictures Colour Library; 149 AA/P Enticknap; 155 Pictures Colour Library; 161 AA/P Kenward; 164 AA/J Smith; 166/167 AA/J Tims; 166/167 AA/A Kouprianoff; 185 AA/P Kenward; 186 AA/P Baker; 188 Digitalvision; 192 AA/C Sawyer; 193 AA/R Strange

Every effort has been made to trace the copyright holders, and we apologise in advance for any accidental errors. We would be happy to apply any corrections in the following edition of this publication.

Contents

REYKJAVÍK
ICELAND
Norwegian Sea
0 200 400 600 800 km
0 100 200 300 400 500 miles
ATLANTIC OCEAN
NORWAY
OSLO
Inverness
Aberdeen
NORTHERN IRELAND
Glasgow
Londonderry
Edinburgh
Belfast
Galway
REPUBLIC OF IRELAND
Killarney
DUBLIN
Newcastle upon Tyne
North Sea
York
Liverpool
Manchester
Cork
BRITAIN
Birmingham
Bristol
Oxford
LONDON
Plymouth
Southampton
English Channel
Aalborg
Gothenburg
DENMARK
Esbjerg
Malmö
Odense
Hamburg
NETHERLANDS
AMSTERDAM
The Hague
BERLIN
Bruges
Calais
Ghent
BRUSSELS
BELGIUM
GERMANY
Cologne
Le Havre
Brest
LUXEMBOURG
Frankfurt-am-Main
PRAGUE
PARIS
Nantes
Strasbourg
Stuttgart
Bay of Biscay
FRANCE
Munich
Salzburg
BERN
Zürich
Innsbruck
AUSTRIA
Geneva
SWITZERLAND
La Coruña-A Coruna
Bordeaux
Clermont-Ferrand
Lyon
Santiago de Compostela
Santander
Milan
SLOVENIA
Trieste
Biarritz
Toulouse
Venice
Porto
Genoa
ANDORRA
Bologna
PORTUGAL
Marseille
Nice
Zaragoza
Florence
LISBON
MADRID
ITALY
Corsica
Barcelona
Pescara
SPAIN
Ajaccio
ROME
Olbia
Foggia
Valencia
Sardinia
Naples
Seville
Balearic Islands
Cádiz
Málaga
Murcia
Tyrrhenian Sea
Cagliari
Gibraltar
Mediterranean Sea
Messina
Palermo
Sicily
MOROCCO
ALGERIA
TUNISIA
MALTA

Coverage map

Introduction

This essential handbook, now covering 42 European countries, has been compiled to ensure you are well prepared for motoring in Europe, whether you are an experienced motorist or adventuring abroad with your car for the first time.

We have included information on requirements by country (see pages 16–165) – from Andorra to Ukraine – with local rules for drivers, including seat-belt and drink-driving laws, speed limits and headlight requirements. There are also details of the documents you should take, equipment to carry in your car and what toll charges you will encounter. Useful quick-reference charts detail compulsory requirements, winter motoring information and distances. Principal mountain passes are also included. Easy-to-read maps, showing both toll and toll-free motorways, will help with route planning and budgeting. The words and phrases section is tailored to assist if you encounter difficulties on the road, from asking directions to reading traffic signs (see pages 166–185).

With all this information at your fingertips, *The European Driver's Handbook* is your passport to a safe and enjoyable trip. We have tried to ensure accuracy, but things do change, so please let us know if you have any comments or corrections. You can also visit theAA.com/motoring_advice/overseas for the latest information on driving in Europe.

Before you go

Documents and insurance

Documents you should take with you

- A valid full driving licence (not provisional), with paper counterpart if you have a photocard licence.
- An International Driving Permit where necessary.
- The original vehicle registration document.
- Your motor insurance certificate.
- Your passport.
- You may need a visa for certain countries, too. It is your responsibility to ensure that you have all documentation needed to comply with the requirements of immigration, customs, health and other regulations.
- If you're travelling in a vehicle other than a motor car or motorcycle or taking a boat, make sure you have any additional documentation that may be required.
- If the vehicle you're driving is company owned, hired or borrowed, try to obtain the original V5 registration document together with a letter of authorisation from the owner. If you can't get the V5 then obtain a Vehicle on Hire Certificate, also known as the VE103b, available from BVRLA/All fleet services on **01452 881037**. This is the only legal alternative to the vehicle registration document. The Vehicle on Hire Certificate must be carried in addition to a letter of authorisation from the registered keeper.

Breakdown cover

Make sure that you have adequate cover. AA European Breakdown Cover provides cover for many European countries, **tel: 0800 072 3279** or visit **theAA.com** and follow the link **European Breakdown Cover** for information.

Car insurance

Contact your insurer for advice at least a month before taking a vehicle overseas. Ensure that you're adequately covered and have the necessary documents to prove it. A Green Card (proof of insurance cover while using your vehicle abroad) is compulsory in Bosnia and Herzegovina.

Credit cards

Occasionally we hear that UK-issued credit cards are not accepted at stores or petrol stations in other countries. Check with your card company to confirm that it can be used in the countries you are visiting.

Driving licence

You must always carry your full UK driving licence, and other qualified drivers in your party should take their licences in case of an emergency.

European Health Insurance Card

National Health treatment is not available outside the UK but you may be able to get free or reduced-cost treatment within the EU with the European Health Insurance Card (EHIC). The EHIC entitles UK residents who are travelling in Europe to reduced-cost, sometimes free, state-provided emergency healthcare when visiting a European Union (EU) country, Iceland, Liechtenstein, Norway or Switzerland. The card is available free of charge and is valid for up to five years. Each person needs their own card. You can apply online at **www.nhs.uk/NHSEngland/Healthcareabroad**, or by phoning the EHIC

Application Line on **0845 606 2030**. Postal application packs are available from post offices. The EHIC may not cover you for all medical costs incurred (the cost of bringing a person back to the UK in the event of illness or death is never covered) so you are strongly advised to arrange travel insurance also to ensure that you are covered for all possible eventualities.

Passports

Each person (including children and babies) must hold an up-to-date passport. Some countries require a passport to remain valid for a minimum period (usually at least six months) beyond the date of entry – check before you travel. Information and application forms are available from main post offices and from Passport Offices or you can apply for an application form online at **www.gov.uk/browse/driving/passports-travelling-abroad.** Allow at least three weeks (six weeks for a first adult passport) for your application to be processed. Holders of passports from outside the UK should check regarding any visa requirements with the appropriate embassy or consulate. Note down your passport number and the date of issue and keep this information in a safe place, separate from your passport. Carry your passport at all times as proof of identity and take one other form of photo ID with you.

Personal insurance

It is essential that you are fully covered by travel insurance. Make sure you have at least the minimum cover for medical expenses, theft and losses abroad.

Pets

If you intend to take your pet abroad contact the Pet Travel Scheme (PETS) helpline **tel: 0870 241 1710** or visit the PETS website **www.gov.uk/take-pet-abroad**

Travel advice

For up-to-date travel advice from the Foreign and Commonwealth Office **tel: 0845 850 2829** or visit **www.gov.uk/foreign-travel-advice**

Your documents

You may be asked to produce your documents at any time. To avoid a police fine and/or confiscation of your vehicle, be sure that they are in order and readily available for inspection.

Preparing your car

Child restraints

Never fit a rear-facing car seat in any seat with an active air bag. Use only an approved restraint suitable for the child's weight and height. Visit **theAA.com/motoring_advice/child_safety/carseats.html** for further information.

Fire extinguisher/first-aid kit

In some countries it is compulsory to equip your vehicle with these items (see individual country sections).

Headlights

If you're driving to the Continent you must adjust the headlamp beam pattern to suit driving on the right so that the dipped beam doesn't dazzle oncoming drivers. Headlamp beam converter kits are widely available, but a dealer may need to make the adjustment, especially if your car has high-intensity discharge (HID), halogen-type or xenon headlamps – check the car's handbook. Remember to remove the converters as soon as you return to the UK.

Keys

Many modern cars have a 'transponder' key to prevent theft. If you lose the key, recovery to an authorised dealer is usually the only answer. Even a dealer may take several days to obtain a replacement, which will be expensive, so always carry a spare set of keys.

Loading your car

Visit **theAA.com/motoring_advice/loading-your-car-safely.html** for rules on how to pack your car. Overloading your car can incur fines and possibly invalidate your insurance.

Nationality plate/GB sticker

Vehicles must display a nationality plate/GB sticker of the approved pattern, design and size. UK registration plates displaying the GB Euro symbol (Euro plates) make display of a conventional sticker unnecessary when driving within the EU. In some countries outside the EU a conventional sticker is required even if you have Euro plates, so it is always safer to display one on your vehicle.

Rear-view mirrors

It is essential to have clear all-round vision. If your vehicle is not equipped with a door or wing-mirror on the left-hand side we recommend that you get one fitted to aid driving on the right.

Reflective jacket/waistcoat

It is now compulsory in many European countries for visiting motorists to carry/wear reflective jackets (see individual country sections). We recommend that you carry at least two jackets/waistcoats in the passenger compartment – one for the driver and one for a passenger, who may assist in changing a wheel. If you intend to hire a car, be aware that not all rental firms provide jackets with their cars. Check with the car hire company before you travel.

Seat belts

If seat belts are fitted to your vehicle it is compulsory to wear them.

Servicing

Service your car well in advance of your journey to reduce the chance of expensive breakdowns when abroad.

Speed-trap detection devices

The use or possession of devices to detect police radar is illegal in most European countries. Penalties can include a fine, driving ban and even imprisonment. Some countries now also prohibit the use of GPS-based navigation systems that have maps indicating the location of fixed speed cameras, meaning that you must deactivate or remove the 'fixed speed camera PoI (Points of Interest)' function. See individual country sections.

Toolkit

Check the handbook for the location of the basic toolkit for the car, which should contain at least a jack and wheel-removal tools. If locking wheel nuts are fitted make sure that the toolkit includes the key or removal tool.

Tyres

Like in the UK, most countries require a minimum tread depth of 1.6mm over the central three-quarters of the tread and around the whole circumference. We recommend a minimum of 2mm but consider changing tyres if the tread is down to 3mm before you go. Tyres wear out quickly after they get down to 3mm. See pages 24–25 for information on winter tyre and snow chain requirements.

Warning triangle

The use of a warning triangle is compulsory in many European countries in the event of an accident or breakdown (not always required for two-wheeled vehicles). In certain circumstances, in some countries two triangles are required.

Wheel chains

Wheel chains are important for any winter motoring and compulsory in some countries even when using winter tyres (see the individual country sections). Snow chains are available from the AA's Dover and Folkestone shops (Dover **tel: 01304 208122**; Folkestone **tel: 0800 072 4372**).The Folkestone shop is beyond the customs point. Telephone ahead to check availability. You will be asked for the vehicle make and model and the tyre size, read from the sidewall of the tyre

A selection of travel and emergency kits are available from accessory stores, theAA.com/shop and the AA Travelshops at Folkestone (Eurotunnel) and Dover.

Driving in

Countries

General motoring information

Accidents

If you are involved in an accident, you must stop, switch on your hazard warning lights and place a warning triangle on the road at a suitable distance. If the accident necessitates calling the police, leave the vehicle in position and phone them, also obtaining medical assistance if needed. Notify your insurance company within 24 hours, making sure all the essential particulars are noted. If you can, take photographs of the scene of the accident. (See the individual country sections for emergency telephone numbers.) In Serbia and, in certain circumstances, in Switzerland, you are required to carry and complete a European Accident Statement form (available from some insurers).

Blue Badge users

The Blue Badge is recognised in all European countries. When displayed on the dashboard

of a car, it allows you to make use of the same parking concessions provided for the country's own citizens with a disability.

The concessions do differ from country to country so it's important to know where, when and for how long you can park in each country. Visit **theAA.com/motoring_advice/overseas/ blue-badge-users.html** and click on the FIA world guide to disabled parking.

Remember, if you are in any doubt about your rights, don't park.

Breakdown

Stop your car in a safe place where possible, out of the way of traffic. If you have a reflective jacket, put it on. Switch on your hazard warning lights and side lights and place a warning triangle to the rear of the vehicle at a suitable distance (this varies widely from country to country). Find the nearest telephone to call for assistance. On motorways, emergency telephones are generally located every 2km (1.24 miles) and automatically connect you to the authorities.

Car crime

Never leave handbags and other attractive items in obvious view even when you are in the car, and never leave anything in an unattended car. For advice on car crime or personal safety in specific countries, contact the Foreign Office Travel Advice Unit on **0845 850 2829** or visit **www.fco.gov.uk**

Crash or safety helmets

The wearing of crash or safety helmets by motorcyclists and their passengers is compulsory in all countries.

Delays and diversions

Roadworks and major events can mean that roads are sometimes closed completely. If this is the case, follow locally signed detours. There may be delays at peak travel periods, delays on some main routes and at frontier crossing points. Mountain passes and alpine roads may be closed during the winter months (see pages 224–235 for more information on Mountain passes).

Drinking and driving

There is only one safe rule – if you drink, don't drive. Laws are strict and the penalties are severe.

Emergency contact

Telephone **112**, the European emergency number you can use in the all the member states of the European Union, in case of accident, assault or in any other distress situation. See individual country entries for contact numbers in non-EU countries.

Fines

Some countries impose on-the-spot fines for minor traffic offences. Fines are generally paid in the currency of the country concerned. You must obtain a receipt as proof of payment.

Leaded petrol

Leaded petrol is no longer generally available in northern European countries and Lead Replacement Petrol (LRP) is getting more difficult to find. If LRP is not on sale, an anti-wear additive (for treating unleaded petrol) can be bought from the filling station shop.

Low Emission Zones

More than 70 cities and towns in eight countries around Europe already have in place, or are preparing to launch, Low Emission Zones (LEZs) – areas where the most polluting vehicles are regulated in some way. Currently most of these zones affect only vans and lorries but some, including those in Germany and Italy, affect passenger cars too. To find out where these LEZs are, what kinds of vehicles are affected, what emission standards are required and whether registration is required or not visit **www.lowemissionzones.eu** (in English). Low Emission Zones are also known as Environment Zones, *Umweltzonen* (Germany), *Milieuzones* (Netherlands), *Lavutslippssone* (Norway), *Miljozone* (Denmark), *Miljözon* (Sweden).

Mobile phones

Before you take your phone abroad ask your network provider whether your phone is enabled for international roaming, what it charges for international roaming services in the countries you will be visiting and whether your handset will work in these countries. It may be worth buying a new SIM card when you arrive at your destination (the SIM card will work only on that country's network) and you can top it up as you

would a 'pay as you go' phone in the UK. The use of hand-held mobile phones while driving is prohibited in many countries.

Rule of the road

In all countries covered in this guide, apart from Cyprus (north and south), Malta, Great Britain and Ireland, the rule of the road is to drive on the right and overtake on the left. For UK drivers it's easy to forget to drive on the right, particularly after doing something familiar, such as leaving a petrol station or car park.

Signposting

Signposting between major towns and along main roads is generally efficient, but on some secondary roads and in open country, advance direction signs may be less frequent. Signs are often of the pointer type and placed on walls or railings on the far side of the turn; they tend to point across the road they indicate, which can be confusing at first. Difficulties may arise with spellings when crossing frontiers, and place names may not be so easily recognised when written in a different language. Extra difficulties may arise in countries with two or more official languages or dialects, although some towns may have both spellings, e.g. San Sebastian – Donostia in Spain, Antwerpen – Anvers in Belgium, Basel – Bâle in Switzerland.

Size restrictions

Check with your national camping or caravanning club that your vehicle and/or trailer complies with the weight and size legislation in the countries that you intend to visit.

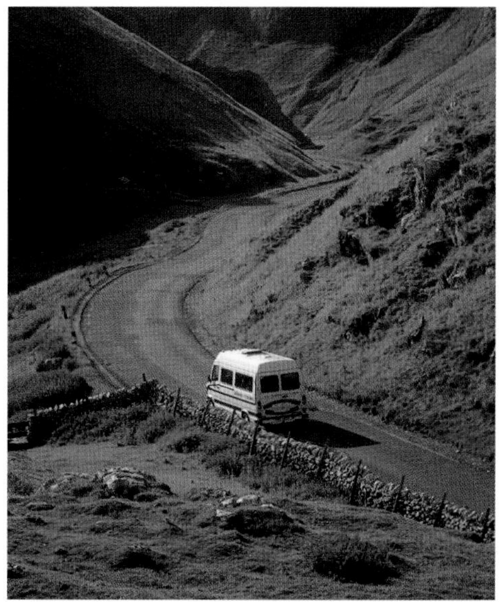

Spectacles

Take a spare pair of spectacles if you wear them – especially if you are the sole driver.

Speed limits

Speed limits for individual countries are listed in the appropriate country sections. Lower limits will apply to motorcycles in some countries and also generally when towing a trailer unless otherwise indicated. Visiting drivers who have held a full licence for under two years may also have to adhere to lower speed limits.

How far in miles? Conversion table: kilometres to miles

kms	1	2	3	4	5	10	15	20	25	30	35	40	45	50
miles	0.62	1.24	1.86	2.49	3.11	6.21	9.32	12.43	15.53	18.64	21.75	24.85	27.96	31.07

Driving requirements chart

DRIVING REQUIREMENTS	Austria	Belgium	Croatia	Denmark	France	Germany
Minimum age/UK licence holders **(1)**	18	18	18	17	18	18
International Driving Permit required for UK licence holders (IDP)	No (2)	No	No	No	No	No
Original registration document	C	C	C	C	C	C
Motor vehicle insurance **(4)**	C	C	C	C	C	C
Motorway tax	C & Tolls	No	Tolls	Tolls	Tolls	No
GB sticker (5)	C	C	C	C	C	C
Warning triangle	C (6)	C (6)	C (6&8)	C	C (6)	R (7)
Reflective jacket/waistcoat	C (6/19)	C (11)	C	R	C (6/10)	No
First-aid kit	C	R (16)	C (6)	R	No	R (16)
Fire extinguisher (6)	No	R (16)	No	R	No	No
Headlamp adjustment (12)	C	C	C	C	C	C
On-the-spot fines	Yes	Yes	Yes (12)	Yes	Yes	Yes
Radar dectectors **(18)**	F	F	F	F	F	F
Daytime headlights/passing lights: cars	No (15)	No (15)	C (15)	C	R (15)	R (15)
Daytime headlights/passing lights: m/cycles	C	C	C	C	C	C
Breathalyser	No	No	No	No	C(20)	No

C = Compulsory **R** = Recommended by AA/respective country **F** = Forbidden.
The above chart covers some of the most popular countries featured in this book. It must be read in conjunction with the 'Driving in' information for the relevant country. The numbers in brackets refer to the notes below. Check **theAA.com/motoring_advice/overseas/compulsory_equipment.html** for the latest information. Items or associated equipment highlighted in **bold** in the chart above can be purchased online from the AA at **theAA.com/shop**.

NOTES

(1) Minimum age at which a visitor may drive a car.
(2) UK driving licences that do not incorporate a photograph are recognised, but drivers must be able to produce photographic proof of identity (e.g. passport).
(3) All valid UK licences should be accepted. However, this cannot be guaranteed on older all-green-style UK licences. Drivers may wish to update them voluntarily before travelling abroad, if time permits. Alternatively, older licences may be accompanied by an IDP.
(4) Before taking a vehicle abroad, contact your motor insurer or broker to notify them of your intentions, and ask their advice. It is important to know what level of cover you will have and what documents you need to prove it.
(5) GB stickers are compulsory within the EU unless your UK registration plates display the GB Euro symbol (Euro plates), which became a legal option from 21 March 2001. The Euro plate must comply with the new British Standard (BS AU 145d). The Euro plate is legally recognised only in the EU; it is still a requirement to display a GB sticker when travelling outside the EU.
(6) Not required for two-wheeled vehicles.
(7) Although it is not compulsory for visiting motorists to carry a warning triangle, its use is compulsory in an accident/breakdown situation.
(8) Spain: One warning triangle is compulsory for non-Spanish-registered vehicles; two for Spanish-registered vehicles. **Note:** Drivers of non-Spanish-registered vehicles should consider carrying two triangles as, regardless of regulations, local officials may impose an on-the-spot fine if only one is available. **Croatia:** Two triangles are compulsory for vehicles towing a trailer. **Switzerland:** Warning triangle must be kept within easy reach (not in the boot).

Ireland	Italy	Netherlands	Norway	Portugal	Spain	Sweden	Switzerland
17	18	18	18	17 (13)	18	18	18
No	No (3)	No	No	No (3)	No (3)	No (2)	No
C	C	C	C	C	C	C	C
C	C	C	C	C	C	C	C
Tolls	Tolls	No	Tolls	Tolls (18)	Tolls	Tolls	C & Tolls
C	C	C	C	C	C	C	C
C	C (6)	R (9&6)	C (6)	R (9)	C (8&6)	R	C (6&8)
No	C (10&6)	No	R (10)	R (10)	C (10)	R	No
No	No	No	R	No	No	R	No
No	No	No	R	No	No	R	No
No	C	C	C	C	C	C	C
Yes (12)	Yes (12)	Yes	Yes	Yes (12)	Yes	Yes (12)	Yes
F	F	F	F	F	F	F	F
No (15)	C (14)	R	C	No (15)	No	C	R
C	C	R	C	C	C	C	R
No	No	No	No	No	No	No	No

(9) The use of hazard warning lights or a warning triangle is compulsory in an accident/breakdown situation. However, a warning triangle should always be carried as hazard warning lights have no effect at bends or rises in the road, or may become damaged or inoperative.
(10) It is compulsory for driver and/or passenger(s) to wear a reflective jacket/waistcoat when exiting a vehicle immobilised on the carriageway, in **Italy** at night or in poor visibility, in **Spain** on all motorways and busy roads. In **Croatia** wearing a jacket is compulsory whenever you have to get out of the vehicle at the roadside in an emergency. In **Portugal** and **Norway** the actual law applies to residents; however, regardless of the regulations local officials may impose an on-the-spot fine. In **Belgium** the wearing of a reflective jacket applies only to the driver; it must be worn should you be stranded on a Belgian motorway or on a major road or should you stop at a place where parking is not allowed. In **France** drivers must have one warning triangle and one reflective jacket in their vehicle (the requirement does not apply to two- or three-wheeled vehicles). In **Austria** the regulation applies only to the driver.
(11) The legal requirement is to 'not dazzle oncoming drivers' rather than specifically to adjust/convert the headlamp beam pattern. Without adjustment the dipped beam will dazzle oncoming drivers and this could result in a fine. Headlamp beam converter kits are widely available but may not be suitable for all types of headlights. The AA shop sells beam converters suitable for all vehicles and individual fitting diagrams are included for the latest 'clear glass', 'projector and xenon' headlamps inside the packaging. In some countries it is compulsory to use dipped headlights at all times when driving during the day. Note: This adjustment is not required for two-wheeled vehicles as the beam pattern is more symmetrical, but check that any extra loading has not affected the beam height. On some cars it is inadvisable or impossible for anyone other than a qualified technician to change a headlamp bulb unit e.g. high-intensity discharge (HID) headlamps and carrying spares is not an option. However, it is recommended that spare bulbs are carried for any lights that may be easily and/or safely replaced by the owner/driver. Spare bulbs are compulsory for **Croatia**.
(12) Sweden: Police are not actually authorised to collect fines, which must be paid in accordance with notice instructions. **Italy:** Police will collect a quarter of the maximum fine amount from drivers of foreign registered vehicles. **Ireland:** Police are not actually

authorised to collect fines; they will issue a notice, which must be paid within 28 days. **Croatia:** The fine does not have to be paid on the spot; however it does need to be paid within eight days. **Portugal:** Some traffic police carry ATMs.

(13) Portugal: Visiting drivers of 17 years of age may encounter problems even though they hold a valid driving licence in the UK.

(14) Outside built-up areas, during snow or rain causing poor visibility.

(15) Compulsory during daylight hours if visibility is poor. For **France** the use of dipped headlights are recommended throughout the year. Also for **Croatia** during daylight hours from the last Sunday in October to the last Sunday in March.

(16) Recommended as their carriage is compulsory for vehicles registered in that country.

(17) Many countries stipulate that GPS-based navigation systems that have maps indicating the location of fixed speed cameras must have the 'fixed speed camera PoI (Point of interest)' function deactivated.

(18) In order to use some motorways in Portugal, a temporary electronic toll device (DEM) or the pre-payment of tolls is required.

(19) Recommended for two-wheeled vehicles.

(20) In principle all drivers should possess a breathalyser, however, as of 25 January 2013 a driver cannot be penalised for not carrying one – the possibility of imposing a fine has been postponed indefinitely. The breathalyser has to be a certified by the French authorities, showing an 'NF' number. The official text states that one unused breathalyser should be produced. We recommend that two single-use breathalysers are carried, so if one is used or damaged you will still have a replacement to produce.

Tyre tread/snow chains

Check all tyres for condition, pressure and tread depth. Where winter tyres are fitted, a minimum tread depth of 3mm is required in most countries (the **Czech Republic** now requires 4mm). For other tyres, while the legal minimum is 1.6mm the AA recommends at least 3mm of tread for winter motoring, and certainly no less than 2mm.
If you've left it to the last minute, snow chains can be purchased from **AA Travelshops** (Dover & Eurotunnel Folkestone). Call 01303 273576 to check they have chains in stock that are suitable for your vehicle.

The information in the table below applies to vehicles not exceeding 3500kg and shows only specific winter requirements and should be read in conjuction with the general compulsory equipment chart and the general Driving in information for the country of interest. The abbreviations used in the table are as follows:

P = Permitted
R = Recommended
M = Mandatory
C = Carry chains and use them as dictated by local signs or road conditions. Reduced speed limits may apply.

Winter tyre/snow chain requirement chart

	Andorra	Austria	Finland	France	Germany
Winter tyres	**R**	**M (1)**	**M (3)**	–	**M (4)**
Snow chains **(5)**	**C**	**C**	**P**	**C**	**C**

NOTES

(1) All vehicles driving on snow covered roads must have winter tyres (or all-season tyres marked M&S/mud and snow) during the winter season (from 1 November to 15 April) and if roads have a covering of snow, slush or ice outside these dates. Tyres must have a minimum tread depth of 4mm. Theoretically snow chains on summer tyres can be used as an alternative to winter tyres where the entire road is heavily covered with snow and no damage to the road is caused by the snow chains. In practice though, because road conditions and the weather cannot be predicted, use of winter tyres is effectively compulsory.

(2) Snow tyres are not compulsory but vehicles not equipped to travel through snow and that impede traffic are liable to a fine.

(3) From 1 December to the end of February (in practice from November to April) unless otherwise indicated by road signs. Tyres must be marked M&S on the sidewall. Spiked/studded tyres may be used from 1 November to the first monday after Easter.

(4) Germany has introduced new regulations requiring all passenger cars and motorbikes including vehicles from foreign countries to be fitted with winter tyres or all season tyres on all axles when conditions are wintry. Winter tyres (or 'all season' tyres) should bear the mark M&S or the snowflake symbol on the side wall.

(5) Snow chains must be fitted on at least two drive wheels. In any country Snow chains may only be used where there's sufficient snow covering to avoid any possibility of damage to the road surface. A fine may be imposed if damage is caused.

(6) Winter tyres, marked M+S (with or without spikes/studs), with a tread depth of at least 3mm are compulsory from 1 December until 31 March for Swedish registered vehicles and trailers and also for foreign registered vehicles.

(7) Between 15 October and 15 April or at other times if conditions dictate. Provinces can introduce their own legislation making the use of winter tyres and snow chains compulsory.

General advice

In any country the driver is responsible for equipping and controlling their vehicle correctly. Drivers may be liable to a fine if they impede the normal flow of traffic or cause an accident as a consequence of not adapting their vehicle (tyres/snow chains) to suit the prevailing weather and road conditions. Road conditions in winter in many resorts will be much more severe than anything encountered in the United Kingdom. The AA recommends driving in extreme winter conditions only if the driver is confident and the vehicle suitably equipped.

Great Britain	Italy	Norway	Sweden	Switzerland
–	R (7)	R	M (6)	R (2)
P	C (7)	C	R	C

Driving in Andorra *(South West Europe)*

The regulations below should be read in conjunction with the General motoring information on pages 18–21.

Drinking and driving

The permitted level of alcohol in the bloodstream is 0.05 per cent.

Driving licence

The minimum age at which a UK licence holder may drive temporarily a imported car and/or motorcycle is 18.

Fines

On-the-spot fines can be imposed.

Fuel

Leaded (98 octane), unleaded petrol (95 and 98 octane) and diesel *(gasoil)* is available, but not LPG. It is forbidden to carry petrol in a can. Credit cards are accepted at most filling stations; check with your card issuer for usage in Andorra before travel.

Lights

Dipped headlights should be used in poor daytime visibility.

Motorcycles

The use of dipped headlights during the day is compulsory. The wearing of a crash helmet is compulsory.

Motor insurance

Third-party insurance is compulsory.

Passengers/children in cars

Children under 10 years and measuring less than 1.5m must be placed in a restraint system adapted to their size, of an EU-approved design. If they are travelling in the front of the car, the airbag must be deactivated.

Seat belts

It is compulsory for front-seat occupants to wear seat belts, if fitted.

Speed limits

The standard legal limits, which may be varied by signs, for **private vehicles with or without trailers** are: in built-up areas 50km/h (31mph), outside built-up areas between 60 and 90km/h (37 and 55mph).

Additional information

- It is compulsory to carry spare bulbs, a warning triangle and a reflective yellow waistcoat.
- Winter tyres are recommended.
- Snow chains must be used when road conditions or signs indicate.

Travel facts: Andorra

Embassy of Andorra
63 Westover Road
London SW18 2RF
Tel: 020 8874 4806.
www.andorra.ad
Information for UK residents planning a trip to Andorra. By appointment only.

Banking hours
Banks are generally open Monday to Friday 9pm to 1pm and 3pm to 5pm and Saturday 9am to 12pm. In the summer months all banks close on Saturday.

Credit/debit cards
Banks have money exchange facilities and automatic cash machines. International credit cards such as Visa, MasterCard and American Express are widely accepted.

Currency
The euro (€) is the currency of Andorra. It is not a member of the EU, does not issue its own euros and therefore uses euros from other European countries.

Electricity
The power supply is 220/230 volts AC. Round two-hole sockets take two-round-pin plugs. British visitors will need an adaptor.

Health care
Comprehensive travel insurance is essential for all visitors.

Pharmacies
The pharmacies in Andorra, identified by a green cross, stock cosmetics, perfumes, and recognised international pharmaceutical products. They offer specialist advice from expert staff.

Post offices
There are two conventional postal systems in Andorra: Spanish post (post offices open Monday to Friday 8.30am to 2.30pm, Saturday 9am to 1pm) and French post (post offices open Monday to Friday 8.30am to 2.30pm, Saturday 9am to 12pm). All parishes have post offices for stamps and related postal items.

Safe water
Bottled mineral water is cheap and widely available.

Telephones
All telephone numbers in Andorra comprise six digits. There are no area codes. The country code for Andorra is 376. To call home from Andorra dial the international code (00) followed by the country code. To call the UK from Andorra dial 00 44.

Time
Andorra is on Central European Time, one hour ahead of Greenwich Mean Time (GMT + 1). From late March, when the clocks are put forward one hour, until late October, Summer Time (GMT + 2) operates.

Emergency telephone numbers
Police **110**
Ambulance/Fire Brigade **118**
Mountain Rescue **112**
Medical Emergency Service **116**

Driving in Austria *(Central Europe)*

The regulations below should be read in conjunction with the General motoring information on pages 18–21.

Drinking and driving

The maximum permitted level of alcohol in the blood is 0.049. If between 0.05 per cent and 0.079 per cent there is a fine, 0.08 per cent or more a severe fine and/or a driving ban for Austria. A limit of 0.01 applies to new drivers who have held a licence for under two years.

Driving licence

The minimum age at which a UK licence holder may drive a temporarily imported car is 18, motorcycle (up to 50cc) with a maximum design speed of 45km/h (27mph) 16 and motorcycle (over 50cc) 18. **Note:** UK driving licences that do not incorporate a photograph are valid only when accompanied by photographic proof of identity, e.g. passport.

Fines

On-the-spot fines can be imposed. The officer collecting the fine should issue an official receipt. For higher fines the driver will be asked to pay a deposit and the remainder of the fine within two weeks. Parked vehicles obstructing traffic may be towed away.

Fuel

Unleaded petrol (95 and 98 octane) and diesel are available; there is limited LPG. Leaded petrol is not sold, although you can buy a lead-substitute additive. Carrying petrol in a can is permitted. Credit cards are accepted by the larger filling stations; check with your card issuer for usage in Austria before you travel.

Lights

Passing lights (dipped headlights) must be used when visibility is poor due to bad weather conditions. It is prohibited to drive only with side lights (position lights).

Motorcycles

The wearing of crash helmets is compulsory for the driver and passenger. It is prohibited to drive only with side lights (position lights). The use of dipped headlights during the day is compulsory.

Motor Insurance

Third-party insurance is compulsory, including cover for trailers.

Passengers/children in cars

Children under 14 and less than 1.5m (4ft 11in) in height cannot travel as a front- or rear-seat passenger unless using suitable restraint system for their height/weight. Vehicles without such protection (e.g. two-seater sports cars or vans/lorries) may not carry children under 14 years. Children under 14 but over 1.5m (4ft 11in) in height must use the adult seat belt. Children 14 or over and over 1.35m (4ft 5in) in height are allowed to use a *Dreipunktgurt* (three-point seat belt) without a special child seat, if the belt does not cover the child's throat/neck.

Seat belts

It is compulsory for front- and rear-seat occupants to wear seat belts, if fitted. If you do not comply there is a fine of €35.

Speed limits

The standard legal limits, which may be varied by signs, for **private vehicles without trailers** are: in built-up areas up to 50km/h (31mph), outside built-up areas 100km/h (62mph) and motorways up to 130km/h (80mph). Lower limits apply to a **car towing a trailer (not over 750kg)**: in built-up areas areas 50km/h (31mph), outside built-up areas and motorways 100km/h (62mph). For a **car towing a trailer over 750kg (not exceeding 3500kg)** it is 100km/h (62mph) on motorways and 80km/h (49mph) on other roads. The speed limit for the total weight of a **car towing a trailer over 3500kg** is 70km/h (43mph) on motorways and 60km/h (37mph) on other roads.

Vehicles not capable of sustaining a minimum speed of 60km/h (37mph) are not permitted on motorways. Mopeds must not exceed 45km/h (28mph). The maximum recommended speed limit for vehicles with snow chains is 40km/h (24mph). Vehicles equipped with spiked tyres must not exceed 100km/h (62mph) on motorways and 80km/h (49mph) on other roads.

Additional information

- It is compulsory to carry a warning triangle conforming to EC regulation 27 (for vehicles with more than two wheels) and a first-aid kit which must be in a strong dirt-proof box..
- Every car driver has to carry a reflective jacket/waistcoat (compliant with European regulation EN471) to be used in the case of a breakdown or accident and when setting up a warning triangle on the road. This regulation does not apply to mopeds/motorcycles, although it is recommended.
- All motorists have the legal obligation to adapt their vehicle to winter weather conditions.
- Between 1 November and 15 April vehicles must be fitted with winter tyres (which must be marked M&S (mud and snow) on the sidewalls and have a minimum tread depth of 4mm) or all-season tyres, which must be marked M&S, and if roads have a covering of snow, slush or ice outside these dates. Theoretically, snow chains on summer tyres can be used as an alternative to winter tyres where the road is heavily covered with snow and no damage to the road surface is caused by the snow chains. In practice, because conditions and the weather are unpredictable, use of winter tyres is effectively compulsory. **Note:** It is the driver's legal responsibility to carry the required winter equipment; therefore, it is essential to check that it is included in any hire car.
- All vehicles using Austrian motorways and expressways must display motorway tax sticker *(vignette)*. The stickers, valid for one year, two months or 10 days, may be purchased at some petrol stations close to the border and in Austria at the frontier, at petrol stations, post offices or in ÖAMTC offices. A *Korridor Vignette* is required for vehicles travelling from Hohenehms to Horbranz on the German border if you don't have a standard *vignette*. The minimum fine for driving without a *vignette* is €120.
- Tolls are also payable when passing through certain motorway tunnels, see page 30.
- The use of the horn is generally prohibited in Vienna and in the vicinity of hospitals.
- Drivers are not permitted to overtake a school bus that has stopped to let children on and off (indicated by a yellow flashing light).
- Spiked tyres may be used from 1 October until 31 May; special local regulations may extend this period.
- It is prohibited to use radar detectors.
- Parking vouchers can be obtained from tobacconists, banks and petrol stations.

Travel facts and toll charges: Austria

Austrian National Tourist Office
The tourist office in London is for press and marketing purposes only; however, you can make enquiries by phone direct to Austria.
Tel: 0845 101 1818 (local UK call charges apply)
www.aboutaustria.org

Banking hours
Banks are generally open Monday to Friday 8am to 3pm and up to 5.30pm on Thursday.

Credit/debit cards
Visa, MasterCard, Amex and Diners Club are accepted by the larger hotels, restaurants and some garages, but smaller establishments prefer cash.

Currency
The euro (€) is the currency of Austria. Euro coins are issued in denominations of 1, 2, 5, 10, 20 and 50 cents and €1 and €2. Banknotes are issued in denominations of €5, €10, €20, €50, €100, €200 and €500.

Electricity
Electric current is 220 volts AC and appliances need two-round-pin continental plugs.

Health care
Free or reduced-cost medical treatment is available in Austria to European visitors on production of a valid European Health Insurance Card (EHIC). See page 10. Comprehensive travel insurance is still advised and is essential for all other visitors.

Pharmacies
Pharmacies *(apotheken)* are the only places that sell over-the-counter medicines. Take all prescription medicines with you.

Post offices
Post office *(postamt)* opening times are generally Monday to Friday 8am to12 and 2 to 6pm. In major cities hours extend through lunchtime and into Saturday morning and at least one office will be open 24 hours. Stamps are sold at post offices and tobacco kiosks *(tabak-trafik)*. Post boxes are yellow.

Safe water
Tap water throughout Austria is safe to drink. Bottled mineral water from local springs is available – look out for well-known brands Vöslauer and Römerquelle.

Telephones
Phone booths are generally dark green with yellow roofs. All boxes, even the new glass ones, display the symbol of a post horn. Most boxes will accept phone cards that are sold by post offices and tobacconists only. The country code for Austria is 43. To call home from Austria dial the international code (00) followed by the country code. To call the UK from Austria dial 00 44.

Time
Austria is on Central European Time, one hour ahead of GMT (GMT + 1). Daylight Saving Time comes into effect from the end of March to the end of October (GMT + 2).

Emergency telephone numbers
Police **133** or **112** Fire **122** or **112** Ambulance **144** or **112**

Toll charges in euros
For details of where to buy the motorway tax sticker *(vignette)* see page 29.

General		**Car towing caravan/ trailer**	**Car**
10-day *vignette*		8.30	8.30
2-month *vignette*		24.20	24.20
Annual *vignette*		80.60	80.60
Road			
A10	Tauern Autobahn	10.00	10.00
A13	Innsbruck – Brenner pass	8.00	8.00
A16	Arlberg Expressway	8.50	
Grossglockner Alpine Road		33.00	not permitted
Bridges and tunnels			
Bosruck Tunnel on **A9**		4.50	4.50
Gleinalm Tunnel on **A9**		7.50	7.50
Karawanken Tunnel on **A11**		6.50	6.50

Driving in Belarus *(Eastern Europe)*

The regulations below should be read in conjunction with the General motoring information on pages 18–21.

Drinking and driving

It is strictly forbidden to drink and drive; nil percentage of alcohol is allowed in the driver's blood.

Driving licence

The minimum age at which a visitor may drive a temporarily imported car and/or motorcycle is 18. National driving licences that bear the photo of the holder are recognised for three months, but an International Driving Permit (IDP) is recommended. An IDP is compulsory for licences not incorporating a photograph.

Fines

The police can fine motorists and demand payment on the spot for minor traffic offences.

Fuel

Unleaded petrol (80, 92, 95 and 98 octane) is available; diesel *(solyarka)* and LPG are available. Leaded petrol is not available. Up to 20 litres of fuel can be imported free of duty if held in a metal container (must be declared on entry). Credit cards are accepted at large filling stations; check with your card issuer for usage in Belarus before travel.

Lights

Vehicles must use lights in poor visibility and when towing or being towed.

Motorcycles

The wearing of crash helmets is compulsory. It is compulsory to use dipped headlights at all times.

Motor insurance

Third-party insurance is compulsory, but fully comprehensive insurance is recommended. A Green Card is accepted. Short-term insurance is available at the border.

Passengers/children in cars

A child under 12 cannot travel as a front-seat passenger. Children under the age of 12 must be seated in a suitable child-restraint system.

Seat belts

It is compulsory for front-seat occupants to wear seat belts, if fitted.

Speed limits

The signs indicating speed limits must be strictly adhered to. Standard legal limits, which may be varied by signs, for **private vehicles without trailers** are: in residential zones 20km/h (12mph), in built-up areas 60km/h (37mph), outside built-up areas 90km/h (55mph) and up to 110km/h (68mph) on different sections of the Brest–Moscow motorway. All motorists who have held a driving licence for less than two years must not exceed 70km/h (43mph).

Additional information

- It is compulsory to carry a first-aid kit and a fire extinguisher. A warning triangle is also cumpulsory but not required for two-wheeled vehicles.
- A road tax is payable at the frontier.
- State Traffic Inspectorate officials will stop vehicles to check documents, especially if they are displaying foreign plates. Motorists entering Belarus are advised to ignore 'private facilitators' who offer to help travellers pass through checkpoints and border crossings.
- It is recommended that visitors carry an assortment of spares for their vehicles such as a fan belt, replacement bulbs and spark plugs.
- It is against the law to drive a dirty car.
- Radar detectors are strictly prohibited.
- It is advisable to pre-plan itineraries and book accommodation before departure.
- All foreign visitors are required to purchase health insurance on arrival.
- Poor road signs between small towns.
- Winter tyres are not a compulsory requirement, although they are highly recommended. All-year tyres and snow chains may be used instead of winter tyres.

Travel facts: Belarus

Belarus Embassy
6 Kensington Court
London
W8 5DL
Tel: 020 7937 3288
http://belarus.embassyhomepage.com
www.belintourist.com/eng

Banking hours
In Belarus banks are generally open Monday to Friday 9 or 10am to 1 or 5pm.

Credit/debit cards
Credit cards are not widely accepted but can be used to withdraw cash at major hotels and banks. Some large stores and restaurants will take them. The number of ATMs is steadily increasing in major cities. Amex is not accepted.

Currency
The unit of currency in Belarus is the Belarusian rouble (BYR). Notes are in denominations of BYR100,000, 50,000, 20,000, 10,000, 5,000, 1,000, 500, 100, 50, 20 and 10. Sterling is not widely accepted for exchange into Belarusian roubles. The US dollar or euros are the preferred foreign currencies. Foreign currency should be exchanged only at Government-licensed booths. These can be found in or near major stores, hotels, banks and shopping centres. Non-compliance can result in fines and/or arrest. Make sure you have enough money for the duration of your stay.

Electricity
The power supply is 220 volts AC, 50Hz. Plugs have two round pins.

Health care
The UK has a reciprocal health-care agreement with Belarus. If you're visiting Belarus and need urgent or immediate medical treatment it will be provided at a reduced cost or, in some cases, free. The range of medical services available may be more restricted than under the NHS, therefore it is essential for all visitors to have comprehensive travel insurance.

Visit **www.nhs.uk/NHSEngland/Healthcareabroad** for a country-by-country guide.

Pharmacies
You should bring essential personal medications as the availability of local supplies cannot be guaranteed.

Post offices
The Central Post Office in Minsk, near the railway station, is open Monday to Friday 8.30am to 5.30pm, Saturday and Sunday 10am to 5pm. Airmail to Western Europe takes a minimum of 10 days.

Safe water
Don't drink village well water. In cities, you should first boil, then filter tap water before drinking it. It is advisable to buy bottled water, which is widely available in shops.

Telephone
Public telephones take cards. Grey booths are for national calls and blue ones for international calls. Calls from Belarus to some countries must be booked through the international operator. The country code for Belarus is 375. To call home from Belarus dial the international code (00) followed by the country code. To call the UK from Belarus dial 00 44.

Time
Belarus is two hours ahead of Greenwich Mean Time (GMT + 2). From late March to late October it is three hours ahead of Greenwich Mean Time (GMT + 3).

Emergency telephone numbers
Police **102**
Fire **101**
Ambulance **103**

Road
M1 Brest-Orsha

Driving in Belgium *(Western Europe)*

The regulations below should be read in conjunction with the General motoring information on pages 18–21.

Drinking and driving

The maximum permitted level of alcohol in the bloodstream is 0.049 per cent. If the level of alcohol in the bloodstream is between 0.05 and 0.08 per cent you will be banned from driving for three hours and issued an on-the-spot fine of €150. If you refuse to pay the fine the public prosecutor will prosecute and impose a fine up to €3,000; if it is 0.08 per cent or more there is an on-the-spot fine of up to €550 and a ban from driving for at least six hours; if prosecuted (more than 0.15 per cent alcohol) the fine is up to €12,000 and your licence suspended for up to five years. However, if you have held your licence for less than two years an on-the-spot fine will not be imposed, and you will automatically be prosecuted.

Driving licence

The minimum age at which a UK driving licence holder may drive a temporarily imported car and/or motorcycle is 18.

Fines

The officer collecting an on-the-spot fine must issue an official receipt showing the amount of the fine. Motorists can refuse to pay an on-the-spot fine; a foreign motorist refusing to do so may be invited to make a *consignation* (deposit). If he does not, his vehicle will be impounded by the police and permanently confiscated if the deposit is not paid within 96 hours. Fines can be paid in cash (euros) or by debit/credit card.

Fuel

Unleaded petrol (95 and 98 octane), diesel and LPG are available. Leaded petrol is not sold, although an anti-wear additive is available. Petrol in a can is permitted, but forbidden aboard ferries and Eurotunnel. Credit cards are accepted at filling stations; check with your card issuer for usage in Belgium before you travel.

Lights

Dipped headlights should be used in poor daytime visibility.

Motorcycles

The use of dipped headlights during the day is compulsory. The wearing of crash helmets is compulsory for both driver and passenger.

Motor insurance

Third-party insurance is compulsory. The police can impound an uninsured vehicle.

Motorways

Motorways are toll-free. See map page 36.

Passengers/children in cars

Children under 18 and less than 1.35m (4ft 5in) must use a suitable child-restraint system , whether seated in the front or rear seat of a vehicle. When two child-restraint systems are used on the rear seats and there isn't adequate room for a third child-restraint system, then the third child may travel on the back seat protected by the adult seat belt. A child under three can not be transported in a vehicle without a child seat/restraint. It is prohibited to use a rear-facing child seat on a front seat with a front air bag unless it is deactivated.

Seat belts

It is compulsory for front- and rear-seat occupants to wear seat belts, if fitted.

Speed limits

The standard legal limits, which may be varied by signs, for **private vehicles with or without trailers (up to a maximum combined weight of 3.5 tonnes)** are: in built-up areas up to 50km/h (31mph), outside built-up areas 90km/h (55mph) and on motorways and dual carriageways separated by a central reservation 120km/h (74mph). The minimum speed on motorways is 70km/h (43mph). A limit of 30km/h (19mph) may be indicated at the entrance to a built-up area. Vehicles with spiked tyres must not exceed 60km/h (37mph) on normal roads and 90km/h (55mph) on motorways/dual carriageways.

Additional information

- Drivers stranded on a Belgian motorway or on a major road (usually four-lane roads, called *route pour automobiles* – sign E17), or stopping at places where parking is not allowed, must wear a reflective safety jacket as soon as they leave their vehicle. The fine for non-compliance is €50, but the amount can be much higher (€60–€1,500) if the driver refuses to pay or when he must go to court (e.g. in the event of an accident).
- A warning triangle is compulsory for vehicles with more than two wheels.
- A first-aid kit and fire extinguisher are recommended as their carriage is compulsory for Belgian-registered vehicles.
- The majority of roundabouts have signs showing that traffic on the roundabout has priority. If no sign is present, traffic joining from the right has priority.
- A road sign has been introduced banning the use of cruise control on congested motorways and can also appear during motorway roadworks.
- A white disc bordered in red, bearing the word *'Peage'* in black, indicates that drivers must stop. The Dutch word *'Tol'* sometimes replaces *'Peage'*.
- Any stationary vehicle must have its engine switched off, unless absolutely necessary.
- A car navigation system with maps indicating the location of fixed speed cameras is permitted but equipment that actively searches for speed cameras or interferes with police equipment is prohibited.
- The police can impound a vehicle with an unsafe load.
- Spiked tyres are permitted from 1 November until 31 March on vehicles weighing up to a maximum of 3.5 tonnes. Snow chains are permitted only on snow- or ice-covered roads. Winter tyres are permitted from 1 October to 30 April; a lower speed limit applies and the maximum design speed for the tyres must be displayed on a sticker on the dashboard.
- Vehicles with spiked tyres must display at the rear a white disc with a red reflectorised border showing the figure '60', when the spiked tyres are applied.

BELGIUM, NETHERLANDS & LUXEMBOURG

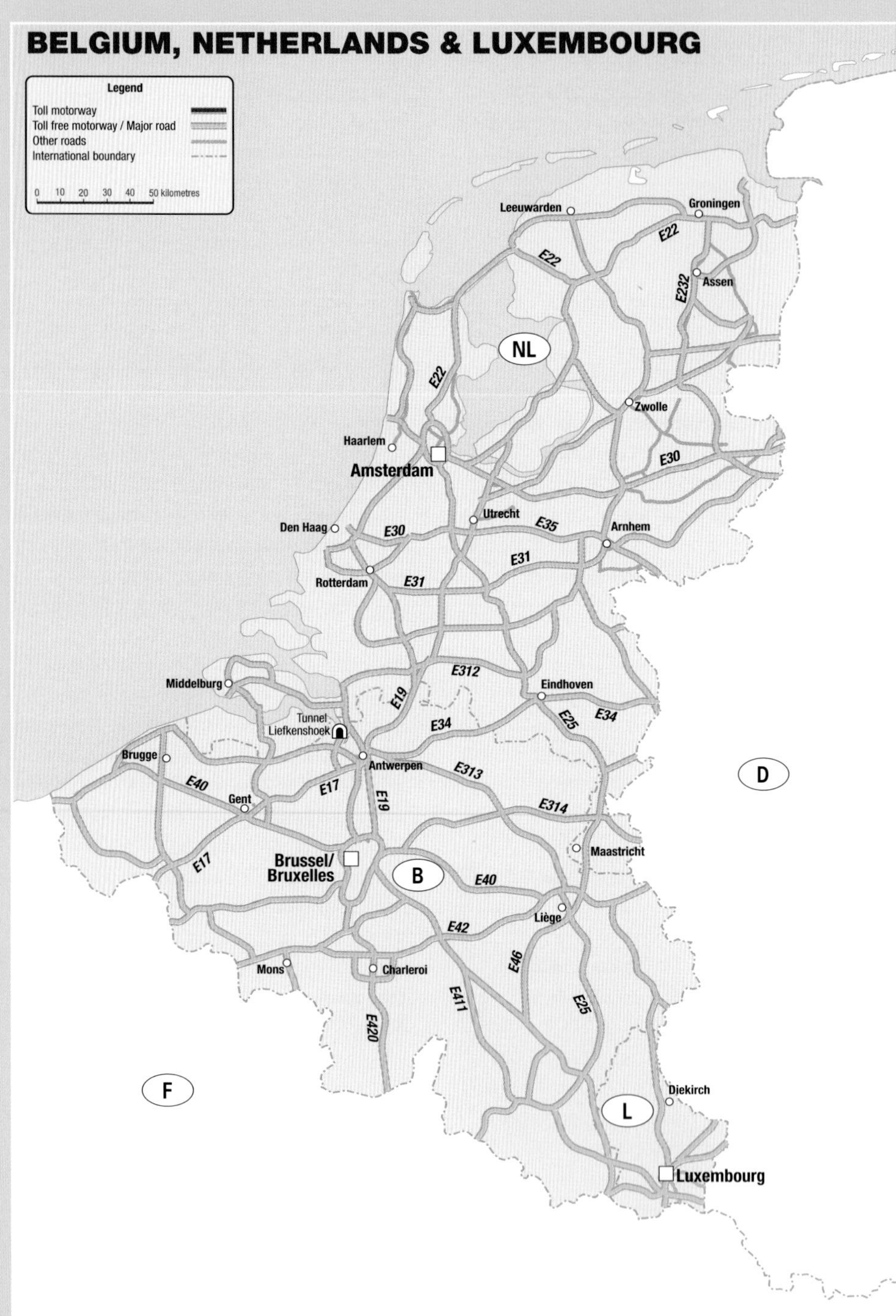

Travel facts and toll charges: Belgium

Tourism Flanders – Brussels
Flanders House
1a Cavendish Square
London W1G 0LD
Tel: 020 7307 7738
www.visitflanders.co.uk

Belgian Tourist Office Brussels & Wallonia
217 Marsh Wall
London E14 9FJ
Tel: 020 7537 1132
Tel: 0800 9545 245 (brochure line)
www.belgiumtheplaceto.be

Banking hours
Banks are generally open Monday to Friday 9am to 4pm. Some banks close for lunch.

Credit/debit cards
Most major credit cards are accepted by larger hotels, restaurants and some garages but smaller establishments prefer cash. ATMs for cash advances can be found outside banks in all the major towns.

Currency
The unit of currency in Belgium is the euro (€). Euro coins are issued in denominations of 1, 2, 5, 10, 20 and 50 cents and €1 and €2. Banknotes are issued in denominations of €5, €10, €20, €50, €100, €200 and €500.

Electricity
The power supply is 220 volts AC. Plugs are round with two pins. British appliances will need an adaptor.

Health care
Free or reduced-cost medical treatment is available in Belgium to European visitors on production of a valid European Health Insurance Card (EHIC). See page 10. Comprehensive travel insurance is still advised and is essential for all other visitors.

Pharmacies
Belgian pharmacies have many medicines available. Nevertheless, it is handy to take a supply of the medicines that you need regularly. It is also advisable to take a leaflet or list of active components, so that the pharmacy can find an alternative under a different product name, if necessary. Pharmacies are open weekdays 9am to 6pm. At night and at weekends at least one local pharmacy will be open.

Post offices
Stamps can be bought at the post office, machines, news-stands and souvenir shops. Most post offices are open Monday to Friday 9am to 5pm (some may close for lunch), Saturday 9am to noon. Post boxes are red and marked *'Poste'*.

Safe water
It is safe to drink tap water, but sometimes bottled water may taste better. Café-restaurants usually offer still or sparkling mineral water.

Telephones
For most public telephones you need a phone card, available from post offices, kiosks and some supermarkets. Public phones displaying stickers showing flags of different countries can be used to make international calls with operator assistance. The country code for Belgium is 32. To call home from Belgium dial the international code (00) followed by the country code. To call the UK from Belgium dial 00 44.

Time
Belgium is on Central European Time, one hour ahead of GMT (GMT + 1). Daylight Saving Time comes into effect from the end of March to the end of October (GMT + 2).

Emergency telephone numbers
Police **101** or **112** Fire and Ambulance **100** or **112**

Toll charges in euros

Bridges and tunnels	Car	Car towing caravan/ trailer
Liefkenshoek Tunnel on **R2**	6.00	19.00

Driving in Bosnia and Herzegovina *(South East Europe)*

The regulations below should be read in conjunction with the General motoring information on pages 18–21.

Drinking and driving

If the level of alcohol in the bloodstream is 0.031 per cent or more, severe penalties include a fine, imprisonment and/or suspension of the driving licence.

Driving licence

The minimum age at which a UK licence holder may drive a temporarily imported car and/ or motorcycle (exceeding 125cc) is 18. We recommend that you obtain an International Driving Permit (IDP) to accompany your UK driving licence.

Fines

On-the-spot fines can be imposed or, for more serious violations, sentence by a local court. An official receipt should be obtained.

Fuel

Leaded petrol (98 octane), unleaded petrol (95 and 98 octane) and diesel *(dizel)* are available. LPG is available at approximately 60 filling stations throughout the country. Carrying petrol in a can is permitted. Credit cards are widely accepted throughout Bosnia and Herzegovina; check with your card issuer for usage before you travel.

Lights

The use of dipped headlights during the day is compulsory throughout Bosnia and Herzegovina.

Motorcycles

The use of dipped headlights during the day is compulsory. The wearing of crash helmets is compulsory for both driver and passenger.

Motor insurance

A Green Card is compulsory.

Passengers/children in cars

A person visibly under the influence of alcohol is not permitted to travel in a vehicle as a front-seat passenger. Children under 12 cannot travel as front-seat passengers. Children under five must use a suitable child-restraint system.

Seat belts

It is compulsory for front- and rear-seat occupants to wear seat belts, if fitted.

Speed limits

The standard legal limits, which may be varied by signs, for **private vehicles without trailers** are: in built-up areas 50km/h (31mph), outside built-up areas 80km/h (49mph) but 100km/h (62mph) on dual carriageways and 130km/h (80mph) on motorways. The maximum speed for a **vehicle with trailer or caravan** under 3.5 tonnes combined weight, is 80km/h (49mph).

Additional information

- It is compulsory for visitors to equip their vehicle with a set of replacement bulbs and a spare tyre.
- A first-aid kit and a warning triangle are also compulsory; two triangles are required if towing a trailer.
- Winter tyres or M&S tyres are compulsory between 15 November and 15 April.
- The authorities at the frontier must certify any visible damage to a vehicle entering Bosnia and Herzegovina and a certificate obtained; this must be produced when leaving.
- A fire extinguisher is compulsory for LPG vehicles.
- Reflective jackets are compulsory.
- It is recommended that snow chains are carried as their use is compulsory if the relevant road sign is displayed or the snow covering is over 5cm (2in) deep. Spiked tyres are forbidden.
- During winter conditions, drivers are obliged to remove all snow and ice from their vehicles. Failure to comply will result in a fine.
- A GPS-based navigation system that has maps indicating the location of fixed speed cameras must have the 'fixed speed camera PoI (Points of Interest)' function deactivated.
- The use of radar detectors is prohibited.

Travel facts: Bosnia and Herzegovina

Embassy of Bosnia & Herzegovina
5–7 Lexham Gardens
London W8 5JJ
Tel: 020 7373 0867
www.bhembassy.co.uk/
www.bhtourism.ba

Banking hours
Banks are generally open Monday to Friday 8am to 7pm.

Credit/debit cards
Most transactions are in cash. The acceptance of major credit and debit cards outside of Sarajevo is becoming more widespread (check with your card provider), but it is advisable to carry enough cash when travelling outside major cities. Cashing traveller's cheques is possible at some banks. ATMs are available in increasing numbers in the larger cities.

Currency
The official currency is the convertible mark (Konvertibilna Maraka or KM), abbreviated as BAM. It is linked to the euro (1.95KM = 1 euro). Notes are in denominations of BAM1, 5, 10, 20, 50, 100 and 200 and 1 and 50 pfenings. Coins are in denominations of BAM1 and 2, and 10, 20 and 50 pfenings. Some euro notes (but not coins) are widely accepted. Expect your change in KM.

Electricity
The power supply is 230 volts AC, 50Hz. Two-round-pin plugs are in use.

Health care
The UK has a reciprocal healthcare agreement with Bosnia and Herzegovina. If you're visiting Bosnia and Herzegovina and need urgent or immediate medical treatment it will be provided at a reduced cost or, in some cases, free. The range of medical services available may be more restricted than under the NHS, therefore it is essential for all visitors to have comprehensive travel insurance.
Visit **www.nhs.uk/NHSEngland/Healthcareabroad** for a country-by-country guide.

Language
The official languages are Bosnian, Serbian and Croatian. The Croats and Bosniaks use the Latin alphabet, whereas the Serbs use the Cyrillic. Most young people will know some English.

Pharmacies
To find a pharmacy, ask for *apoteka*. In major cities they will generally have regular prescription drugs readily available; there is usually at least one that is open 24 hours a day. Not all villages and smaller towns have a pharmacy. Contact your embassy if you need medical attention, as they will be able to recommend a doctor.

Post offices
You have to go to a post office to buy stamps and to send letters or postcards abroad.

Safe water
The water is generally considered safe to drink, although bottled water is recommended.

Telephones
Phone booths, at bus stations and post offices, accept 10KM and 20KM phone cards, which can be bought from post offices or small newspaper kiosks. Different phone companies provide services in different parts of the country and a phone card may not be valid once you leave the town you bought it in. It is cheaper to phone after 7pm. The country code for Bosnia and Herzegovina is 387. To call home from here dial the international code (00) followed by the country code. To call the UK from Bosnia and Herzegovina dial 00 44.

Time
Bosnia is on Central European Time, one hour ahead of GMT (GMT + 1). Daylight Saving Time comes into effect from the end of March to the end of October (GMT + 2).

Emergency telephone numbers
Police **122**
Fire **123**
Medical emergency **124**

Driving in Bulgaria *(South East Europe)*

The regulations below should be read in conjunction with the General motoring information on pages 18–21.

Drinking and driving

If the level of alcohol in the bloodstream is 0.05 per cent or more the driver will be prosecuted and receive a fine and driving suspension. The police carry out random breath tests and can test for drugs at the roadside.

Driving licence

The minimum age at which a UK driving licence holder may drive a temporarily imported car and/or motorcycle is 18. It is recommended that an International Driving Permit (IDP) accompanies an older licence that is not a European Community model.

Fines

On-the-spot fines are issued. An official receipt should be obtained. Wheel clamps are in use for illegally parked cars. Vehicles causing an obstruction will be towed away.

Fuel

Leaded petrol is no longer available in Bulgaria. Unleaded petrol (95 and 98 octane), diesel and LPG are available. Credit cards are accepted at most filling stations but not all local stations in small towns accept international cards; check with your card issuer for usage in Bulgaria before travel.

Lights

The use of dipped headlights during daylight hours throughout the year is recommended; however their use is compulsory from 1 November to 31 March.

Motorcycles

The wearing of crash helmets is compulsory for both driver and passenger. Motorcyclists must have their lights on at all times.

Motor insurance

Green Cards are recognised. Third-party insurance is compulsory.

Passengers/children in cars

Children under the age of 3 may not travel in vehicles without a child restraint. Children aged 3 or over measuring less than 150cm may travel without a restraint but must occupy a rear seat.

Seat belts

It is compulsory, for front- and rear-seat occupants to wear seat belts, if fitted.

Speed limits

The standard legal limits, which may be varied by signs, for **private vehicles without trailers** are: in built-up areas 50km/h (31mph), outside built-up areas 90km/h (55mph) and motorways 130km/h (80mph). Lower limits apply to **cars towing a caravan or trailer**: outside built-up areas 70km/h (43mph), motorways 100km/h (62mph).

Additional information

- A first-aid kit is compulsory.
- A fire extinguisher and a warning triangle are compulsory (neither are required for two-wheeled vehicles).

- It is compulsory to wear a reflective jacket when leaving a car, day or night, in case of breakdown or emergency on a motorway. This regulation applies to all occupants and to motorcyclists.
- In built-up areas it is prohibited to use the horn between 10pm and 6am (9am on public holidays), and between midday and 4pm.
- Visiting motorists are required to drive through a liquid disinfectant on entry for which the charge is (approx.) €12, and to purchase a *vignette* (road tax). The *vignette* is available at the border, most petrol stations and offices of the CI and DZI bank, and are available for periods of one week, one month or a year. Heavy fines are imposed for non-compliance.
- Snow chains are permitted. They can become compulsory according to road conditions and will be indicated by the international road sign. Spiked tyres are forbidden.
- Drivers of luxury or 4 x 4 vehicles are advised to use guarded car parks.
- A GPS-based navigation system that has maps indicating the location of fixed speed cameras must have the 'fixed speed camera PoI (Points of Interest)' function deactivated. The use of radar detectors is prohibited.
- In one-way streets parking is on the left only.

Helpful road signs

Recommended maximum speed

U-turn allowed

Travel facts: Bulgaria

Embassy of the Republic of Bulgaria
Commercial Section
186–188 Queen's Gate
London SW7 5HL
Tel: 020 7584 9400
Email: tourism@bulgarianembassy.org.uk
www.bulgariatravel.org
www.travel-bulgaria.com

Banking hours
Banks are generally open Monday to Friday 9am to 12 noon and 3pm to 5pm.

Credit/debit cards
Major international credit cards (Visa, MasterCard or American Express) are accepted in larger hotels and car hire offices, and in some restaurants and shops, mainly in Sofia. Check with your provider for details. Bulgaria is still a country that operates mainly on cash rather than credit cards.

Currency
Bulgarian lev (Lv) = 100 stotinki. Notes are in denominations of Lv50, 20, 10, 5, 2 and 1. Coins are in denominations of 50, 20, 10, 5, 2 and 1 stotinki. The lev is pegged to the euro. €1 = 1.955 BGN. Many banks will cash euro cheques.

Electricity
The power supply is 220 volts AC, 50Hz. Appliances need two-round-pin continental plugs.

Health care
Free or reduced-cost medical treatment is available in Bulgaria to European visitors on production of a valid European Health Insurance Card (EHIC). See page 10. Comprehensive travel insurance is still advised and is essential for all other visitors.

Pharmacies
Many pharmacies are not as widely stocked as at home. Minor complaints can be solved at a pharmacy *(apteka)*, but if you need a doctor *(lekar)* or dentist *(zâbolekar)* visit the nearest health centre *(poliklinika)*, where staff might speak English, German or French, and will almost certainly understand Russian.

Post offices
Post offices in large towns are open 8.30 or 9am to 5.30pm. Postage stamps and postcards are sold in post offices and at newspaper kiosks.

Safe water
Drinking water in major towns is generally safe to drink, though you may prefer to buy bottled mineral water.

Telephones
Public phones on the streets operate with tokens (0.20 lev) and phone cards, which are available from post offices and newspaper kiosks. The country code for Bulgaria is 359. To call home from here dial the international code (00) followed by the country code. To call the UK from Bulgaria dial 00 44.

Time
Bulgaria is on Eastern European Time. It is two hours ahead of Greenwich Mean Time (GMT + 2) and from late March to late October it is three hours ahead of Greenwich Mean Time (GMT + 3).

Emergency telephone numbers
Police **166** or **112** Fire **160** or **112**
First aid **150** or **112** Road assistance **146**

Toll charges in lev
General

7-day *vignette*	10.00
1-month *vignette*	25.00
Annual *vignette*	67.00

Driving in Croatia *(South East Europe)*

The regulations below should be read in conjunction with the General motoring information on pages 18–21.

Drinking and driving

Drinking and driving is strictly forbidden for all drivers under the age of 24. Nil percentage of alcohol is allowed in a driver's blood. The legal limit for alcohol in the blood of drivers aged 24 years and over is 0.05 per cent. Exceptions to this rule apply to professional drivers. Tests for narcotics may be applied; if they prove positive, severe consequences include confiscation of the vehicle, a severe fine and removal of the driving licence. It is prohibited to drive after taking any medicine where the side effects may affect the ability to drive a motor vehicle.

Driving licence

The minimum age at which a UK licence holder may drive a temporarily imported car and/or motorcycle (exceeding 125cc) is 18.

Fines

The police officer will impose a fine on the spot; the fine must be paid within eight days at a post office or bank. The police may hold your passport until evidence of payment is produced. The driving licence of a foreign motorist can be suspended for up to eight days for driving under the influence of excess alcohol, driving without prescribed medical aids e.g. glasses, driving in a state of exhaustion or when ill. The driving licence must be collected within three days of the end of suspension. Illegally parked cars can be wheel clamped.

Fuel

Unleaded petrol (95 and 98 octane) and diesel *(dizel)* are available; LPG is available at most motorway filling stations. It is forbidden to carry petrol in a can. Credit cards are accepted at filling stations; check with your card issuer for usage in Croatia before travel.

Lights

It is compulsory for all vehicles to use dipped headlights when visibility is reduced; a fine is imposed for non-compliance. Dipped headlights are compulsory in the daytime from the last Sunday in October to the last Sunday in March (out of the Daylight Saving Time period); there is a fine for non-compliance.

Motorcycles

The use of dipped headlights during the day is compulsory. The wearing of crash helmets is compulsory for both the driver and passenger. A child under 12 cannot travel as a passenger. A fine will be imposed if the passenger on a motorcycle is found to be under the influence of alcohol or narcotics.

Motor insurance

Third-party insurance is compulsory. It is recommended that all visitors obtain a green card prior to travel to facilitate insurance formalities. The green card must cover Croatia (HR) as well as Boznia Herzegovina if travelling on a 20km section of coastline at Neum, along the Dalmatian Coastal highway.

Passengers/children in cars

A child under 12 cannot travel as a front-seat passenger, with the exception of a child under two years seated in a suitable child seat. The seat must be fitted facing in the opposite direction of travel with the passenger air bags deactivated. Children aged two to five must be seated in a suitable child seat; other children must be seated using a suitable child restraint, using a booster seat where necessary.

Seat belts

It is compulsory for front- and rear-seat occupants to wear seat belts, if fitted.

Speed limits

The standard legal limits, which may be varied by signs, for **private vehicles without trailers** are: in built-up areas 50km/h (31mph), outside built-up areas 90km/h (55mph) but 110km/h (68mph) on expressways and 130km/h (80mph) on motorways, unless otherwise indicated by road signs. If **towing a trailer or caravan** the speed limit is reduced to 80km/h (49mph) on expressways and 90km/h (55mph) on motorways. All motorists under 24 years of age must not exceed 80km/h (49mph) on normal roads outside built-up areas, 100km/h (62mph) on expressways and 120km/h (74mph) on motorways. The minimum speed on motorways is 60km/h (37mph).

Additional information

- It is compulsory for visitors to equip their vehicle with a set of replacement bulbs (this does not apply if the vehicle is fitted with xenon, neon, LED or similar lights); a first-aid kit (excluding motorcycles); a warning triangle (excluding motorcycles) – two triangles required if towing a trailer.
- During winter, especially in the Gorski Kotar and Lika regions, carrying a shovel and the use of snow chains is compulsory (see winter equipment below).
- All drivers of motor vehicles (except motorcycles with sidecars and mopeds under 50cc) must have a reflective safety jacket (EN471) in the vehicle and wear it whenever they have to get out of the vehicle at the roadside, in an emergency. Be aware, however, that car hire companies may not supply them to persons hiring vehicles.
- The use of spiked tyres is prohibited.
- It is prudent to have winter equipment ready between November and the end of April. This may consist of winter tyres marked M&S on the sidewalls or snow chains for the driving wheels. Vehicles not adapted to winter conditions may be prohibited from driving and can encounter a fine. Snow tyres must have a minimum tread depth of 4mm.
- The authorities at the frontier must certify any visible damage to a vehicle entering Croatia and a certificate obtained; this must be produced when leaving the country.
- Radar detectors are forbidden.

Travel facts and toll charges: Croatia

Croatian National Tourist Office
2 The Lanchesters
162–164 Fulham Palace Road
London W6 9ER
Tel: 020 8563 7979
www.visit-croatia.co.uk; http://gb.croatia.hr

Banking hours
Banks are generally open Monday to Friday 7am to 4 or 7pm, Saturday until 1pm. In the larger cities some banks open on Sundays.

Credit/debit cards
Major credit cards are accepted in hotels, larger shops and restaurants. Large cities, towns and resorts have ATMs in banks, supermarkets, airports and elsewhere.

Currency
The currency in Croatia is the kuna (1 kuna = 100 lipa). There are 1, 2, 5, 10, 20, 50 lipa coins, 1, 2, 5 and 25 kuna coins and 5, 10, 20, 50, 100, 200, 500 and 1,000 kuna banknotes.

Electricity
Electric current is 220 volts AC, 50Hz. Appliances need two-round-pin continental plugs.

Health care
The UK has a reciprocal health-care agreement with Croatia. If you're visiting Croatia and need urgent or immediate medical treatment it will be provided at a reduced cost or, in some cases, free. The range of medical services available may be more restricted than under the NHS, therefore it is essential for all visitors to have comprehensive travel insurance.
Visit **www.nhs.uk/NHSEngland/Healthcareabroad** for a country-by-country guide.

Pharmacies
Pharmacies sell over-the-counter medicines; most have English speaking staff.

Post offices
Post offices are open from 7am to 7pm, Saturday until 1pm. In larger cities some are open until 9pm in summer.
Postage stamps *(marke)* are sold in post offices and at newspaper and tobacco kiosks.

Safe water
The tap water in Croatia is chlorinated and safe to drink; however, it is advisable to drink bottled water.

Telephones
Public telephones are operated by phone cards, available from post offices, newspaper and tobacco kiosks and in hotel and tourist complexes. The country code for Croatia is 385. To call the UK from Croatia dial the international code (00) followed by the country code. To call the UK from Croatia dial 00 44.

Time
Croatia is on Central European Time, one hour ahead of GMT (GMT + 1). Daylight Saving Time comes into effect from the end of March to the end of October (GMT + 2 hours).

Emergency telephone numbers
Police **92** or **112** Fire **93** or **112** Ambulance **94** or **112**

Toll charges in kunas

Road		Car	Car towing caravan/ trailer
E59 (A2)	Zagreb – Macelj	42.00	62.00
E65 (A1)	Zagreb – Split – Dubrovnik	220.00	339.00
E65 (A6)	Zagreb – Rijeka	60.00	108.00
E70 (A3/ A5)	Zagreb – Lipovac (Slovenian border)	121.00	184.00
E71 (A4)	Zagreb – Gorican	41.00	62.00
E73 (A5)	Osijek – Sredanci Int.	39.00	
A7	Rupa – Rijeka	8.00	15.00
Bridges and tunnels			
	Krk Bridge	35.00	46.00
A8	Kanfanar – Matuiji (Ucka Tunnel)	28.00	40.00
A9	Kastel – Pula (Mirna Bridge)	12.00	21.00

Driving in Republic of Cyprus

(Eastern Mediterranean)

The regulations below should be read in conjunction with the General motoring information on pages 18–21.

Drinking and driving

The maximum legal level of alcohol in the blood is 0.049 per cent. Persons suspected of driving under the influence of alcohol may be subject to a blood test.

Driving licence

All national driving licences are accepted. The minimum age for driving a temporarily imported car and/or motorcycle is 18.

Fines

The Cyprus traffic police are empowered to impose on-the-spot fines for traffic offences, however, they cannot collect them.

Fuel

Unleaded petrol (95 and 98 octane) and diesel are available. There is no LPG or leaded petrol, but you can buy lead-substitute additive. It is forbidden to carry petrol in a can. Credit cards are accepted at most filling stations; check with your card issuer for use in Cyprus before you travel.

Lights

Vehicle lights must be used between half an hour after sunset and half an hour before sunrise. Spotlights are prohibited.

Motorcycles

The wearing of crash helmets is compulsory for the rider and pillion passenger.

Motor insurance

Third-party insurance is compulsory.

Passengers/children in cars

Children under five cannot travel as a front-seat passenger. Children over five and under 10 must use a suitable child-restraint system.

Seat belts

It is compulsory for front- and rear-seat occupants to wear seat belts, if fitted.

Speed limits

The standard legal limits, which may be varied by signs, for **private vehicles without trailers** are: in built-up areas 50km/h (31mph) or 65km/h (40mph) depending on the road, outside built-up areas 80km/h (49mph) and 100km/h (62mph) on motorways. The minimum speed on motorways is 65km/h (40mph).

Additional information

- It is compulsory to carry two warning triangles.
- The rule of the road is drive on the left, overtake on the right.

- The use of the vehicle horn is prohibited between 10pm and 6am, and in the vicinity of hospitals.
- Spiked tyres and snow chains are permitted on mountain roads in winter.
- A GPS-based navigation system with maps indicating the location of fixed speed cameras must have the 'fixed speed camera PoI (Points of Interest)' function deactivated.
- The use of radar detectors is prohibited.
- Eating and drinking while driving is prohibited.
- Smoking in a car with a person that is under 16 is prohibited. A fine is imposed for non-compliance.

Travel facts: Republic of Cyprus

Cyprus Tourism Organisation
17 Hanover Street
London W1S 1YP
Tel: 020 7569 8800
www.visitcyprus.com

Banking hours

Banks are generally open Monday to Friday 8.30am to 1.30pm (some branches open in the afternoon).

Credit/debit cards

Hotels, large shops and restaurants normally accept major credit cards and traveller's cheques.

Currency

The currency of the Republic of Cyprus is the euro (€), introduced 1 January 2008, which is divided into 100 cents. Notes are issued in denominations of €5, €10, €20, €50, €100, €200 and €500; coins in 1, 2, 5, 10, 20 and 50 cents, and €1 and €2.

Electricity

The power supply is 240 volts AC, 50Hz and the type of socket is generally a European two-round-pin style, but there are some older buildings with UK-style three rectangular pins.

Health care

Free or reduced-cost medical treatment is available in Cyprus to European visitors on production of a valid European Health Insurance Card (EHIC). See page 10. Comprehensive travel insurance is still advised and is essential for all other visitors.

Language

The official language is Greek. English is widely spoken and French and German are spoken within the tourism industry.

Pharmacies

Minor ailments can be dealt with at pharmacies *(farmakio)*, which sell most branded medicines. Local newspapers list pharmacies that are open at night and on weekends/holidays, as well as the names of doctors who are on call on weekends/holidays.

Post offices

There are main post offices in large towns and sub-post offices in the suburbs. Post offices are open Monday to Friday 7:30am to 1:30pm (Thursday also 3 to 6pm). Post boxes are painted yellow.

Safe water

Tap water in hotels, restaurants and public places is generally safe to drink in Cyprus. Bottled mineral water is inexpensive and widely available.

Telephones

Phone cards for public phone boxes and mobile phones are sold in kiosks all over the island and are generally available in €5, €10, €20 and €50 units.The country code for Cyprus is 357. To call home from here dial the international code (00) followed by the country code. To call the UK from Cyprus dial 00 44.

Time

Cyprus is on Eastern European Time. It is two hours ahead of Greenwich Mean Time (GMT + 2) and from late March to late October it is three hours ahead of Greenwich Mean Time (GMR + 3).

Emergency telephone numbers

Police **199** or **112**
Fire **199** or **112**
Ambulance **199** or **112**

Driving in Turkish Republic of Northern Cyprus *(Eastern Mediterranean)*

The regulations below should be read in conjunction with the General motoring information on pages 18–21. Please check the current position with local authorities.

Drinking and driving

Current laws are subject to change. Drivers should refrain from drinking and driving.

Driving licence

A UK licence is acceptable. The minimum age for driving a temporarily imported car and/or motorcycle is 18.

Fines

There are no on-the-spot fines.

Fuel

Leaded (98 octane), unleaded petrol (95 and 97 octane), diesel *(mazot)* and Euro-diesel are available but not LPG. It is permitted to carry petrol in a can, but not aboard ferries. Credit cards are accepted at most filling stations; check with your card issuer for use in Cyprus before you travel.

Lights

Vehicle lights must be used between half an hour after sunset and half an hour before sunrise.

Motorcycles

The wearing of crash helmets is compulsory.

Motor insurance

Third-party insurance is compulsory. A Green Card is not accepted. Short term insurance may be purchased at the port of arrival.

Passengers/children in cars

A child under 12 cannot travel as a front-seat passenger; children over five and under 10 must use a suitable child restraint system.

Seat belts

It is compulsory for front seat occupants to wear seat belts.

Speed limits

The standard legal limits, which may be varied by signs, for **private vehicles without trailers** are: in built-up areas 50km/h (31mph), outside built-up areas 70km/h (43mph), 80km/h (49mph), 90km (56mph) or 100km (62mph).

Additional information

- The rule of the road is drive on the left, overtake on the right.
- Two warning triangles are compulsory.
- Road signs are predominately in English.
- Do not use a mobile phone while driving.

Travel facts: Northern Cyprus

Northern Cyprus Tourism Centre
29 Bedford Square
London WC1B 3ED
Tel: 020 7631 1930
www.cypnet.co.uk/ncyprus

Banking hours
In North Cyprus banks are open Monday to Friday 8.30am to 12 noon and 1.30 to 4pm throughout the year. Most major banks have ATMs which accept main credit and debit cards.

Credit/debit cards
Most major credit and debit cards are accepted by hotels, restaurants and shops.

Currency
The unit of currency in North Cyprus is Turkish lira (TL) divided into 100 kurus (Kr). Banknotes are issued in denominations of 5, 10, 20, 50, 100 and 200TL. Coins in 1, 5, 10, 25 and 50Kr and 1TL and 2TL. Most businesses will accept the euro, pound sterling, US dollars.

Electricity
The power supply is 240 volts AC, 50Hz. Sockets take UK-style three rectangular pins.

Health care
Comprehensive travel insurance is essential for all visitors.

Language
Turkish is the official language; English is widely spoken and understood.

Pharmacies
Pharmacies *(eczane)* sell many prescription drugs over the counter. Many pharmacists, provided they speak English, will advise you which medicine to take for your condition

Post offices
There are main post offices in large towns and sub-post offices in the suburbs. Post offices are open Monday to Friday 8am to 3.30pm except on Thursdays, when they open 8am to 1pm and 2 to 6pm (5pm in winter). Post boxes are painted yellow. Mail posted in Northern Cyprus has to travel via Turkey.

Safe water
Tap water is not always safe to drink. If you are in any doubt, it is best to stick to bottled water that has either been opened in front of you or purchased by you.

Telephones
The international dialling code 90 392 should precede the seven-digit local telephone numbers when calling North Cyprus from abroad. Public telephone booths are available and telephone cards can be purchased from the Telecommunications Office. To call home from here dial the international code (00) followed by the country code. To call the UK from Cyprus dial 00 44.

Time
Cyprus is on Eastern European Time. It is two hours ahead of Greenwich Mean Time (GMT + 2) .

Emergency telephone numbers
Police **155**
Fire **199**
Forest fire **177**
Ambulance **112**

Driving in Czech Republic *(Central Europe)*

The regulations below should be read in conjunction with the General motoring information on pages 18–21.

Drinking and driving

Drinking and driving is forbidden. Nil percentage of alcohol is allowed in the driver's blood. A fine of between 25,000 and 50,000CZK will be imposed and the driving licence withdrawn for up to two years. Random breath testing takes place frequently. Police can also test for drugs by testing saliva.

Driving licence

The minimum age at which a UK licence holder may drive a temporarily imported car is 18, a motorcycle up to 125cc 17 years, over 125cc (max 25kW) 18 years. Photocard licences are accepted; licences not incorporating a photo must be accompanied by an International Driving Permit (IDP).

Fines

On-the-spot fines of up to 5,000CZK can be imposed; the maximum fine for a traffic offence is 100,000CZK. An official receipt should be obtained. The police are empowered to retain the driving licence when a serious traffic offence has been committed. Illegally parked vehicles may be clamped or towed away.

Fuel

Unleaded petrol *(natural)*, (95 and 98 octane), diesel *(nafta)* and LPG *(autoplyn* or *plyn)* are available. It is permitted to carry up to 10 litres of petrol in a can. Credit cards are accepted at filling stations; check with your card issuer for usage in Czech Republic before you travel.

Lights

You must use dipped headlights during the day throughout the year. The fine for non-compliance is approximately 2,000CZK. Any vehicle warning lights, other than those supplied with the vehicle as original equipment, must be made inoperative.

Motorcycles

The use of dipped headlights during the day is compulsory throughout the year. The wearing of crash helmets is compulsory for the driver and passenger of motorcycles. It is forbidden for motorcyclists to smoke while riding their machine.

Motor insurance

Third-party insurance is compulsory.

Passengers/children in cars

All passengers must use seat belts. Children (persons with a weight under 36kg/79lb and under 1.5m/4ft 11in in height) are not permitted to travel in a vehicle unless using a suitable restraint system. A child in the front seat of a vehicle using a suitable child-restraint system and where the air bag is activated must travel facing forward.

Seat belts

It is compulsory for front- and rear-seat occupants to wear seat belts, if fitted.

Speed limits

The standard legal limits, which may be varied by signs, for **private vehicles without trailers** are: in built-up areas 50km/h (31mph), outside built-up areas 90km/h (55mph) and motorways (for vehicles not exceeding 3.5 tonnes and buses) 130km/h (80mph). On expressways that pass through built-up areas the limit is 80km/h (50mph). **Towing combinations** under 3.5 tonnes combined weight are limited by the maximum permissable speed of the slower part of the combination. The maximum speed with snow chains is 50km/h (31mph). At railway crossings drivers must not exceed 30km/h (18mph) for 50 metres before the crossing. The arrival of a train is indicated by red flashing lights/red or yellow flag. Vehicles constructed with a maximum speed of 80km/h (49mph) or under are not permitted to travel on motorways.

Additional information

- A first-aid kit is compulsory.
- A warning triangle (not required for two-wheeled vehicles) is compulsory.
- A set of replacement bulbs and fuses is compulsory.
- Winter tyres are compulsory from 1 November to 31 March (or longer, dependent on weather conditions) on all wheels of passenger vehicles and must be marked M&S when there is compacted snow or ice on the road. They are also compulsory whenever the temperature falls below 4 degrees celsius and there is a possibility of snow or ice on the road. These regulations also apply during winter periods to roads where the sign right is placed, even if it is free of snow and ice. The minimum depth on winter tyres is 4mm. As snow chains can only be used when roads are completely covered, we recommend that winter tyres are fitted.
- The driver of a vehicle with two or more axles must carry a reflective waistcoat (EU standard EN471), which must be used in a breakdown or emergency outside a built-up area on expressways and motorways. It must be worn when exiting the vehicle and therefore must be kept in the car (not in the boot). The waistcoat is recommended for passengers and riders of mopeds and motorcycles.
- Motorway tax is payable for the use of motorways and express roads. A windscreen sticker must be displayed on all four-wheeled vehicles up to 3.5 tonnes as evidence of payment. The sticker can be purchased at the Czech frontier, UAMK branch offices, petrol stations or post offices for periods of one year, one month or 10 consecutive days. Fines are imposed for non-display.
- The authorities at the frontier must certify any visible damage to a vehicle entering the Czech Republic. If any damage occurs inside the country a police report must be obtained at the scene of the accident. Damaged vehicles may be taken out of the country only on production of this evidence.
- The use of an audible warning device is permitted only in built-up areas to avoid imminent danger; they are prohibited between 8pm and 6am, and in Prague.
- The use of spiked tyres is prohibited.
- A GPS-based navigation system with maps indicating the location of fixed speed cameras must have the 'fixed speed camera Pol (Points of Interest)' function deactivated. The use of radar detectors is prohibited.

Compulsory winter tyres

End of compulsory winter tyres zone

Travel facts and toll charges: Czech Republic

Czech Tourist Authority
13 Harley Street
London W1G 9QG
Tel: 020 7631 0427
www.czechtourism.com
www.pis.cz/en

Banking hours
Banks are normally open Monday to Friday from 9am to 5pm. Some open Saturday morning.

Credit/debit cards
Payment by credit/debit card in the Czech Republic is not as widespread as it is in other European countries. There are plenty of ATMs throughout the country.

Currency
The local currency is the Czech koruna, or Czech Crown, (Kč) which is divided into 100 heller. Notes are issued in denominations of Kč50, 100, 200, 500, 1,000, 2,000, 5,000; coins in hellers 50 and Kč1, 2, 5, 10, 20, 50.

Electricity
The electrical supply is 220 volts AC, as in the rest of Europe. Czech plugs have two round pins.

Health care
Free or reduced-cost medical treatment is available in Czech Republic to European visitors on production of a valid European Health Insurance Card (EHIC). See page 10. Comprehensive travel insurance is still advised and is essential for all other visitors.

Pharmacies
Pharmacies *(lékánat* or *apothéka)* are the only places to sell over-the-counter medicines. They also dispense many drugs *(leky)* normally available only on prescription in other Western countries. Take a supply of your own prescription medicines with you as you may not be able to find exactly the same in Czech Republic.

Post offices
Post offices have distinctive orange *Posta* signs outside. They are normally open Monday to Friday 8am to 5pm and Saturday until noon. Stamps *(známky)* can be bought from news kiosks, tobacconists, some hotels and shops, as well as post offices.

Safe water
Tap water may not be particularly palatable, but it is safe to drink, though most people drink mineral water *(minerální voda* or *minerálka)*.

Telephones
Most pay phones accept only telephone cards, which can be obtained from post offices, newsagents and any establishment displaying the blue and yellow *Ceský Telecom* logo. They come in denominations of 50 units upwards. The country code for Czech Republic is 420. To call home from here dial the international code (00) followed by the country code. To call the UK dial 00 44.

Time
The Czech Republic is on Central European Time (GMT + 1), but from late March, when clocks are put forward one hour, until late October, Czech Summer Time (GMT + 2) operates.

Emergency telephone numbers
General **112**
Police **158** or **112**
Fire **150** or **112**
Ambulance **155** or **112**

Toll charges in Czech koruna
For details of where to buy the motorway tax see page 53. You may be charged more if your vehicle is over 3,500kg.

General	**Car (with or without trailer)**
10-day *vignette*	310.00
1 month *vignette*	440.00
1 year *vignette*	1,500.00

Driving in Denmark *(Northern Europe)*

The regulations below should be read in conjunction with the General motoring information on pages 18–21.

Drinking and driving

If the level of alcohol in the bloodstream is 0.05 per cent or more severe penalties can be imposed including licence suspension, fines or imprisonment, depending on the level of excess.

Driving licence

The minimum age at which a UK licence holder may drive a temporarily imported car and/or motorcycle is 17.

Fines

Visitors who infringe traffic regulations can expect to be fined on the spot. If you do not accept the fine, the police will take the matter to court to be settled by a judge. The police may retain the vehicle until such time. Vehicles parked against regulations will be taken away by the police at the owner's expense.

Fuel

Unleaded petrol (92 and 95 octane) and diesel are available. There is limited availability of LPG. Leaded petrol is no longer available; a leaded petrol substitute called *'Millenium'* is available. It is permitted to carry petrol in a can, but not aboard ferries. Credit cards are accepted at most filling stations; check with your card issuer for use in Denmark before travel.

Lights

The use of dipped headlights is compulsory during the day.

Motorcycles

The use of dipped headlights is compulsory during the day. The wearing of crash helmets with straps is compulsory for both driver and passenger.

Motor insurance

Third-party insurance is compulsory.

Passengers/children in cars

Children under three years must be seated in a child-restraint system adapted to their size. Children over three and less than 1.35m (4ft 5in) must be seated in a child-restraint system suitable for their height and weight. A child must not be placed in the front seat with their back to the road if the vehicle is fitted with an active air bag. As all rear-seat passengers must wear a seat belt it is not possible to transport three children if there are only two seat belts.

Seat belts

It is compulsory for front- and rear-seat occupants to wear seat belts.

Speed limits

The standard legal limits, which may be varied by signs, for **private vehicles without trailers** are: in built-up areas 50km/h (31mph), outside built-up areas 80km/h (49mph) or 90km/h (55mph), and motorways 110km/h (68mph) or 130km/h (80mph). Lower limits apply to **private cars towing a trailer or caravan**: outside built-up areas 70km/h (43mph) and on motorways 80km/h (49mph).

Additional information

- A red warning triangle is compulsory in case of an accident or breakdown. It is recommended that visitors equip their vehicle with a fire extinguisher and a first-aid kit.
- Generally there is a duty to give way to traffic approaching from the right.
- A bold line, a line of white triangles (shark's teeth) painted across the road or a white triangle with a red border indicate that you must stop and give way to traffic on the road you are entering.
- When roads are wet or slushy, speed must be reduced as far as possible to prevent other road users from being splashed.
- It is prohibited to use radar detectors.
- Spiked tyres may be used between 1 November and 15 April; they must be fitted to all four wheels.
- Right-hand drive vehicles must have wing-mirrors on both sides of the vehicle.
- Private cars must be equipped with an exterior side mirror and an interior rear-view mirror.
- Motorists must always yield to bicycles.

Road signs (a selection of standard and non-standard)

Traffic merges

Minimum speed limit

Recommended speed limit

Compulsory slow lane

1 hour parking zone

Place of interest

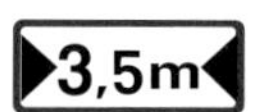

Maximum width

Travel facts and toll charges: Denmark

Danish Tourist Board
55 Sloane Street
London SW1X 9SR
Tel: 020 7259 5959
www.visitdenmark.com

Banking hours
Banks are normally open Monday to Friday from 10am to 4pm, and until 6pm on Thursday.

Credit/debit cards
Most shops accept major credit cards. The most common are Visa and MasterCard.

Currency
The monetary unit is the Danish kroner (DKK), which is divided into 100 øre. Banknotes are issued in denominations of DKK50, DKK100, DKK200, DKK500 and DKK1,000. Coins are found in DKK20, DKK10, DKK5, DKK2, DKK1 and 50 øre and 25 øre. Some shops, hotels and restaurants, particularly in larger cities, display prices in both Danish kroner and euros and many are likely to accept payment in euros. It is advisable to ask beforehand if you wish to pay in anything other than Danish kroner.

Electricity
The electricity supply in Denmark is 220 volts AC (50Hz). Appliances need two-round-pin continental plugs.

Health care
Free or reduced-cost medical treatment is available in Denmark to European visitors on production of a valid European Health Insurance Card (EHIC). See page 10. Comprehensive travel insurance is still advised.

Pharmacies
Only medicine prescribed by Danish or other Scandinavian doctors can be dispensed at a chemist *(apotek).* Many medicines that can be bought over the counter in the UK can be obtained only with prescriptions in Denmark. If you take prescribed medication, you should bring a supply large enough to last throughout the trip since some medicines may not be on the market in Denmark.

Post offices
Post offices are generally open Monday to Friday from 9 or 10am to 5 or 6pm. Some are closed on Saturdays. Opening hours for those that are open are usually from 9 or 10am to noon or 2pm. You can buy stamps from newsagents and post offices.

Safe water
The tap water in Denmark is safe to drink. Bottled mineral water is widely available.

Telephones
Most Danish public telephone boxes are operated by means of phonecards, but also by means of Danish currency and euros. Some of the public coin phones also accept credit cards. There are no area codes. The country code for Denmark is 45. To call home from Denmark dial the international code (00) followed by the country code. To call the UK dial 00 44.

Time
Denmark follows Central European Time (CET), which is one hour ahead of Greenwich Mean Time (GMT + 1). From the last Sunday in March to the last Sunday in October, clocks are put forward one hour (GMT + 2).

Emergency telephone numbers
Police **112**
Fire **112**
Ambulance **112**

Toll charges in Danish kroner

Bridges and tunnels	Car	Car towing caravan/ trailer
Øresund Bridge (one way)	335.00	670.00
Storebaelt Bridge (one way)	230.00	350.00

Driving in Estonia *(Eastern Europe)*

The regulations below should be read in conjunction with the General motoring information on pages 18–21.

Drinking and driving

The level of alcohol allowed in the driver's blood is 0.02%. A fine and/or imprisonment can be imposed for non-compliance.

Driving licence

The minimum age at which a UK licence holder may drive a temporarily imported car and/or motorcycle is 18.

Fines

Police can impose fines on the spot. They monitor speeds closely and will impose fines for even the smallest speeding offences. Illegally parked cars will be clamped and heavy fines imposed for unlawful parking.

Fuel

Unleaded petrol (95 and 98 octane), diesel and LPG are available. Leaded petrol is no longer available. Carrying petrol in a can is permitted, subject to payment of excise duty at the frontier. Credit cards are accepted at most filling stations; check with your card issuer before travel. Special winter diesel with a high congealing point is available in winter months.

Lights

Dipped headlights during the day is compulsory.

Motorcycles

Dipped headlights during the day is compulsory. The wearing of crash helmets is compulsory for both the driver and passenger.

Motor insurance

Third-party insurance is compulsory.

Passengers/children in cars

Children too small to wear seat belts must travel in a child seat adapted to their size.

Seat belts

It is compulsory for front-seat occupants to wear seat belts. Rear seat belts must be worn if fitted.

Speed limits

The standard legal limits, which may be varied by signs, for **private vehicles without trailers** are: in built-up areas 50km/h (31mph), outside built-up areas 90km/h (55mph) but up to 110km/h (68mph) on some roads during the summer months. Motorists who have held a driving licence for less than two years must not exceed 90km/h (55mph) outside built-up areas.

Additional information

- A first-aid kit, fire extinguisher, two wheel chocks (blocks of wood or plastic to put under a vehicle's wheels when parked, to prevent it from moving) and a warning triangle (not required for two-wheeled vehicles) are compulsory.
- Winter tyres (with a minimum tread depth of 3mm) are compulsory between 1 December and 1 March; however these dates may vary from October to April according to the weather conditions.

- It is recommended that visitors carry an assortment of spares for their vehicle, such as fan belt, replacement bulbs and spark plugs.
- In addition to the original vehicle registration document, it is recommended that an International Certificate for Motor Vehicles (ICMV) is also carried if visiting any Russian-speaking areas outside Estonia.
- The border police may ask visitors for proof of sufficient personal insurance cover on entry.
- It is prohibited to overtake a tram that has stopped to let passengers on or off.
- Motorists must pay a toll to enter the city of Tallinn.

Travel facts: Estonia

Estonian Embassy
16 Hyde Park Gate
London SW7 5DG
Tel: 020 7589 3428

Estonia does not have a tourist office in the UK, but the embassy can help tourists with information. You can collect tourist brochures from the embassy Monday to Friday 9am to 5pm.
www.estonia.gov.uk
www.visitestonia.com

Banking hours
Banks are generally open from Monday to Friday from 9am to 3 or 4pm. Most banks are closed on Saturday and Sunday. Currency exchange offices are open from Monday to Friday from 9am to 6pm; on Saturday from 9am to 3pm. Some are also open on Sunday.

Credit/debit cards
Credit cards such as Visa and MasterCard/Eurocard, are accepted in most of the major hotels, restaurants and shops. Most banks will give cash advances on credit cards supported by a valid passport. Check with the credit card company for further details before travelling.

Currency
The national currency is the kroon (EEK). The smaller unit is the cent, 1 kroon = 100 cents. The kroon is pegged to the euro at €1 = 15.65EEK. Foreign currencies can be easily exchanged in banks and exchange offices.

Electricity
The electricity supply in Estonia is 220 volts AC, 50Hz. Continental-style two-pin plugs are in use.

Health care
Free or reduced-cost medical treatment is available in Estonia to European visitors on production of a valid European Health Insurance Card (EHIC). See page 10. Comprehensive travel insurance is still advised and is essential for all other visitors.

Pharmacies
Over-the-counter medicines are available in pharmacies *(apteek)*, which can be found in every town. However, it may be more convenient to bring enough medicines to last throughout your trip.

Post offices
Post offices are generally open during normal shopping hours: Monday to Friday from 9am to 6pm, and Saturday 9.30am to 3pm. The Central Post Office in Tallinn, at Narva mnt, is open seven days a week.

Safe water
The tap water is safe to drink but you may prefer bottled mineral water.

Telephones
Pay phones accept phone cards, which can be purchased from hotel reception desks, tourist information offices, post offices, news-stands and some shops. The country code for Estonia is 372. To call home from Estonia dial the international code (00) followed by the country code. To call the UK dial 00 44.

Time
Estonia is on Eastern European Time. It is two hours ahead of Greenwich Mean Time (GMT + 2) and from late March to late October it is three hours ahead of Greenwich Mean Time (GMT + 3).

Emergency telephone numbers
Police **110** or **112**
Fire **112**
Ambulance **112**

Driving in Finland *(Northern Europe)*

The regulations below should be read in conjunction with the General motoring information on pages 18–21.

Drinking and driving
The police can carry out random breath tests and blood tests. If the level of alcohol in the bloodstream is 0.05 per cent or more the driver will be penalised, which could include a daily fine or imprisonment and withdrawal of driving licence. The police test for alcohol and narcotics.

Driving licence
The minimum age at which a UK licence holder may drive a temporarily imported car is 18, a motorcycle (not exceeding 125cc) 16, exceeding 125cc 18. Motorists banned from driving in an EU or EEA country are not permitted to drive in Finland.

Fines
Police may impose, but not collect, on-the-spot fines up to €115 for parking and other minor infringements. The fine is payable at a bank within two weeks. For more serious offences there is a system of daily fines with a minimum of €6 per day. The police can remove an illegally parked vehicle; the release fee is up to €170.

Fuel
Unleaded petrol (95 and 98 octane) and diesel is available. Leaded petrol and LPG are not available. Carrying up to 10 litres of petrol in a can is permitted. Credit cards are accepted at most filling stations; check with your card issuer before travel. A new type of fuel, the SP95-E10 is now being sold throughout Finland. It is not suitable for use in all cars; check with your manufacturer before using it. If in doubt, use the standard SP98 octane unleaded fuel which continues to be available.

Lights
All vehicles must use headlights inside and outside built-up areas at all times.

Motorcycles
The use of dipped headlights during the day is compulsory. Drivers and passengers of mopeds or motorcycles must wear a crash helmet.

Motor insurance
Third-party insurance is compulsory.

Passengers/children in cars
A child less than 1.35m (4ft 5in) travelling in a car, van or lorry must be seated in a child seat or child restraint. A child under three years old may not be transported in a vehicle without a child restraint/seat, except in a taxi. Where a child restraint/seat is not available, a child three years and over must travel in the rear seat of the vehicle using a seat belt or other safety device attached to the seat. All child restraints/seats have to conform with the ECE standard 44/03 or EU directive 77/541EEC. It is the responsibility of the driver to ensure that all children under 15 are safely restrained.

Seat belts
It is compulsory for front- and rear-seat occupants to wear seat belts, if fitted.

Speed limits

The standard legal limits, which may be varied by signs, for **private vehicles without trailers** are: inside built-up areas 50km/h (31mph), outside built-up areas 80km/h (49mph) or 100km/h (62mph), according to the quality of road, with 80km/h (49mph) being the upper limit where there are no signs. On motorways the limit is 120km/h (74mph). There is no minimum speed on motorways. Temporary speed limits may be enforced on some or all roads by the local road districts. Reduced speed limits apply during the winter months, October to March (generally 20km/h or 12mph less than standard limits). Lower limits apply to **private cars towing a trailer or caravan:** outside built-up areas and on motorways 80km/h (49mph) and for a trailer without brakes 60km/h (37mph).

Additional information

- A warning triangle is compulsory.
- Winter tyres, marked M&S on the sidewall, are compulsory between 1 December and end of February. The recommended minimum tread depth is 3mm for winter tyres, but in difficult weather conditions it is 5mm.
- Pedestrians must use reflectors in the hours of darkness (any type of reflector is accepted). A car driver/passenger who steps out of a vehicle becomes a pedestrian and therefore must have a reflector, such as a jacket/waistcoat.
- Radar detectors are prohibited.
- Spiked tyres may be used from 1 November to the first Monday after Easter; if used they must be fitted on all wheels.
- Snow chains may be used temporarily when required by conditions. Drivers must be careful to avoid damaging the road surface.
- Beware of game (elk, reindeer, etc.) as they constitute a very real danger on some roads.
- It is prohibited to sound a horn in towns and villages except in cases of immediate danger.

Travel facts: Finland

Finnish Tourist Board
PO Box 33213
London W6 8JX
Tel: 020 7365 2512
www.visitfinland.com/uk

Banking hours
Finnish banks are open Monday to Friday 9.15am to 4.15pm. ATMs are fairly widespread and marked by the sign OTTO.

Credit/debit cards
Most major credit cards, including Visa, MasterCard and EuroCard, can be used for payment in many shops and restaurants.

Currency
The Euro (€) is the official currency of Finland. Banknotes are issued in €5, €10, €20, €50, €100, €200 and €500; coins in denominations of €1 and €2 and 1, 2, 5, 10, 20 and 50 cents.

Electricity
The electric current in Finland is 220V (230V) AC, 50Hz. A two-round-pin continental plug system is used.

Health care
Free or reduced-cost medical treatment is available in Finland to European visitors on production of a valid European Health Insurance Card (EHIC). See page 10. Comprehensive travel insurance is still advised and is essential for all other visitors.

Pharmacies
Medicines are available over the counter at pharmacies *(apteekki)*. Some have late opening hours.

Post offices
Post offices are open Monday to Friday 9am to 6pm. Post offices in grocery stores and petrol service stations may stay open until 8 or 9pm. Yellow post boxes on walls are for daily collections. Stamps are available at post offices, book and newspaper shops, R-kiosks, stations and hotels.

Safe water
Tap water is of the highest quality and can be consumed throughout the country. Bottled mineral water is available in shops and restaurants.

Telephones
Telephone calls can be made from booths, hotels and post offices. Many public telephones operate using a pre-paid card purchased from R-kiosks, Sonera shops and some post offices. The country code for Finland is 358. To call home from Finland dial the international code (00) followed by the country code. To call the UK dial 00 44.

Time
Finland is on Eastern European Time. It is two hours ahead of Greenwich Mean Time (GMT + 2) and from late March to late October it is three hours ahead of Greenwich Mean Time (GMT + 3).

Emergency telephone number
Emergency **112**

Driving in France and Monaco

(Western Europe)

The regulations below should be read in conjunction with the General motoring information on pages 18–21.

Drinking and driving

If the level of alcohol in the bloodstream is 0.05 per cent or more (0.02 per cent for bus/coach drivers), severe penalties include fine, imprisonment and/or confiscation of driving licence. Saliva tests will be used to detect drivers under the influence of drugs – severe penalties are as above. See also page 66.

Driving licence

The minimum age at which a UK licence holder may drive a temporarily imported car is 18, a motorcycle (up to 80cc) 16, a motorcycle (over 80cc) 18.

Fines

On-the-spot fines or 'deposits' are severe. An official receipt should be issued. Vehicles parking contrary to regulations may be towed away and impounded.

Fuel

Unleaded petrol (95 and 98 octane), diesel and LPG are available. Leaded petrol is no longer available – lead replacement petrol *(super carburant)* is available or a lead-substitute additive can be bought. Carrying petrol in a can is permitted, but not aboard ferries. A new type of fuel, the SP95-E10 *(Sans Plomb 95 octane, ethanol 10%: lead-free 95 octane containing 10 per cent of ethanol)* is now sold throughout France. This fuel is not suitable for all cars and you should check with your vehicle manufacturer before using it. If in doubt use the standard SP95 or SP98 octane unleaded fuel, which continues to be available alongside the new fuel. Credit cards are accepted at most filling stations; check with your card issuer for usage in France and Monaco before travel. Many automatic petrol pumps are operated by credit/debit card. However, cards issued outside France are not always accepted by these pumps.

Lights

Dipped headlights must be used in poor daytime visibility. It is highly recommended by the French government that four-plus wheeled vehicles use dipped headlights day and night (this is already compulsory for motorcycles).

Motorcycles

The use of dipped headlights during the day is compulsory for motorcycles. The wearing of crash helmets is compulsory for both driver and passenger of any two-wheel motorised vehicle.

Motor insurance

Third-party insurance is compulsory.

Motorways

See motorway map, page 68. To join a motorway follow signs with the international motorway symbol or signs with the words *'par Autoroute'* added. Signs with the words *'péage'* or *'par péage'* lead to toll roads. Motorcycles under 80cc are prohibited. Use green alternative routes to avoid traffic jams on major highways.

Most motorways charge tolls (see pages 69–70) except on certain sections in the immediate vicinity of towns such as Paris, Bordeaux, Lille, Lyon, Marseille and Metz.

On the majority of toll motorways in France a travel ticket is issued on entry and the toll is paid on leaving the motorway and also at occasional intermediate points. The travel ticket gives all relevant information about toll charges, including the toll category of the vehicle. At the exit point the ticket is handed in. On some motorways the toll collection is automatic; ensure you have the correct change ready to throw in the collecting basket. If change is required use the marked separate lane. **Note:** toll booths will not exchange traveller's cheques – ensure you have sufficient euros with you to meet the high toll charges (alternatively, credit cards are now accepted at most toll booths).

It is usually possible to obtain 24-hour service for a car and/or occupants every 40km (25 miles). Rest stops, most with toilet facilities, can be found every 15km (9 miles). Free emergency telephones are sited every 2km (1.24 miles) on most motorways.

Passengers/children in cars

Children under the age of 10 are not permitted to travel in the front seat of a vehicle, unless there are no rear seats or the rear seats are already occupied with children under 10, or there are no seat belts. Children under 10 must travel in an approved child seat or restraint adapted to their size according to European regulations, which classify child restraints in five different groups according to the child's weight. Group 0 to 10kg must be carried in a rear-facing car seat, placed either at the front passenger seat or the back (if placed at the front, the airbag must be switched off). Babies can also travel in a carry cot on the rear seat only. A child up to 13kg must be seated in a bigger version of the restraints used for the first weight group, installed under the same conditions. Children 9-18kg must be seated in a restraint with a harness or protection tray, children of 15-25kg and 22-36kg need a booster seat with a cushion or adult seat belt. Taxis are exempt but in other vehicles a fine is levied if a child is not restrained. It is the driver's responsibility to ensure all passengers under 18 are appropriately restrained.

Seat belts

It is compulsory for front- and rear-seat occupants to wear seat belts, if fitted.

Speed limits

The standard legal limits, which may be varied by signs, for **private vehicles with and without trailers** are: in built-up areas 50km/h (31mph), outside built-up areas 90km/h (55mph), but 110km/h (68mph) on urban motorways and dual-carriageways separated by a central reservation and 130km/h (80mph) on motorways. Lower limits of 80km/h (49mph) outside built-up areas, 100km/h (62mph) on dual carriageways and 110km/h (68mph) on motorways apply in wet weather and to visiting motorists who have held a driving licence for less than two years. Additionally, speed limits are reduced on motorways in built-up areas. The minimum speed limit on motorways is 80km/h (49mph). **Note:** Holders of EU driving licences exceeding the speed limit by more than 40km/h (25mph) will have their licences confiscated on the spot.

Additional information

- It is compulsory to carry a warning triangle (excludes motorcycles).

- Snow chains must be fitted to vehicles using snow-covered roads in compliance with the relevant road sign. Maximum speed limit 31mph (50km/h).
- It is compulsory to carry one reflective jacket (EN471) in the vehicle. This must be kept within the passenger compartment and put on before exiting the vehicle in emergency/breakdown situations.
- It is recommended that visitors equip their vehicle with a set of replacement bulbs.
- In built-up areas, give way to traffic coming from the right – *'priorité a droite'*. At signed roundabouts bearing signs *'Vous n'avez pas la priorité'* or *'Cédez le passage'* traffic on the roundabout has priority; where no such sign exists traffic entering the roundabout has priority.
- Overtaking stationary trams is prohibited when passengers are boarding/alighting.
- 'Blue zone' parking discs are available from police stations, tourist offices and shops.
- In built-up areas the use of the horn is prohibited except in immediate danger.
- Any apparatus with a screen that could distract the driver (such as TV, video, DVD equipment) should be positioned where the driver is unable to see it. This excludes GPS systems. It is prohibited to touch or program the device unless parked in a safe place. Road signs indicating the location of fixed speed cameras are being removed and additional fixed speed cameras added. A GPS-based navigation system with maps indicating camera locations should ideally be updated or deactivated as a minimum measure.
- It is prohibited to carry, transport or use radar detectors. Failure to comply with this regulation involves a fine of up to €1,500, and the vehicle and/or device may be confiscated.
- It is compulsory for all drivers including motorcyclists, but excluding mopeds, to carry a breathalyser in their vehicle. Failure to produce one will incur an on-the-spot fine of €11. The breathalyser has to be certified by the French authorities, showing an NF number. We recommend that two single-use breathalysers are carried, so if one is used or damaged you will still have a replacement to produce.

Road signs (a selection of standard and non-standard)

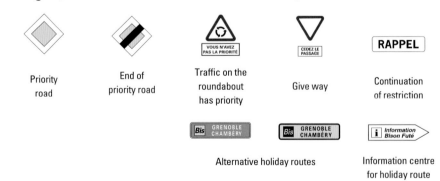

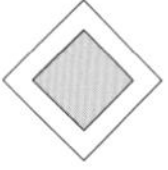
Priority road

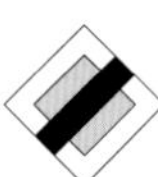
End of priority road

Traffic on the roundabout has priority

Give way

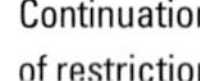
Continuation of restriction

Alternative holiday routes

Information centre for holiday route

Travel facts: France and Monaco

Atout France/The French Tourist Board
Lincoln House
300 High Holborn
LONDON WC1V 7JH
Tel: 090 68 244 123 (60p per minute at all times)
uk.franceguide.com

Banking hours
Banks are generally open Monday to Friday 9am to 4.30pm. Some open extended hours including Saturday morning, but may close on Monday instead. Banks close at noon on the day before a national holiday, as well as on the holiday itself.

Credit/debit cards
Credit cards are widely accepted in shops, restaurants and hotels. Visa (Carte Bleue), MasterCard (Eurocard) and Diners Club can be used in most ATM cash dispensers. Some smaller shops and hotels may not accept credit cards – always check first.

Currency
The currency in France is the euro (€). Euro coins are issued in denominations of 1, 2, 5, 10, 20 and 50 cents and €1 and €2. Banknotes are issued in denominations of €5, €10, €20, €50, €100, €200 and €500.

Electricity
The power supply in France is 220 volts. Sockets accept two-round-pin (or increasingly three-round-pin) plugs, so an adaptor is needed for most non-continental appliances. A transformer is needed for appliances operating on 110–120 volts AC.

Health care
Free or reduced-cost medical treatment is available in France and Monaco to European visitors on production of a valid European Health Insurance Card (EHIC). See page 10. Comprehensive travel insurance is still advised and is essential for all other visitors.

Toll Payments
UK motorists can now pre-pay tolls. Further information can be found at http://www.saneftolling.co.uk/

Pharmacies
Pharmacies – recognised by their green cross sign – have highly qualified staff able to offer medical advice, provide first aid and prescribe a wide range of drugs, although some are available by prescription *(ordonnance)* only.

Post offices
Post offices *(bureaux de poste)* are well signed, and generally open Monday to Friday 8am to 5pm, Saturday 8am to noon. In smaller places, opening hours may be shorter and offices may close for lunch. Main post offices sometimes stay open until later in the evenings. Post boxes are yellow.

Safe water
It is safe to drink tap water served in hotels and restaurants, but never drink from a tap marked *eau non potable* (not drinking water). Bottled water is cheap and widely available.

Telephones
All telephone numbers in France comprise 10 digits. There are no area codes; simply dial the number. In addition to coin-operated models, an increasing number of public phones take phone cards *(télécartes)*. These can be bought from France Telecom shops, post offices, tobacconists and at railway stations. Some cards give cheaper overseas calls than standard *télécartes*, so ask before you buy if you need to phone abroad. The country code for France is 33. To call home from France dial the international code (00) followed by the country code. To call the UK from France dial 00 44.

Time
France is on Central European Time, one hour ahead of Greenwich Mean Time (GMT + 1). From late March, when clocks are put forward one hour, until late October, French Summer Time (GMT + 2) operates.

Emergency telephone numbers
Police **17** or **112**
Fire **18** or **112**
Ambulance **15** or **112**

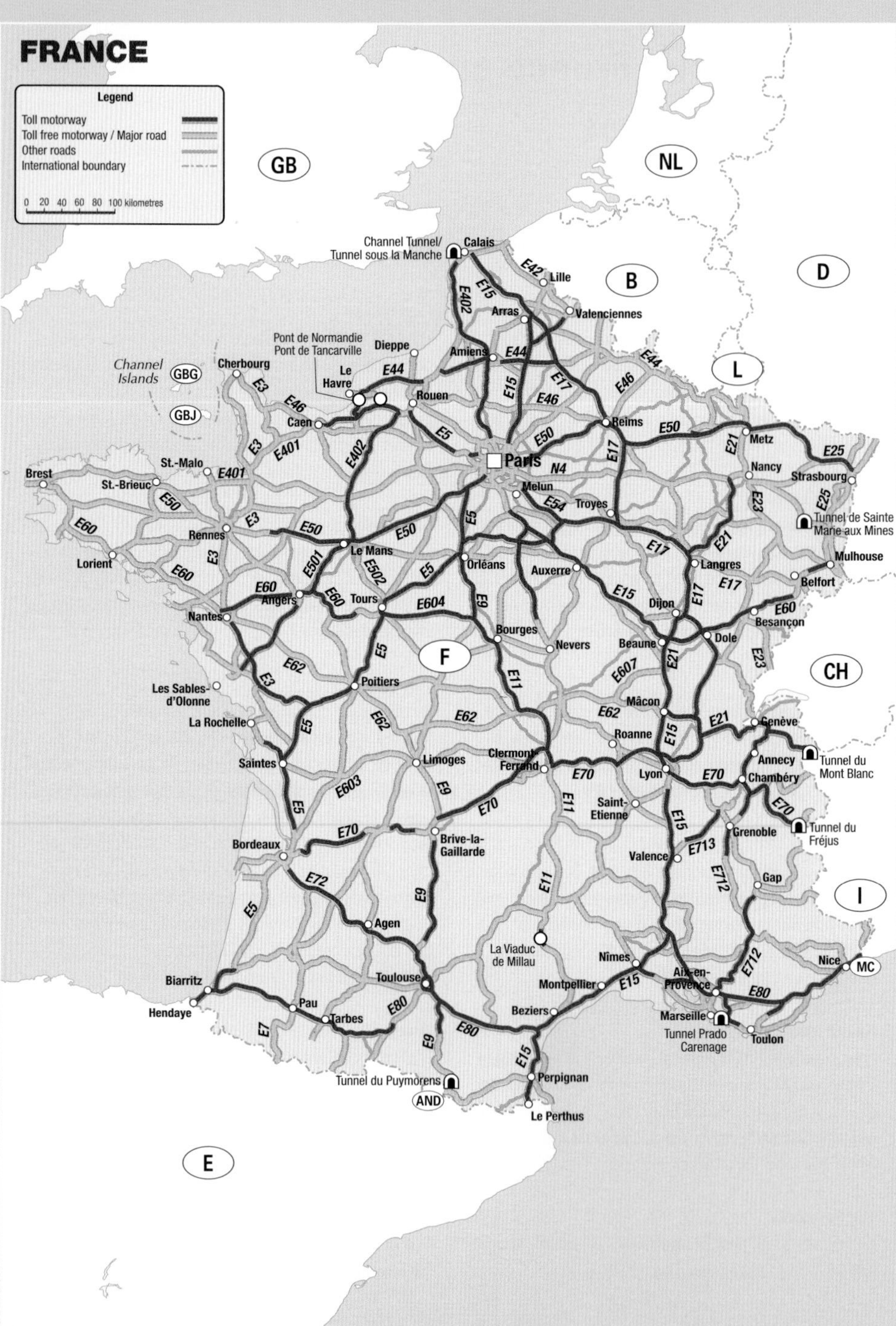
FRANCE
Legend
Toll motorway
Toll free motorway / Major road
Other roads
International boundary
0 20 40 60 80 100 kilometres
GB
NL
B
D
L
CH
I
E
F
AND
MC
GBG
GBJ
Channel Islands
Channel Tunnel/
Tunnel sous la Manche
Calais
Lille
Arras
Valenciennes
Pont de Normandie
Pont de Tancarville
Dieppe
Amiens
Cherbourg
Le Havre
Rouen
Caen
Reims
Metz
Paris
St.-Malo
Brest
St.-Brieuc
Melun
Troyes
Nancy
Strasbourg
Tunnel de Sainte Marie-aux Mines
Rennes
Le Mans
Orléans
Auxerre
Langres
Mulhouse
Belfort
Lorient
Angers
Tours
Dijon
Besançon
Nantes
Bourges
Nevers
Beaune
Dole
Les Sables-d'Olonne
Poitiers
Mâcon
La Rochelle
Roanne
Genève
Annecy
Tunnel du Mont Blanc
Saintes
Limoges
Clermont-Ferrand
Lyon
Chambéry
Saint-Etienne
Tunnel du Fréjus
Bordeaux
Brive-la-Gaillarde
Grenoble
Valence
Gap
Agen
La Viaduc de Millau
Nîmes
Nice
Biarritz
Toulouse
Montpellier
Aix-en-Provence
Hendaye
Pau
Tarbes
Beziers
Marseille
Tunnel Prado Carenage
Toulon
Tunnel du Puymorens
Perpignan
Le Perthus
E3
E5
E7
E9
E11
E15
E17
E21
E23
E25
E42
E44
E46
E50
E54
E60
E62
E70
E72
E80
E401
E402
E501
E502
E603
E604
E607
E712
E713
N4

Toll charges in euros

Road	Car	Car towing caravan/ trailer
E3/E5 (A83/A10) Nantes – Bordeaux	24.50	38.60
E5 (A10/A837) Bordeaux – La Rochelle	13.80	20.80
E5 (A63) Bordeaux – Hendaye (Spanish border)	7.30	11.10
E5 (A10) Paris – Tours	22.20	35.00
Tours – Bordeaux	31.70	49.60
Tours – Poitiers	10.50	16.60
Poitiers – Saintes	11.30	17.70
E5 (A13/A14) Rouen – Paris	6.20	9.70
E5/E11(A10/A71) Paris – Clermont-Ferrand	36.10	56.90
E9 (A66) Toulouse – Tunnel du Puymorens	4.80	7.30
Brive la Gaillarde – Toulouse	15.10	23.70
E15 (A26/A1) Calais – Paris	21.40	32.80
E15 (A1) Lille – Paris	15.70	22.90
E15 (A7/A9) Lyon – Montpellier	24.40	38.30
E15 (A6) Paris – Beaune	21.00	32.40
Paris – Mâcon	27.40	42.30
Paris – Lyon	32.90	51.50
E15 (A9) Orange – Montpellier	7.70	12.20
Montpellier – Le Perthus (Spanish border)	13.80	22.00
E15/E17 (A26) Calais – Reims	21.70	32.20
A4/A26 Reims – Troyes	9.60	14.20
E15/E17 (A4/A26/A5/A6) Reims – Lyon	40.00	60.70
E15/E80 (A7/A8) Lyon – Aix-en-Provence	24.20	38.00
E17 (A31) Dijon – Beaune	2.80	4.10
E17 (A31) Langres – Dijon	3.80	5.70
E17/E21/E62 (A26/A5/A39/A40) Reims – Chamonix Mont Blanc	54.80	84.00
E19 (A1/A2) Valenciennes – Paris	13.80	20.20
E19/E17 (A2/A26) Valenciennes – Reims	12.50	18.80
E21 (A39) Dijon – Dole	2.90	4.50
Dole – Bourg-en-Bresse	10.70	16.50
E21 (A31) Nancy – Langres	8.30	13.00
E25 (A4) Metz – Strasbourg	12.90	19.90
E25 (A40) Genève – Tunnel du Mont Blanc	5.70	10.20
E44 (A29) Le Havre – St Saens **(E402)**	7.80	11.60
E44 (A29/A16) Neufchâtel-en-Bray – Amiens	4.60	7.00
E44/E17 (A29/A26) Amiens – Reims	12.70	19.30
E46/E5 (A13/A14) Caen – Paris	23.20	38.90
E50 (A4) Paris – Reims	10.40	15.80
E50 (A4) Paris – Metz	24.50	37.30
E50 (A11/A81) Paris – Rennes	28.60	43.60
E50/E25 (A4) Paris – Strasbourg	37.40	55.80
E50/E501 (A11) Paris – Angers	25.50	41.90
E54/E15 (A5/A6/A31) Paris – Lyon (via Troyes)	38.20	58.50
E60 (A11) Angers – Nantes	8.40	13.20
E60 (A85) Angers – Tours	9.60	13.70
E60 (A36) Beaune – Besançon	7.30	11.30
Besançon – Belfort	7.40	11.40
Belfort – Mulhouse (German border)	2.80	4.40
E62 (A40) Mâcon – Genève	15.60	25.30
E70 (A89) Bordeaux – Brive-la-Gaillarde	16.80	26.40
Brive-la-Gaillarde – Clermont-Ferrand	11.90	19.30
E70 (A72) Clermont-Ferrand – Lyon	13.80	21.40
E70 (A43) Lyon – Chambéry	11.00	17.20

Toll charges in euros *continued*

Road	Car	Car towing caravan/ trailer
E70 (A43/A430)		
Chambéry – Albertville	16.20	25.30
E70/E711		
(A43/A48) Lyon – Grenoble	10.20	16.50
E72 (A62) Bordeaux – Toulouse	18.00	28.80
E80 (A8) Aix-en-Provence – Cannes	23.80	36.30
Cannes – Nice	2.90	4.40
Nice – Menton		
(Italian border)	2.30	3.50
E80 (A64) Bayonne – Toulouse	19.00	30.70
E80 (A9/A54) Montpellier – Arles	5.40	8.30
E80 (A8/A54) Montpellier –		
Aix-en-Provence	9.70	14.90
E80/E15		
(A61/A9) Toulouse – Montpellier	20.20	31.30
Toulouse – Le Perthus		
(Spanish border)	18.90	29.00
E402 (A28) Rouen – Le Mans	22.50	37.50
Le Mans – Tours	7.50	11.50
E402/401 (A16) Calais – Paris	18.90	27.00
E604 (A85) Tours – Bourges	13.50	21.70
E611/E62		
(A42/A40) Lyon – Genève	15.60	25.00
E712 (A51) Aix-en-Provence – Gap	12.60	18.70
E712 (A41) Chambéry – Genève	11.10	18.30
Grenoble – Chambéry	5.80	8.50
E712 (A51) Grenoble – Sisteron	13.30	5.00
E712/E25		
(A41/A40) Chambéry – Chamonix	12.70	20.30
E713 (A49) Valence – Grenoble	8.80	13.80
A14 Orgeval – Paris (La Défense)	8.10	16.10

Road	Car	Car towing caravan/ trailer
A52/A50 Aix-en-Provence – Toulon	7.80	11.80
A57 Toulon – Le Cannet des Maures	3.90	6.00
A87 Angers – Les Sables d'Olonne	9.60	15.70
A13/E5 Le Havre – Paris	19.50	33.30

Bridges and tunnels

La Rochelle (high season)	16.00	27.00
(La Rochelle – Ilede Ré on D735)		
Summer tariff		
Pont de Normandie (Le Havre)	5.30	6.10
Pont de Tancarville (Le Havre)	2.50	3.10
Tunnel du Puymorens		
(near Andorra/Spanish border)	6.40	13.00
Tunnel Prado Carenage (Marseille)		
(cars only)	2.70	
Tunnel du Fréjus (French/		
Italian border)	40.90	54.10
Tunnel du Mont Blanc (French/		
Italian border)	40.90	54.50
Le Viaduc de Millau (July & August)	8.90	13.30
(rest of year)	7.00	10.50
Tunnel de Sainte Marie		
aux Mines (on the A159 near Colmar)	8.00	17.10

Driving in Germany *(Central Europe)*

The regulations below should be read in conjunction with the General motoring information on pages 18–21.

Drinking and driving

If the level of alcohol in the bloodstream is 0.050 per cent or more, penalties include fines and the licence holder can be banned from driving in Germany. The blood alcohol level is nil per cent for drivers under 21 and those who have held a licence for less than two years; if even a small amount of alcohol is detected in the blood the fine is €250.

Driving licence

The minimum age at which a UK licence holder may drive a temporarily imported car and/or motorcycle is 18.

Fines

On-the-spot fines or a deposit can be imposed. Should a foreign motorist refuse to pay, their vehicle can be confiscated. Motorists can be fined for offences such as exceeding speed limits, abusive language, making derogatory signs and running out of petrol on a motorway. Wheel clamps are not used but vehicles causing obstruction can be towed away.

Fuel

Unleaded petrol (95 and 98 octane) and diesel are available. LPG is available from more than 5,000 stations. There is no leaded petrol, but you can buy a lead-substitute additive. It is permitted to carry petrol in a can in Germany, but it is forbidden aboard ferries. Credit cards are accepted at most filling stations; check with your card issuer before travel. High Ethanol Petrol (petrol containing 10% ethanol) is now widely available in Germany but is not suitable for all vehicles. Check with your manufacturer.

Lights

It is recommended to use dipped headlights or daytime running lights at all times. It is compulsory during daylight hours if fog, snow or rain restrict visibility. Driving with side lights (parking lights) alone is not allowed. Vehicles must have their lights on in tunnels.

Motorcycles

The use of dipped headlights during the day is compulsory. The wearing of a crash helmet is compulsory for both driver and passenger of a moped or motorcycle. Drivers of trikes and quads capable of exceeding 20km/h (12mph) must wear a helmet unless the vehicle is constructed with seat belts and they are worn.

Motor insurance

Third-party insurance is compulsory.

Passengers/children in cars

A child less than 1.5m (4ft 11in) and under 12 must sit in an approved child seat or restraint. It is prohibited to use a child seat in the front of a vehicle if the airbag has not been deactivated. All restraints/seats must confirm to ECE 44/03 or ECE 44/04. It is the responsibility of the driver to ensure that all children are safely restrained.

Seat belts

It is compulsory for front- and rear-seat occupants to wear seat belts, if fitted.

Speed limits

The standard legal limits, which may be varied by signs, for **private vehicles without trailers** are: in built-up areas 50km/h (31mph), outside built-up areas 100km/h (62mph) and on dual carriageways and motorways a recommended maximum of 130km/h (80mph). The minimum speed on motorways is 60km/h (37mph). Different speed limits apply in bad weather conditions. Lower limits apply for **private vehicles with a caravan or trailer** (up to 3.5 tonnes): outside built-up areas the maximum limit is 80km/h (49mph) and on motorways 100km/h (62mph). UK and Irish caravanners wanting to travel at 100Km/h on motorways have to pass a TÜV (MOT) test in Germany to confirm outfit suitability. A 100km/h sticker will then be fixed to the back of the caravan/trailer. However, problems may be experienced when encountering officials in different regions. The maximum speed limit for vehicles with snow chains is 50km/h (31mph).

Tyres

- All motorists are obliged to adapt their vehicles to winter weather conditions. This includes, but is not limited to, winter tyres and anti-freeze fluid for the washer system. Extreme weather may additionally require snow chains.
- It is prohibited to use summer tyres during winter weather conditions. Summer tyres are predominantly fitted to vehicles in the UK. Winter weather conditions include black ice, snow, ice, slush and hoarfrost. These conditions may be present even if the temperature is above 0 degrees. German law specifies that the tyres must be winter tyres or all-season tyres designed for use in wintry conditions. Suitable tyres will normally be marked 'M+S' or have a snowflake or snowy mountains symbol. Motorists in violation face fines of €40. If they actually obstruct traffic, the fine is €80. You may also be prevented from continuing your journey.

Additional information

- Visiting UK motorists are strongly advised to carry a warning triangle, as all drivers must signal their vehicle in case of breakdown; this is a compulsory requirement for residents.
- It is recommended that visitors carry a first-aid kit and set of replacement bulbs.
- Slow-moving vehicles must stop at suitable places and let others pass.
- It is prohibited to overtake or pass a school bus that is approaching a stopping point. Pass buses with caution. A fine will be imposed for non-compliance.
- Spiked tyres and the use of radar detectors are prohibited.
- A GPS-based navigation system that has maps indicating the location of fixed speed cameras must have the 'fixed speed camera PoI (Points of Interest)' function deactivated. Should you be unable to deactivate this function the GPS system must not be carried.
- All vehicles entering certain German cities, indicated by signs *'Umweltzone'*, must display a coloured sticker *(plakette)* on the windscreen. These can be obtained from technical inspection centres or approved garages in Germany for a fee of €5 to €10, on production of the registration certificate. The fine for non-compliance is €40. The fee is a 'one-off' charge and is valid in any German city as long as it remains fixed in the vehicle i.e. not transferred to another vehicle. Visit **www.umweltbundesamt.de/umweltzonen** for maps and detailed information.

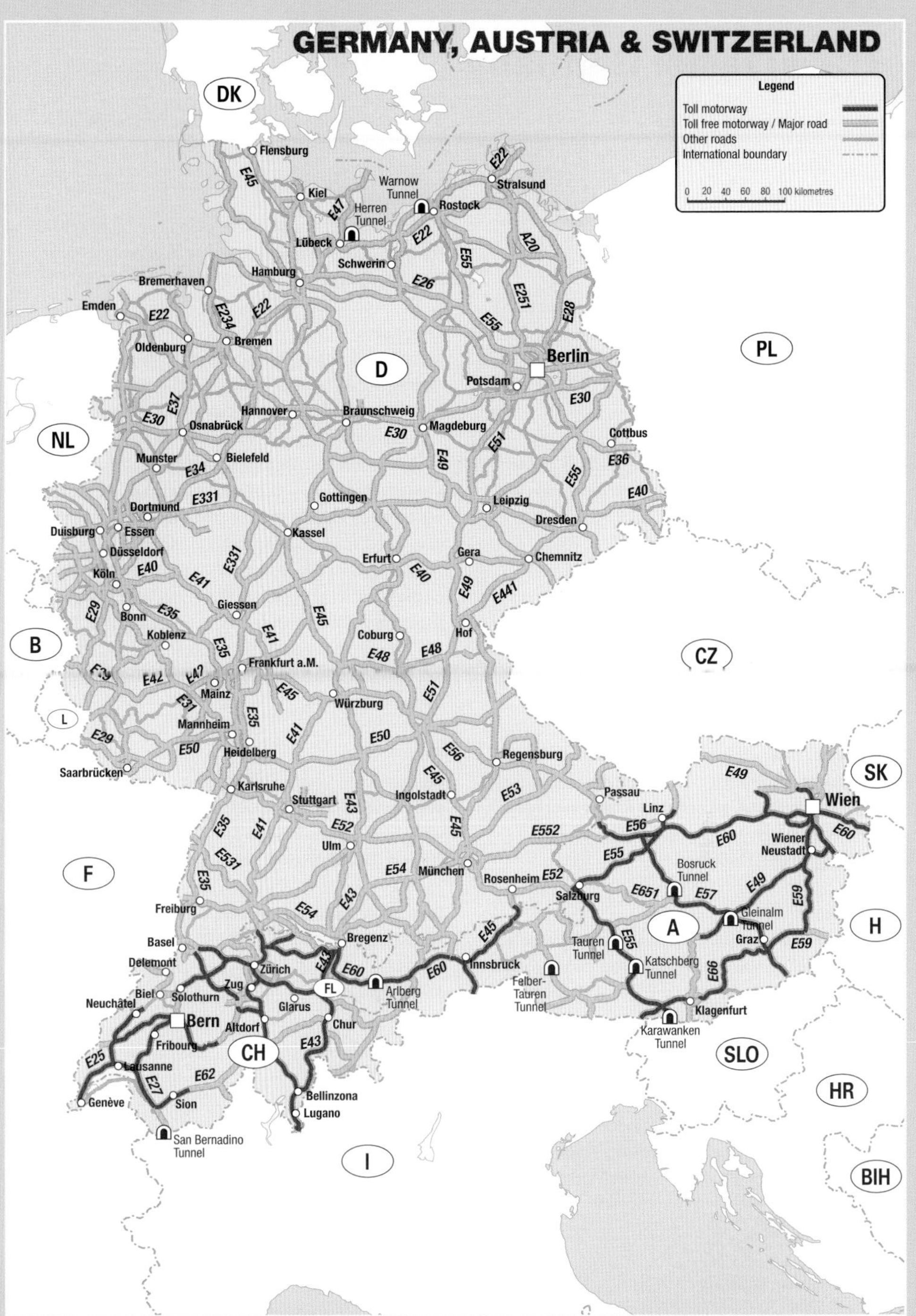
GERMANY, AUSTRIA & SWITZERLAND
Legend
Toll motorway
Toll free motorway / Major road
Other roads
International boundary
0 20 40 60 80 100 kilometres
DK
NL
B
L
F
D
PL
CZ
SK
H
A
CH
FL
SLO
HR
BIH
I
Flensburg
Kiel
Warnow Tunnel
Herren Tunnel
Rostock
Stralsund
Lübeck
Schwerin
Hamburg
Bremerhaven
Emden
Oldenburg
Bremen
Berlin
Potsdam
Hannover
Braunschweig
Magdeburg
Osnabrück
Munster
Bielefeld
Cottbus
Dortmund
Duisburg
Essen
Düsseldorf
Köln
Bonn
Koblenz
Gottingen
Kassel
Leipzig
Dresden
Erfurt
Gera
Chemnitz
Giessen
Coburg
Hof
Frankfurt a.M.
Mainz
Würzburg
Mannheim
Heidelberg
Saarbrücken
Karlsruhe
Stuttgart
Ingolstadt
Regensburg
Passau
Linz
Wien
Wiener Neustadt
Ulm
München
Rosenheim
Salzburg
Bosruck Tunnel
Gleinalm Tunnel
Graz
Tauren Tunnel
Katschberg Tunnel
Felber-Tauren Tunnel
Klagenfurt
Karawanken Tunnel
Freiburg
Basel
Delemont
Bregenz
Innsbruck
Arlberg Tunnel
Zürich
Zug
Biel
Solothurn
Neuchâtel
Glarus
Bern
Altdorf
Chur
Fribourg
Lausanne
Genève
Sion
Bellinzona
Lugano
San Bernadino Tunnel
E45
E47
E22
E55
A20
E26
E251
E28
E234
E30
E37
E51
E49
E34
E36
E331
E40
E41
E441
E29
E35
E48
E42
E31
E50
E56
E43
E53
E52
E531
E552
E54
E60
E57
E651
E59
E66
E62
E27
E25

Travel facts: Germany

German National Tourist Office
PO Box 2695
London W1A 3TN
Tel: 020 7317 0908
www.germany-tourism.co.uk

Banking hours
Opening hours can vary greatly although banks tend to open at 8.30 or 9am and close at 4pm (6pm Thursday). They are closed at weekends although many have a foyer with ATMs that can be accessed 24 hours a day.

Credit/debit cards
Credit cards with a Maestro, Cirrus, Delta or Plus logo can be used to withdraw cash and pay for goods and services all over the country.

Currency
The currency in Germany is the euro (€). Euro coins are issued in denominations of 1, 2, 5, 10, 20 and 50 cents and €1 and €2. Banknotes are issued in denominations of €5, €10, €20, €50, €100, €200 and €500.

Electricity
The power supply in Germany is 220 volts AC. Sockets accept two-round-pin (or increasingly three-round-pin) plugs, so an adaptor is needed for most non-continental appliances. A transformer is needed for appliances operating on 110–120 volts.

Health care
Free or reduced-cost medical treatment is available in Germany to European visitors on production of a valid European Health Insurance Card (EHIC). See page 10. Comprehensive travel insurance is still advised and is essential for all other visitors.

Pharmacies
Pharmacies *(apotheken)* can be found in every town and most villages throughout Germany. German pharmacists are highly trained and can offer excellent advice and over-the-counter medicines.

Post offices
Post offices are generally open Monday to Friday 8am to 6pm, Saturday 8am until noon. Post boxes are bright yellow.

Safe water
It is safe to drink the tap water in Germany, although mineral water *(Mineralwasser)* is also widely available. It's sold *mit Kohlensäure* (carbonated) or *still* (still).

Telephones
Most pay phones in Germany accept only phone cards *(telefonkarten)*, which can be bought at tourist or post offices, fuel stations, newspaper kiosks and elsewhere. International calls can be made from all pay phones except for those marked *National*. Phone calls can also be made from main post offices, where the connection will be made for you; you pay after the call has been completed. If you're using a phone card to call abroad, shop around for the best rates (these are usually printed on the back of the cards), as these vary from company to company. The country code for Germany is 49. To call home from Germany dial the international code (00) followed by the country code. To call the UK from Germany dial 00 44.

Time
Germany is on Central European Time, one hour ahead of Greenwich Mean Time (GMT + 1). From late March, when clocks are put forward one hour, until late October, Daylight Saving Time (GMT + 2) operates.

Emergency telephone numbers
Police **110**
Fire **112**
Ambulance **112**

Charges in euros

Bridges and tunnels	Car	Car towing caravan/ trailer
Warnow Tunnel (Rostock)	3.50	4.50
Herren Tunnel (Lübeck)	1.50	1.50

Driving in Gibraltar *(South West Europe)*

The regulations below should be read in conjunction with the General motoring information on pages 18–21.

Drinking and driving

The maximum level of alcohol in the bloodstream is 80mg of alcohol in 100ml of blood, 35mcg of alcohol on 100ml of breath and 107ml of alcohol in 100ml of urine.

Driving licence

The minimum age at which a UK licence holder may drive a temporarily imported car and or motorcycle is 18.

Fines

There are no on-the-spot fines, except when a vehicle is clamped or towed away.

Fuel

Leaded petrol and LPG is not available. Unleaded petrol (97 octane) and diesel is available. Carrying petrol in a can (in a purpose made steel container) is permitted on payment of duty. Credit cards are accepted at most filling stations; check before you travel.

Lights

The use of full headlights is prohibited; use only dipped headlights during the hours of darkness.

Motorcycles

The wearing of crash helmets is compulsory.

Motor insurance

A Green Card is compulsory (British motorists may, if they wish, produce a British certificate of motor insurance).

Passengers/children in cars

Children under three must use a child restraint appropriate for their weight, in any vehicle. There is only one exception in that they are permitted to travel unrestrained in the rear of a taxi if the right child restraint is not available. A rear-facing baby seat may be used only if the air bag has been deactivated. Children aged three and over and under 1.35m (4ft 5ins) in height must use an appropriate child restraint. A child over 12 or 1.35m (4ft 5ins) may use an adult seat belt.

Seat belts

It is compulsory for front- and rear-seat occupants to wear seat belts, if fitted.

Speed limits

The standard legal limits for cars, motorcycles and **towing combinations** under 3.5 tonnes is 50km/h (31mph) unless otherwise indicated by traffic signs.

Additional information

- The use of a car horn is not permitted within the city limits.
- The Spanish–Gibraltar frontier at La Linea is open to pedestrian and vehicular traffic of all EU nationalities and to nationals who do not require a visa.

Travel facts: Gibraltar

The Gibraltar Government Office
150 Strand
London
WC2R 1JA
Tel: 020 7836 0777
www.gibraltar.gov.uk/holiday.php

Banking hours
Banks are generally open Monday to Thursday from 9am to 3.30pm, and until 4.30pm on Friday. Bureaux de change open from 9am to 6pm.

Credit/debit cards
UK debit cards and all major credit cards are readily accepted in Gibraltar.

Currency
Sterling is the currency in Gibraltar, and British notes and coins circulate alongside Gibraltar pounds and pence. Gibraltar notes and coins are not accepted in the UK, and Scottish and Northern Irish notes are not accepted by most businesses in Gibraltar. Euros are accepted and change normally given in sterling.

Electricity
The power supply in Gibraltar is 230 volts AC, 50Hz. Two-pin plugs are standard.

Health care
If you are a British national resident in the UK you can obtain emergency treatment in Gibraltar by presenting your UK passport as proof of residence. However, as some emergency treatment may require transfer to Spain or the UK, you should obtain a European Health Insurance Card (EHIC). See page 10. Comprehensive travel and medical insurance is advised and is essential for all other visitors.

Pharmacies
Gibraltar has well-stocked pharmacies *(farmacia)* providing for the local community and visitors alike. The range of products is greater than across the frontier in Spain. Pharmacies are identified by a green cross.

Post offices
The General Post Office, 104 Main Street, is open Monday to Friday 9am to 4.30pm (closes 2.15pm mid-June to mid-September) and Saturday 10am to 1pm.

Safe water
The municipal water supply in Gibraltar is considered safe to drink. Bottled water is widely available.

Telephones
The country code for Gibraltar is 350. To call home from Gibraltar dial the international code (00) followed by the country code. To call the UK from Gibraltar dial 00 44.

Time
Gibraltar is on Central European Time (GMT + 1). Clocks are put forward one hour (GMT + 2) between March and October.

Emergency telephone numbers
Ambulance **190** or **112**
Fire **190** or **112**
Police **199** or **112**

Driving in Great Britain *(Western Europe)*

The regulations below, which cover England, Scotland, Northern Ireland and Wales, should be read in conjunction with the General motoring information on pages 18–21.

Drinking and driving

The maximum permitted level of alcohol in the blood is 0.08 per cent. The police can ask a driver suspected of having committed an offence to undergo a breath test. A penalty of up to £5,000 and/or 6 months' imprisonment and 12 months' withdrawal of driving licence, if the first time, can be imposed. The police may also carry out tests to detect a driver who may be under the influence of narcotics.

Driving licence

Visitors may use their national driving licence only if they have reached the minimum age to drive a vehicle in the UK; a motorcycle with or without sidecar, up to 25kW and a power to weight ratio not exceeding 0.16kW/kg, 17 years; a motorcycle with or without a sidecar above 25kW, 21years; a temporarily imported car, 17 years. A provisional (learner's) driving licence issued abroad is not valid for use in the UK.

Fines

Drivers without a satisfactory UK address who commit traffic offences will have to pay a financial penalty deposit equal to the amount of the fixed penalty or £300 as a deposit in respect of a potential court fine. The deposit has to be paid on the spot. Those who can provide a satisfactory UK address will be issued with a fixed penalty that has to be paid within 28 working days. The police and examiners from the Vehicle Operator and Services Agency (VOSA) can collect on-the-spot payments. Vehicles illegally parked are liable to a fine and may also be wheel-clamped or removed.

Fuel

Unleaded 95 octane petrol is sold as Premium Unleaded and unleaded 97 octane petrol as Super Unleaded. All UK petrol and diesel contains 10ppm or less sulphur. Leaded 4-star petrol and lead replacement petrol (LRP) are no longer available. Drivers of older cars designed to use leaded petrol are advised to use lead-replacement additives available widely in filling stations and accessory stores. Prices vary according to the region, fuel brand and type of outlet; supermarket prices may be lower. There are approximately 1,300 filling stations that sell Liquefied Petroleum Gas (LPG). If you are visiting the UK please be aware that UK filling stations use a bayonet-type LPG pump attachment that requires an adaptor for use with other European LPG vehicle connectors. UK filling stations do not generally have adaptors available so you should make sure that you have a suitable adaptor before travelling. The following two companies can supply 'European to UK' LPG adaptors: Autogas 2000 Ltd, **www.autogasshop.co.uk/autogaslpg-filling-adapters-1-c.asp**; Gasure LPG conversions and adapters, **www.gasure.co.uk/adaptors.htm**

Lights

Motorists must use side lights between sunset and sunrise and headlights at night (between half an hour after sunset and half an hour before sunrise) on all roads without street lighting and on roads where the street lights are more than 185m apart or are not lit. Motorists must use headlights or front and rear fog lights when visibility is seriously reduced, generally to less than 100m, use dipped headlights at night in built-up areas unless the road is well lit, and use headlights at night on lit motorways and roads with a speed limit in excess of 30mph (48km/h).

Motorcycles

It is compulsory for riders of motorcycles, scooters and mopeds to wear a safety helmet of an approved design. This also applies to passengers, except those in sidecars. The helmet must be manufactured to a standard similar to the British Standard. The use of headlights during the day is recommended.

Motor insurance

It is prohibited to drive an imported vehicle in the UK without adequate motor insurance. If the importer does not hold an insurance certificate valid for the UK, arrangements should be made prior to travel. Minimum third-party insurance, including trailers, is compulsory.

Motorway/bridge tolls

See motorway map on page 82. Tolls are payable when using certain motorway sections and some bridges and tunnels; see chart on page 83. Not all booths accept credit/debit cards. For information on the M6 toll visit **www.m6toll.co.uk**

Passengers/children in cars

Children under three years must use a child restraint appropriate for their weight in any vehicle (including vans and other goods vehicles). The only exception is that a child under three may travel unrestrained in the rear

of a taxi if the right child restraint is not available. Rear-facing baby seats must not be used in a seat with a frontal air bag unless the air bag has been deactivated manually or automatically. In vehicles where seat belts are fitted, children three years to 12 years and under 1.35m in height (4ft 5in) must use the appropriate child restraint. These children may travel in the rear and use an adult belt in a taxi, if the right child restraint is not available, or for a short distance in an unexpected necessity, or where two occupied child seats in the rear prevent the third being fitted. Drivers are responsible for making sure children under 14 years comply with these laws. Fines for non-compliance vary between £30 and £500.

Seat belts

Seat belts must be worn in the front and rear of vehicles, if fitted.

Speed limits

The standard legal limits, which may be varied by signs, for **private vehicles without trailers** are: in built-up areas up to 30mph (48km/h) unless otherwise indicated, outside built-up areas 60mph (96km/h), motorways and dual carriageways up to 70mph (112km/h). Cars **towing trailers or caravans** are limited to 50mph (80kp/h) outside built-up areas, and 60mph (96km/h) on dual carriageways and motorways. Cars **towing a trailer or caravan**, motor caravans with an unladen weight exceeding 3.5 tonnes, and vehicles adapted to carry more than eight passengers as well as the driver must not use the outside lane of a motorway with three or more lanes.

Additional information

- The rule of the road is drive on the left, overtake on the right.
- While it is not compulsory, it is recommended that you carry a warning triangle, first-aid kit and fire extinguisher. Motorists must not use a warning triangle on a motorway. Do not put yourself in danger by attempting even minor repairs. Call for assistance.
- It is an offence to use a hand-held phone or similar device when driving.
- It is prohibited to use the horn when the vehicle is stationary, except at times of danger due to another vehicle in movement, or as an anti-theft device. The use of the horn is prohibited in built-up areas from 11.30pm to 7am.
- A toll (congestion charge) is payable when driving or parking in central London on weekdays (Monday to Friday excluding public holidays) between 7am and 6pm. The entrances to the zone are indicated by the letter 'C' in white on a red background. At present the standard charge for most vehicles is £10 if purchased on or before the date of travel. Visit **www.tfl.gov.uk/roadusers/congestioncharging/** for further information. Tolls are payable on certain motorway sections, bridges and tunnels (see page 83).
- Visiting motorists driving left-hand drive vehicles should ensure that their headlights are adjusted for driving on the left, otherwise they risk being stopped by the police and subsequently fined up to £1,000.
- At some intersections called 'box junctions', criss-cross yellow lines are painted on the roadway. Traffic at these junctions must not enter 'the box' (i.e. the area of yellow lines) unless the exit road or lane is clear.

Travel facts: Great Britain

Britain and London Visitor Centre
1 Regent Street
London SW1Y 4XT
Tel: 0870 156 6366
www.visitbritain.com

Banking hours
Banks are generally open from Monday to Friday 9.30am to 4.30pm. Some banks open Saturday morning. Opening hours can differ considerably from branch to branch. Some banks in Scotland close for an hour at lunchtime. Many banks have 24-hour banking lobbies where you can access a range of services via machines.

Credit/debit cards
All credit/debit cards that bear the Visa, MasterCard or American Express logo are widely accepted in Britain. Retailers can charge more for goods and services bought by credit card, but they must display a notice if any price increase applies.

Currency
Britain's currency is the pound sterling (£), issued in banknotes of £5, £10, £20 and £50. There are 100 pennies or pence (p) to each pound and coins come in denominations of 1p, 2p, 5p, 10p, 20p, 50p, £1 and £2. Scottish £1 notes are still in circulation in Scotland. The Channel Islands and the Isle of Man have different coins and notes from the mainland but the monetary system is the same.

Electricity
The power supply in Britain is 230/240 volts AC. Sockets accept only three-square-pin plugs, so an adaptor is needed for continental appliances. A transformer is needed for appliances operating on 110–120 volts.

Health care
Free or reduced-cost medical treatment is available in Great Britain to European visitors on production of a valid European Health Insurance Card (EHIC). See page 10. Comprehensive travel insurance is still advised and is essential for all other visitors.

Pharmacies
Prescription and non-prescription drugs and medicines are available from chemists/pharmacies. Pharmacists can advise on medication for common ailments. Pharmacies operate a rota so there will always be one that is open 24 hours a day. Notices in pharmacy windows give details.

Post offices
Post offices are generally open Monday to Friday 9am to 5.30pm, Saturday 9am to noon.

Safe water
Tap water is safe to drink. Bottled mineral water is widely available but can be expensive.

Telephones
Traditional red phone booths are now rare; instead they come in a variety of designs and colours. Coin-operated phones take 10p, 20p, 50p and £1 coins (20p is the minimum charge), but phones taking British Telecom (BT) phone cards or credit cards are often more convenient. Phone cards are available from post offices and many shops. The country code for Britain is 44. To call home from Britain dial the international code (00) followed by the country code. To call Germany from Britain dial 00 49.

Time
Britain is on Greenwich Mean Time (GMT) in winter, but from late March to late October British Summer Time BST (GMT + 1) operates.

Emergency telephone numbers
Police **999** or **112**
Fire **999** or **112**
Ambulance **999** or **112**

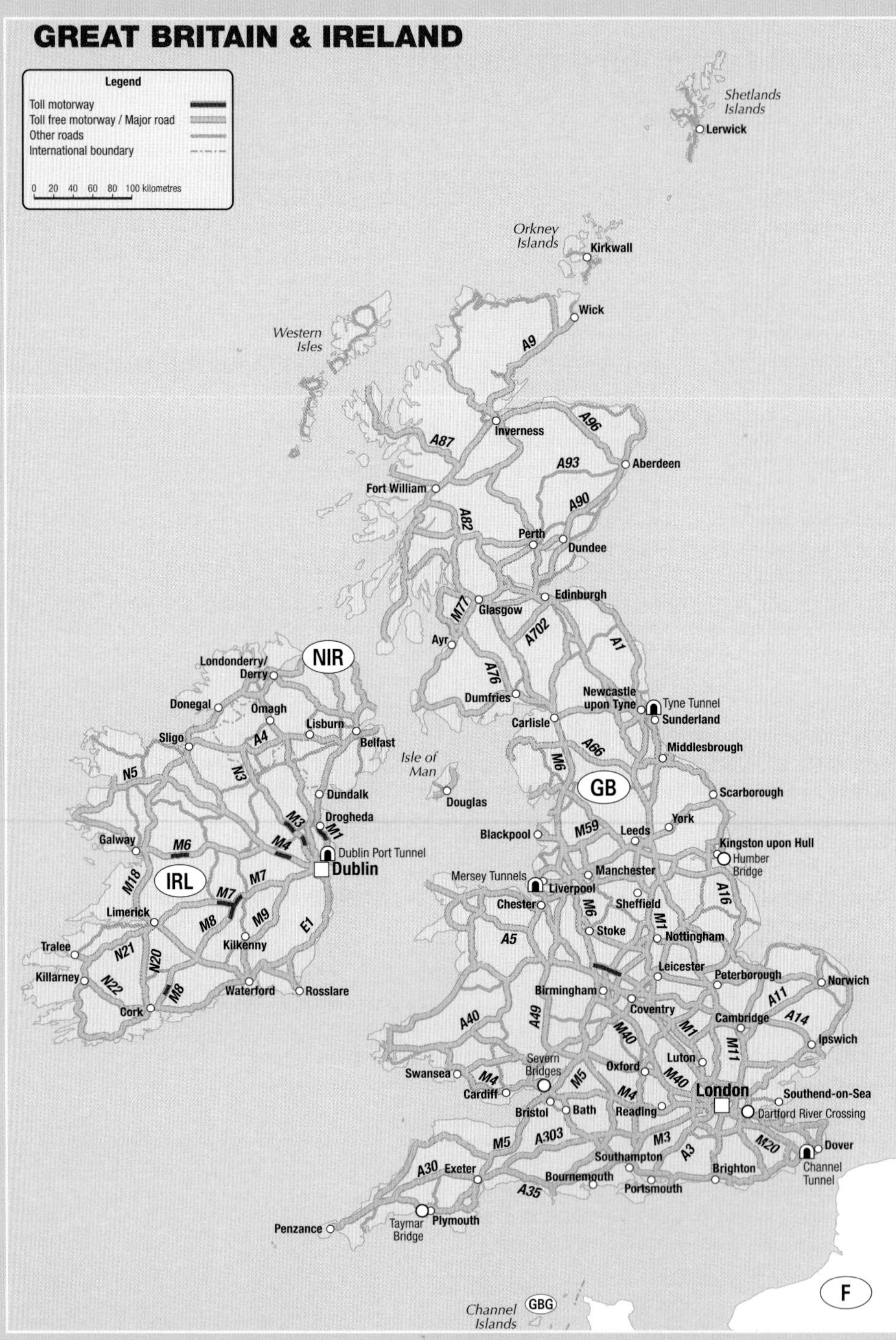

GREAT BRITAIN & IRELAND
Legend
Toll motorway
Toll free motorway / Major road
Other roads
International boundary
0 20 40 60 80 100 kilometres
Shetlands Islands
Lerwick
Orkney Islands
Kirkwall
Wick
Western Isles
A9
Inverness
A96
A87
A93
Aberdeen
Fort William
A90
A82
Perth
Dundee
Edinburgh
M77
Glasgow
A702
Ayr
A1
A76
Dumfries
Newcastle upon Tyne
Tyne Tunnel
Sunderland
Carlisle
A66
Middlesbrough
M6
GB
Scarborough
Isle of Man
Douglas
York
Blackpool
M59
Leeds
Kingston upon Hull
Humber Bridge
Manchester
Mersey Tunnels
Liverpool
A16
Chester
Sheffield
M1
Stoke
Nottingham
A5
Leicester
Peterborough
Norwich
Birmingham
Coventry
A11
A40
A49
Cambridge
A14
M40
M11
Ipswich
Luton
Severn Bridges
Swansea
M4
M5
Oxford
Cardiff
London
Southend-on-Sea
Bristol
Bath
Reading
Dartford River Crossing
A303
M3
M20
Dover
A3
Southampton
Channel Tunnel
A30
Exeter
Bournemouth
Brighton
Portsmouth
A35
Plymouth
Taymar Bridge
Penzance
Channel Islands
GBG
F
NIR
Londonderry/ Derry
Donegal
Omagh
Lisburn
Belfast
Sligo
A4
N3
N5
Dundalk
M3
Drogheda
M1
Galway
M6
M4
Dublin Port Tunnel
Dublin
M18
IRL
M7
Limerick
M8
M9
E1
Kilkenny
Tralee
N21
N20
Killarney
N22
Waterford
Rosslare
Cork

Toll charges in £ sterling

General	Car	Car towing caravan/ trailer
Central London	10.00	10.00

Central London congestion charge zone. Charge applies between 7am and 6pm weekdays and allows unlimited trips into or out of the zone in one day. For more information see page 80.

Durham	2.00	

Durham Peninsula (cathedral area) user charge zone. Charge applies 10am-4pm Mon-Sat (excl BH) Vehicles pay on exit.

Road		
M6 Toll Road		
Weekday night charge (11pm to 6am) (Main Plaza)	3.80	7.60
Weekday night charge (11pm to 6am) (Local Junction)	2.80	7.60
Weekday day charge (6am–11pm) (Main Plaza)	5.30	9.60
Weekday day charge (6am–11pm) (Local Junction)	4.00	9.00
Weekend charge (6am–11pm) (Main Plaza)	4.80	8.60
Weekend charge (6am–11pm) (Local Junction)	3.80	8.60

Bridges and Tunnels		
Aldwark Toll Bridge between Little Ouseburn and Aldwark/ Linton-on-Ouse	0.40	1.00
Batheaston Bridge off **A4** near Bath	0.50	1.00
Cartford Bridge 5 miles (3km) east of Poulton-le-Fylde	0.40	0.80

Bridges and tunnels	Car	Car towing caravan/ trailer
Cleddau Bridge on **A477**	0.75	1.50
Clifton Suspension Bridge on **B3129**. Not suitable for caravans over 4 tons	0.50	0.50
Dartford River Crossing on **A282/M25** (free 10pm–6am)	2.00	3.00
Dunham Bridge on **A57**	0.36	0.45
Humber Bridge on **A15**	1.50	4.00
Itchen Bridge on **A3025** (off-peak 0.50)	0.60	0.60
Mersey Tunnel (Kingsway) between Wallasey and Liverpool	1.40	2.80
Mersey Tunnel (Queensway) between Birkenhead and Liverpool	1.40	2.80
Middlesbrough Transporter on **A178**	1.20	2.00
Newport Transporter B4237 to A48	1.00	
Penrhyndeudraeth Bridge (Briwet Bridge; between **A496** and **A487**)	0.40	0.70
Second Severn Crossing on **M4** (westbound only)	6.20	6.20
Severn Bridge on **M48** (westbound only)	6.20	6.20
Swinford Bridge on **B4044**	0.05	0.10
Tamar Bridge on **A38** (eastbound only)	1.50	3.00
Tyne Tunnel on **A19**	1.20	1.20
Warburton Bridge on **B5159**	0.12	0.12
Whitchurch Bridge on **B471**	0.40	0.40
Whitney-on-Wye Bridge on **B4350**	0.50	0.50

Driving in Greece *(Southern Europe)*

The regulations below should be read in conjunction with the General motoring information on pages 18–21.

Drinking and driving

It is a criminal offence to drive if the level of alcohol in the bloodstream is 0.05 per cent or more. Nil percentage of alcohol is allowed in blood of drivers who have held a licence for less than two years, and to motorcyclists.

Driving licence

The minimum age at which a UK licence holder may drive a temporarily imported car and/or motorcycle (over 50cc) is 17.

Fines

Police can impose fines but not collect them on the spot. The fine must be paid at a Public Treasury office within 10 days. You can be fined for the unnecessary use of a car horn. Vehicles may be towed away if parked illegally, or if violating traffic regulations.

Fuel

Unleaded petrol (95 and 98 octane) and diesel *(petreleo)* is available. Leaded petrol is not available. Lead replacement petrol is sold as Super 2002 (98 octane). It is forbidden to carry petrol in a can in a vehicle. LPG may not be used in private cars, only in taxis. Credit cards are accepted at some filling stations. Check with your card issuer for use in Greece before travel.

Lights

Dipped headlights should be used in poor daytime visibility. The use of undipped headlights in towns is strictly prohibited.

Motorcycles

The use of dipped headlights during the day is compulsory. The wearing of crash helmets is also compulsory.

Motor insurance

Third-party insurance is compulsory.

Passengers/children in cars

Children under three years must be placed in a suitable child restraint. Approved child restraints are those conforming with standard ECE R44/03 (or later). Children between three and 11 years, measuring less than 1.35m must be seated in an appropriate child restraint for their size. From the age of 12, children measuring over 1.35m can wear an adult seat belt. Placing a rear-facing child restraint in the front passenger seat is allowed only on condition that the passenger airbag is deactivated.

Seat belts

It is compulsory for front-seat occupants to wear seat belts.

Speed limits

The standard legal limits, which may be varied by signs, for **private vehicles without trailers** are: in built-up areas 50km/h (31mph) for cars, 40km/h (24mph) for motorcycles; outside built-up areas 90km/h (55mph) or 110km/h (68mph) for cars, 70km/h (43mph) for motorcycles; motorways 130km/h (80mph) for cars and 90km/h (55mph) for motorcycles. When **towing**

a trailer or caravan, the limits outside built-up areas are 80km/h (49mph), and 90km/h (55mph) on motorways.

Additional information

- A fire extinguisher, first-aid kit and warning triangle are compulsory.
- The police are empowered to confiscate the number plates of illegally parked vehicles throughout Greece. Generally this applies only to Greek-registered vehicles, but the drivers of foreign-registered vehicles should beware of parking illegally.
- Snow chains may be used when roads are covered with snow or ice, usually between November and March. The maximum speed limit for cars with chains is 50km/h (31mph).

Travel facts and toll charges: Greece

Greek National Tourism Organisation
4 Conduit Street
London W1S 2DJ
Tel: 020 7495 9300 (enquiries and information)
www.visitgreece.gr

Banking hours
Banks are generally open Monday to Friday 8am to 2pm (Friday 1.30pm) and 8am to 6pm in major tourist areas.

Credit/debit cards
Cash is still the preferred method of payment in Greece. Only the larger and more expensive hotels, restaurants and shops will accept payment by credit card.

Currency
The currency in Greece is the euro (€). Euro coins are issued in denominations of 1, 2, 5, 10, 20 and 50 cents and €1 and €2. Banknotes are issued in denominations of €5, €10, €20, €50, €100, €200 and €500.

Electricity
The power supply in Greece is 230 volts AC, 50Hz. Sockets accept two-round-pin plugs.

Health care
Free or reduced-cost medical treatment is available in Greece to European visitors on production of a valid European Health Insurance Card (EHIC). See page 10. Comprehensive travel insurance is still advised and is essential for all other visitors.

Pharmacies
Pharmacies *(farmakeío)*, indicated by a green cross, give advice and prescriptions for common ailments. Codeine is banned in Greece and you can be fined for carrying it.

Post offices
Post offices, identified by a yellow OTE sign, are generally open Monday to Friday 8am to 2pm (7pm in major tourst areas). Stamps *(ghramatósima)* are also sold at kiosks or shops selling cards. Post boxes are yellow; use the slot marked *Exoterico* for overseas mail.

Safe water
Tap water is chlorinated and is regarded as safe to drink. Bottled mineral water it is cheap to buy and is widely available.

Telephones
Calls from phone booths can be made using a phone card available from kiosks, OTE offices and some shops. They are sold in units of 100, 500 and 1,000. You can also make calls from street kiosks, which have metered phones and charge at the end of the call, although connections tend to be poor. The country code for Greece is 30. To call home from Greece dial the international code (00) followed by the country code. To call Britain from Greece dial 00 44.

Time
Greece is on Eastern European Time. It is two hours ahead of Greenwich Mean Time (GMT + 2) and from late March to late October it is three hours ahead of Greenwich Mean Time (GMT + 3).

Emergency telephone numbers
Police, Fire and Amulance **112**
Tourist Police **171**

Toll charges in euros

Road		Car
A1/E75	Lamia – Inofita	4.90
A1/E75	Katerini – Larisa	3.30
A1/E75	Larisa – Lamia	5.50
A1/E75	Thessaloniki – Katerini	2.80
A1/E75	Lamia – Afidnes	6.05
A1/E75	Afidnes – Athina	2.05
A7/E65	Korinthos – Tripoli	2.90
A8/E65–E55	Korinthos – Patra	6.20
A8/E94	Athina – Korinthos	9.00
E94	Athina – International Airport E. Venizelos	2.80
A8/E65-E55	Rio-Antirio Bridge	12.90
A7/E65	Artemission Tunnel	2.40
E55	Aktion Tunnel	3.00

Driving in Hungary *(Central Europe)*

The regulations below should be read in conjunction with the General motoring information on pages 18–21.

Drinking and driving

Nil per cent of alcohol is allowed in the driver's blood. Amounts of less than 0.08 per cent incur a fine, more than 0.08 per cent incur legal proceedings.

Driving licence

The minimum age at which a UK licence holder may drive a temporarily imported car and/or motorcycle is 17. All valid UK driving licences should be accepted in Hungary. This includes the older all-green paper-style UK licences (in Northern Ireland older paper-style with photographic counterpart) although the EC appreciates that these may be more difficult to understand and that drivers may wish to update them before travelling abroad. Alternatively, older licences may be accompanied by an International Driving Permit (IDP).

Fines

On-the-spot fines can be imposed. The police must hand over the payment order to transfer the amount of the fine to be paid within 30 days. The fine is payable only in the Hungarian forint (HUF) – credit cards are not accepted. Cash should not be given to a policeman at the roadside. Wheel clamps are in use.

Fuel

Unleaded petrol (95 octane), diesel *(dizel or gazolaj)* and LPG are available. Leaded petrol is not available. It is permitted to carry up to 10 litres of petrol in a can. Credit cards are accepted at some filling stations, check with your card issuer for usage in Hungary. Cash is the most usual form of payment.

Lights

The use of dipped headlights is compulsory at all times outside built-up areas. At night the use of full beam in built-up areas is prohibited.

Motorcycles

The use of dipped headlights is compulsory at all times. The wearing of crash helmets is compulsory for both driver and passenger.

Motor insurance

Third-party insurance is compulsory. Should a visitor cause an accident involving a Hungarian citizen they must report it to the Association of Hungarian Insurance Companies.

Passengers/children in cars

A child under three years of age may travel in a vehicle only if using a suitable child-restraint system appropriate for their weight; they are permitted to travel in the front of the vehicle using this restraint if it is rear facing and there is no air bag or it has been deactivated. Children under 1.5m (4ft 11in) and over three years must use a suitable child-restraint system and be seated in the rear of the vehicle.

Seat belts

It is compulsory for front- and rear-seat occupants to wear seat belts, where fitted.

Speed limits

The standard legal limits, which may be varied by signs, for **private vehicles without trailers** are: in built-up areas 50km/h (31mph), outside built-up areas 90km/h (55mph) or 110km/h (68mph) on semi-motorways and 130km/h (80mph) on motorways. When **towing a trailer or caravan** the limits are: 50km/h (31mph) in built-up areas, 70km/h (43mph) outside built-up areas and on semi-motorways, and 80km/h (49mph) on motorways. Vehicles with snow chains must not exceed 50km/h (31mph). In city centres, roads with a 30km/h (18mph) speed limit are increasingly common.

Additional information

- A first-aid kit and warning triangle are compulsory.
- All pedestrians walking on a road, or road shoulder outside a built-up area, must wear a reflective jacket at night and when visibility is poor. Any person exiting a vehicle outside a built-up area in a breakdown situation becomes a pedestrian and therefore must wear a reflective jacket.
- The use of snow chains or their presence in a car can be made compulsory on some roads when weather conditions require.
- It is recommended that the driver of a conspicuously damaged vehicle entering Hungary obtains a police report confirming the damage at the time of entry, otherwise lengthy delays may be encountered at the frontier when leaving Hungary. This report should be obtained from the police of the country where the car was damaged.
- Motorway tax is payable for the use of M1 (Budapest–Hegyeshalom), M3 (Budapest –Gorbehaza–Nyiregyhaza), M5 (Budapest–Kiskunfelegyhaza–Szeged–Roszke/border with Serbia), M6 (M0–Erd–Dunaujvaros), M7 (Budapest–Lake Balaton–Letenye, border with Croatia), M30 (Emod–Miskolc), M35 (Gorbehaza-Debrecen). The electronic *vignette* and any toll charges must be paid in forints. Credit cards accepted: Visa, Eurocard/MasterCard, DKV and UTA. The *vignette* can be purchased in person, online, or by telephone (land line or mobile). When a motorist has purchased an *e-vignette*, a confirmation message will be sent or a coupon issued. This document must be kept for one year after the expiry of validity. The motorway authorities check all vehicles electronically, and verify the registration number, the category of toll paid and the validity of the *e-vignette*. For further information visit **www.motorway.hu.** *Vignettes* are available for four days (vehicles up to 3.5 tonnes only), one week, one month or 13 months. Fines are imposed for non-display. The Hungarian motoring association recommends that foreign motorists wishing to purchase a *vignette* at the border have cash in Hungarian forints. *Vignettes* should be purchased only from outlets where the prices are clearly displayed at the set rate. See toll charges, opposite.
- Motorist should be wary of contrived incidents, particularly on the Vienna–Budapest motorway, designed to stop motorists and expose them to robbery.
- There are restrictions on traffic entering Budapest when air pollution exceeds a fixed level on two consecutive days.
- Spiked tyres are prohibited.
- The use of the horn is prohibited in built-up areas, except in case of danger.

Travel facts and toll charges: Hungary

Hungarian Tourist Office
46 Eaton Place
London SW1X 8AL
Tel: 0800 360 00000
www.gotohungary.co.uk
www.hungary.com

Banking hours
Banks are generally open Monday to Friday 8am to 4pm, and some are open until noon on Saturday.

Credit/debit cards
The acceptance of credit cards is limited; they are becoming increasingly popular but they are not accepted everywhere. Most ATMs in Hungary accept Visa, MasterCard (including Cirrus and Maestro), American Express and Diners Club.

Currency
Hungary's currency is the forint (Ft or HUF). The denominations of forint banknotes are Ft200, 500, 1,000, 2,000, 5,000, 10,000 and 20,000. There are coins of 1, 2, 5, 10, 20, 50 and 100 forints.

Electricity
Hungary has 220–230V AC power supply. Electrical sockets take two-round-pin plugs.

Health care
Free or reduced-cost medical treatment is available in Hungary to European visitors on production of a valid European Health Insurance Card (EHIC). See page 10. Comprehensive travel insurance is still advised and is essential for all other visitors.

Pharmacies
A pharmacy *(gyógyszetár* or *patica)* sells both prescription and non-prescription medicines (bring your own medication if you need a specific product). Information about the nearest 24-hour facility is posted at all pharmacies.

Post offices
Buy stamps *(bélyeg)* at a post office *(posta)*, news kiosk or tobacconist *(dohanyaruds)* or from a hotel. Post boxes are wall mounted and red with a calling-horn emblem.

Safe water
Although tap water is safe, you may find it causes mild upsets. Bottled mineral water and soda water are widely available and advised.

Telephones
The public phones take Ft10, Ft20, Ft50 and Ft100 coins or phone cards available from hotels, post offices, petrol stations, newsagents, kiosks and street vendors. The minimum charge for a call is Ft20.The country code for Hungary is 36. To call home from Hungary dial the international code (00) followed by the country code. To call the UK from Hungary dial 00 44.

Time
Hungary is on Central European Time, one hour ahead of GMT (GMT + 1). Daylight Saving Time comes into effect from the end of March to the end of October, CET + 1 (GMT + 2).

Emergency telephone numbers
Police **107** Fire **105** Ambulance **104**
International emergency number **112**

Toll charges in forints
For details of where to buy the motorway tax see page 88.

General	Car	Car towing caravan/ trailer
1-day *vignette*		3,375.00
7-day *vignette*	2,975.00	8,255.00
1 month	4,780.00	13,970.00
1 year	42,980.00	123,975.00

Driving in Iceland *(North Atlantic)*

The regulations below should be read in conjunction with the General motoring information on pages 18–21.

Drinking and driving

The maximum permitted level of alcohol in the driver's blood is 0.05 per cent. If it is more than 0.049 per cent, severe penalties include the withdrawal of your driving licence, a prison sentence and a fine of up to 160,000 króna.

Driving licence

The minimum age at which a UK licence holder may drive a temporarily imported car and/or motorcycle (over 50cc) is 17. All valid UK driving licences should be accepted in Iceland. This includes the older all-green-style UK licences (in Northern Ireland older paper-style with photographic counterpart). Alternatively, older licences may be accompanied by an International Driving Permit (IDP).

Fines

On-the-spot fines may be imposed by the traffic police. In some circumstances, payment may be made at a police station or the police officer will provide details of the official bank account into which the fine must be paid. Illegally parked cars may be towed away and a parking fine imposed.

Fuel

Unleaded petrol (95 and 98 octane) and diesel are available but not LPG. There is no leaded petrol (lead-substitute petrol is available as 98 octane). It is forbidden to import fuel in a spare can. Some credit cards are accepted at most filling stations; check with your card issuer for usage in Iceland before you travel.

Lights

The use of dipped headlights during the day is compulsory; there are fines for non-compliance.

Motorcycles

The use of dipped headlights during the day is compulsory. The wearing of crash helmets is compulsory for both driver and passenger.

Motor insurance

Third-party insurance is compulsory.

Passengers/children in cars

Children under three must be in an approved restraint system adapted to their size. Children over three years and under 1.5m must be in a child restraint suitable for their height and weight. Children must not be placed on the front seat of a vehicle with an active airbag.

Seat belts

It is compulsory for front/rear-seat occupants to wear seat belts, if fitted.

Speed limits

The standard legal limits, which may be varied by signs, for **private vehicles without trailers** are: in built-up areas 50km/h (31mph), outside built-up areas 80km/h (49mph) on gravel roads and 90km/h (55mph) on asphalt roads. When **towing**, the limit on asphalt is 80km/h (49mph).

Additional information

- It is compulsory to carry a warning triangle,

which must be used in conjunction with hazard warning lights.

- Winter tyres are compulsory on roads affected by winter weather from 1 November–18 April (exact dates vary).
- It is recommended that visitors equip their vehicle with first-aid kit, fire extinguisher and a set of replacement bulbs.
- Snow chains may be used when necessary.
- The use of spiked tyres is permitted between 15 November and 15 April.
- It is prohibited to drive outside marked roads or tracks in order to protect flora and fauna.
- Weather conditions can change rapidly; on a local phone dial 1777 between 7.30am and 10pm for information about road conditions.

Travel facts: Iceland

Embassy of Iceland in the UK
2a Hans Street, London SW1X 0JE
Tel: 020 7259 3999
There is currently no Icelandic tourist board in the UK, but the embassy can deal with enquiries.

Banking hours
Banks are generally open Monday to Friday 9.15am to 4pm. They may stay open later Thursday and Friday.

Credit/debit cards
Credit/debit cards are widely accepted.

Currency
Iceland uses the króna, plural krónur (kr). (International abbreviation: ISK). Notes are in denominations of 500, 1000, 2000 and 5000, and coins of 1, 5, 10, 50, 100.

Electricity
Power supply is 220/240 volts AC, 50Hz. Sockets accept two-round-pin plugs. UK visitors need an adaptor.

Health care
Free or reduced-cost medical treatment is available in Iceland to European visitors on production of a valid European Health Insurance Card (EHIC). See page 10. Comprehensive travel insurance is still advised and is essential for all other visitors.

Pharmacies
Most pharmacies *(apótek)* have English-speaking staff. For 24-hour opening **tel: 118**.

Post offices
Post offices are found in the main communities around Iceland, and opening hours are generally Monday to Friday 8.30am to 4.30pm. Stamps can also be bought in most souvenir outlets where postcards are sold. Icelandic stamps are of particular interest to collectors.

Safe water
Cold tap water is some of the best in the world (beware of the hot, which may come from natural thermal sources and smell sulphurous). In the hills, clean spring water is usually safe to drink but avoid glacial meltwater.

Telephones
Public telephones *(sími)* are usually found outside the post office. They take coins (ISK10, 50 and 100) or phone cards – available from post offices/telephone stations. Iceland's country code is 354. To call home from here dial the international code (00) followed by the country code. To call the UK from Iceland dial 00 44.

Time
Iceland is on GMT all year. It does not go on to Daylight Saving Time. In the north, the sun does not fully set in June; in January there may be only 3.5 hours of daylight.

Emergency telephone number
Police, Fire and Ambulance **112**

Toll charges in Icelandic króna
Bridges and tunnels

Hvalfjörður Tunnel	1.00	1.30

Driving in Ireland (Republic of)

(Western Europe)

The regulations below should be read in conjunction with the General motoring information on pages 18–21.

For regulations covering Northern Ireland see Great Britain, pages 78–80.

Drinking and driving

If the level of alcohol in the bloodstream is more than 0.05 per cent, severe penalties, including a fine and/or imprisonment plus disqualification, can be imposed. The lower limit of 0.02 per cent applies to novice drivers. Random breath testing is in force throughout Ireland.

Driving licence

The minimum age at which a UK licence holder may drive a temporarily imported car or motorcycle (exceeding 150cc) is 17.

Fines

A member of the Garda may hand a person a fixed penalty notice; this will detail that an offender has to pay the fine within 28 days. This may be handed to the offender directly or attached to the windscreen. If a fine is not paid within 28 days, the fine increases by 50%. A person can opt to go to court. Illegally parked cars can be clamped and sometimes towed.

Fuel

Unleaded petrol (95 octane) and diesel are available. There is no leaded petrol. The availability of lead replacement petrol and LPG is extremely limited. Petrol in a can is permitted, but forbidden on board ferries. Credit cards are accepted at most filling stations; check with your card issuer for use in Ireland before travel.

Lights

Dipped headlights should be used in poor daytime visibility.

Motorcycles

The use of dipped headlights during the day is compulsory. The wearing of crash helmets is compulsory for both driver and passenger.

Motor insurance

Third-party insurance is compulsory.

Passengers/children in cars

Children under three years of age may not travel in a car (other than a taxi) unless they are placed in an appropriate child restraint. They can travel on the front seat of the car if they are in a rear-facing restraint system and the air bag is disabled. Children over three who are under 1.5m (4ft 11in) and weigh less than 36kg must use an appropriate child restraint when travelling in cars fitted with seat belts. If the car is not equipped with seat belts they must travel on the rear seats.

Seat belts

It is compulsory for front- and rear-seat occupants to wear seat belts, if fitted.

Speed limits

The standard legal limits, which may be varied by signs, for **private vehicles without trailers** are: in built-up areas 50km/h (31mph), outside built-up areas 60–100km/h (37–62mph) according to road signs and 120km/h (75mph) on motorways.)

Additional information

- A warning triangle is compulsory for vehicles with an unladen weight exceeding 1,524kg (1.5 tonnes).
- The rule of the road is drive on the left, overtake on the right.
- Horns must not be used between 11.30pm and 7am.
- Distances are given in kilometres.
- Some level crossings have manual gates, which motorists must open and close.
- The use of radar detectors is prohibited; they can be confiscated by the Garda (Irish police).
- A barrier-free toll system now operates on the M50 Dublin. Number plates are recorded and the fee must be paid by 8pm the following day at any of the 'payzone' outlets. Further information can be found on **www.eflow.ie**

Travel facts and toll charges: Ireland

Irish Tourist Board
Nations House, 103 Wigmore Street
London W1U 1QS
Tel: 020 7518 0800
www.discoverireland.com
www.visitireland.com

Banking hours
Banks are generally open Monday to Friday 10am to 4pm. Some banks in small towns close 12.30 to 1.30pm. Banks open until 5pm one day a week (Thursday in Dublin).

Credit/debit cards
Credit and debit cards are accepted in major hotels, restaurants and large stores. Check first in small or rural establishments.

Currency
The monetary units in the Republic of Ireland is the euro (€); in Northern Ireland it is the pound sterling (£), see page 81. These are not interchangeable. Euro banknotes come in denominations of €500, €200, €100, €50, €20, €10 and €5; coins in denominations of €2 and €1 and 50, 20, 10, 5, 2 and 1 cents.

Electricity
The power supply in the Republic of Ireland is: 230 volts AC. Electrical sockets take either plugs with two round pins or three square pins.

Health care
Free or reduced-cost medical treatment is available in the Republic of Ireland to European visitors on production of a valid European Health Insurance Card (EHIC). See page 10. Comprehensive travel insurance is still advised and is essential for all other visitors.

Pharmacies
Prescription and non-prescription drugs and medicines are available from pharmacies.

Post offices
Opening hours are generally Monday to Friday 9am to 5.30/6pm, Saturday 9am to 1pm.

Safe water
Tap water in Ireland is safe to drink. Bottled mineral water is widely available.

Telephones
Public telephone boxes are being replaced by glass and metal booths. Lift the handset, insert the correct coins (10, 20 or 50 cents) or phone card and dial. The country code for Ireland is 353. To call home from the Republic dial the international code (00) followed by the country code. To call the UK from the Republic dial 00 44.

Time
Ireland observes Greenwich Mean Time (GMT), but from late March, when clocks are put forward one hour, until late October, Summer Time (GMT + 1) operates.

Emergency telephone numbers
Police, Fire, Ambulance and Coastal Rescue **999** or **112**

Toll charges in euros

Roads	**Car**	**Car towing caravan/ trailer**
M1 Toll Drogheda Bypass	1.90	1.90
M3 (2 Toll plazas) Dublin & Kells	2.80	2.80
M4 Toll Kinnegad – Enfield – Kilcock	2.90	2.90
M6 Toll Galway – Ballinasloe	1.90	1.90
M7/M8 Toll M7 Portlaoise – Castletown, **M8** Portlaoise – Cullahill	1.90	1.90
M8 Toll Rathcormac – Fermoy	1.90	1.90
Bridges and tunnels		
East Link Toll Bridge East of Dublin	1.75	1.75
M50 Dublin Port Tunnel (northbound) 4–7pm	10.00	10.00
M50 Dublin Port Tunnel (southbound) 6–10am	10.00	10.00
M50 West Link Toll Bridge on Dublin Outer Ring (peak time)	3.10	3.10
N18 Limerick Tunnel	1.90	1.90

Driving in Italy and San Marino

(Southern Europe)

The regulations below should be read in conjunction with the General motoring information on pages 18–21.

Drinking and driving

If the level of alcohol in the bloodstream is 0.051 per cent or more, severe penalties, which include fines, confiscation of vehicle and imprisonment, can be imposed. For professional drivers and drivers with less than three years experience the alcohol limit is zero.

Driving licence

The minimum age at which a UK licence holder may drive a temporarily imported car and/or motorcycle (over 125cc or with a passenger) is 18. All valid UK driving licences should be accepted in Italy. This includes the older all-green-style UK licences (in Northern Ireland older paper-style with photographic counterpart) although drivers may wish to update them before travelling, if time permits. Alternatively, older licences may be accompanied by an International Driving Permit (IDP).

Fines

On-the-spot fines can be imposed. Fines for speeding offences are particularly heavy. The police can impose the fine and collect one quarter of the maximum fine; they must give a receipt for the amount paid. Fines for serious offences committed at night between 10pm and 7am are increased by one third; serious offences include speeding, going through a red light etc. Illegally parked vehicles can be clamped or towed away and a fine imposed.

Fuel

Unleaded petrol (95 octane and 98 octane), diesel *(gasolio)* and LPG are available. Leaded petrol is not available, but you can buy a lead-substitute additive. Carrying petrol in a can is permitted. Credit cards are accepted at most filling stations. Check with your card issuer for usage in Italy and San Marino before travel.

Lights

The use of dipped headlights during the day is compulsory outside built-up areas and during snow and rain or poor visibility. Rear fog lights may be used only when visibility is less than 50m or in case of strong rain or intense snow. Lights must be switched on in tunnels.

Motorcycles

The use of dipped headlights during the day is compulsory on all roads. The wearing of crash helmets is compulsory for both driver and passenger. The vehicle can be seized for non-compliance. It is prohibited to carry a child under five years of age on a moped or motorcycle. The registration certificate must state that the moped/motorcycle is designed to carry a passenger. Motorcycles under 150cc are not allowed on motorways.

Motor insurance

Third-party insurance is compulsory.

Motorways

See map, page 98. To join a motorway, follow the green signposts (vehicles that cannot exceed 40kmh/25mph and motorcycles under 150cc are prohibited). On the majority of toll motorways a ticket is issued on entry (do not enter in the yellow TELEPASS lanes) and the toll is paid on leaving the motorway. The entry ticket gives information about the toll charges, including the toll category of the vehicle. At the exit use either the white or blue lanes, return your ticket and pay. Blue lanes are self service and take credit cards or Viacard. White lanes are self service and take cash, credit cards or Viacard. White lanes with operators take cash, credit cards and pre-paid Viacard. Toll booths will not exchange traveller's cheques. If paying with cash ensure you have sufficient euros to meet the high toll charges. Credit cards are accepted at the majority of toll booths. Visit **www. autostrade.it** for further information.

It is usually possible to obtain services for a car and/or occupants every 30–50km (19–31 miles). Emergency telephones are sited every 2km (1.24 miles) on most motorways.

Passengers/children in cars

Children travelling in foreign-registered vehicles, i.e in a UK-registered vehicle, must be secured according to UK legislation.

Seat belts

It is compulsory for front- and rear-seat occupants to wear seat belts, if fitted.

Speed limits

The standard legal limits, which may be varied by signs, for **private vehicles without trailers** are: in built-up areas 50km/h (31mph), outside built-up areas 90km/h (55mph) on ordinary roads, 110km/h (68mph) on dual carriageways and 130km/h (80mph) on motorways. Newly qualified drivers must not exceed a speed limit of 90km/h (55mph) outside built-up areas and 100km/h (62mph) on motorways. This applies for three years after passing their test.

Note: in wet weather lower speed limits of 90km/h (55mph) apply on dual carriageways and 110km/h (68mph) on motorways.

Restrictions apply if vehicles have spiked tyres.

Additional information

- A warning triangle is compulsory for all vehicles with more than two wheels.
- The wearing of a reflective jacket/waistcoat is compulsory if the driver and/or passenger(s) exits a vehicle that is immobilised on the carriageway at night or in poor visibility. This does not apply to two-wheeled vehicles.
- Vehicles must be equipped with winter tyres or snow chains from 15 October until 15 April. Provinces can introduce their own legislation making the use of winter tyres or snow chains compulsory during winter conditions.
- Any vehicle with an overhanging load must display a **fully** reflectorised square panel 50cm x 50cm (20in x 20in) that is red and white diagonally striped; a fine may be imposed if the sign is not displayed. This also applies to vehicles such as cars/caravans carrying bicycles at the rear.
- Tolls are levied on the majority of motorways. See pages 99–100.
- In built-up areas the use of the horn is prohibited except in cases of immediate danger.
- The transportation or use of radar detectors is prohibited; violation of this regulation will result in a fine between of €708 and €2,834 and confiscation of the device.
- A pollution charge is levied in the centre of Milan. Charges apply Monday to Friday

generally from 7.30am until 7.30pm. Drivers must purchase an 'area c' pass (formerly Eco-pass) before entering the restricted zone. Tariffs vary according to the emissions of the vehicle. Further information can be found at https://areac.atm-mi.it/Areac/iweb/Acquisto.aspx.

- Traffic is restricted in many historical centres/major towns known as *'Zone a Traffico Limitato'* or ZTLs; circulation is permitted only for residents. Entering such areas normally results in a fine by post.
- Either winter tyres or snow chains may be used on roads where chains are compulsory.

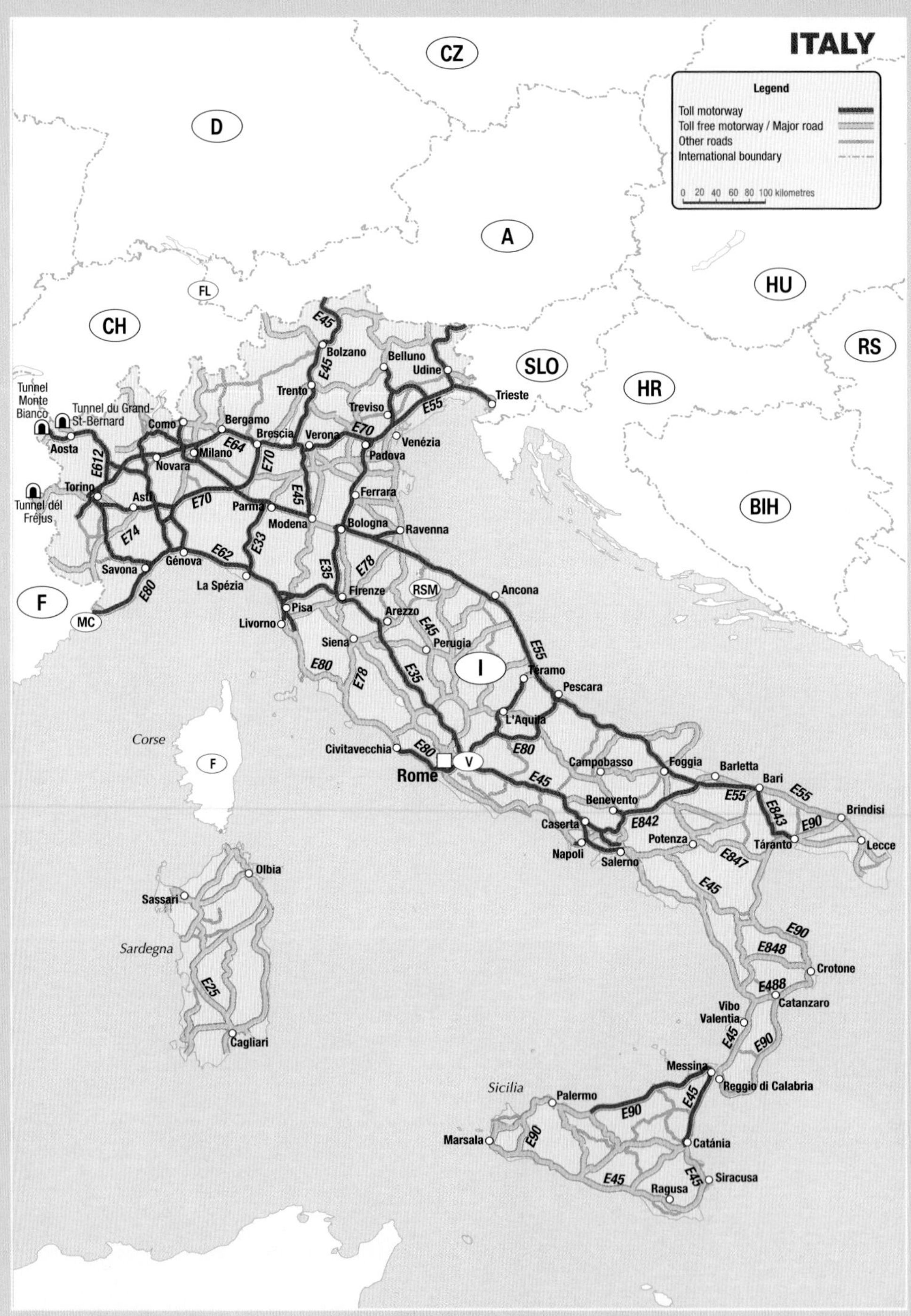
ITALY
Legend
Toll motorway
Toll free motorway / Major road
Other roads
International boundary
0 20 40 60 80 100 kilometres
CZ
D
A
HU
RS
SLO
HR
BIH
CH
FL
F
MC
RSM
I
V
Corse
Sardegna
Sicilia
Tunnel Monte Bianco
Tunnel du Grand-St-Bernard
Tunnel dél Fréjus
Aosta
Torino
Asti
Novara
Como
Milano
Bergamo
Brescia
Verona
Bolzano
Trento
Belluno
Udine
Treviso
Trieste
Venézia
Padova
Ferrara
Parma
Modena
Bologna
Ravenna
Génova
Savona
La Spézia
Pisa
Livorno
Firenze
Arezzo
Siena
Perugia
Ancona
Téramo
Pescara
L'Aquila
Civitavecchia
Rome
Campobasso
Foggia
Barletta
Bari
Brindisi
Lecce
Táranto
Benevento
Caserta
Napoli
Salerno
Potenza
Crotone
Catanzaro
Vibo Valentia
Messina
Reggio di Calabria
Palermo
Marsala
Catánia
Siracusa
Ragusa
Olbia
Sassari
Cagliari
E45
E55
E70
E64
E612
E74
E62
E33
E80
E35
E78
E842
E843
E90
E847
E848
E488
E25

Toll charges in euros

Road	Car	Car towing caravan/ trailer
E25 (A26)		
Génova – Alessandria	5.00	6.70
Génova – Iselle (Swiss border)	15.30	20.90
E25 (A5)		
Santhià – Aosta	20.40	30.90
E33 (A15)		
Parma – La Spézia	13.70	19.70
E35 (A1)		
Milano – Bologna	13.90	19.20
Bologna – Firenze	7.40	10.00
Firenze – Roma	16.80	23.20
E35 (A8/A9)		
Milano – Chiasso (Swiss border)	3.70	6.10
Stelvio Pass	10.00	10.00
E35/E45 (A1)		
Milano – Napoli	52.20	71.80
E45 (A1)		
Roma – Napoli	15.00	20.70
E45 (A3)		
Nápoli – Salerno	3.90	5.50
E45 (A14 Dir)		
Bologna – Ravenna	4.80	6.60
E45 (A18)		
Messina – Catánia	3.60	10.70
E45 (A22)		
Passo del Brennero (Austrian border) Trento	9.90	13.50
Trento – Verona	6.10	8.40
Verona – Modena	6.80	9.40
E45/E55 (A14)		
Bologna – Ancona	13.20	18.20

Road	Car	Car towing caravan/ trailer
E45/E55 (A14)		
Bologna – Taranto	49.30	67.90
E55 (A14)		
Ancona – Pescara	10.10	13.90
Pescara – Bari	21.70	29.70
E55 (A14)		
Pescara – Taranto	26.20	35.90
E55 (A23)		
Udine – Tarvisio (Austrian border)	6.90	9.40
E62 (A7)		
Milano – Tortona	4.10	5.80
Milano – Génova	9.70	13.40
E62 (A8)		
Milano – Varese	3.00	4.20
E64 (A4)		
Torino – Milano	13.10	17.20
Milano – Bréscia	6.00	8.30
E64/E70 (A4)		
Milano – Venézia	18.60	25.90
E70 (A4)		
Bréscia – Verona	3.60	5.00
Verona – Padova	4.80	6.60
Padova – Venézia	3.20	4.50
E70 (A4)		
Venézia – Trieste	10.70	14.70
E70 (A21)		
Torino – Alessandria	7.90	10.90
Alessandria – Piacenza	6.80	9.10
Torino – Piacenza	15.50	20.90
Piacenza – Brescia	5.50	7.70

Toll charges in euros *continued*

Road		Car	Car towing caravan/ trailer
E70 (A32)			
	Torino – Tunnel del Fréjus (France)	11.90	21.90
E74 (A33)			
	Asti – Cuneo	2.50	5.10
E76 (A11)			
	Firenze – Pisa Nord	6.90	9.70
E80 (A10)			
	Génova – Savona	2.70	3.70
	Savona – Ventimiglia (French border)	13.60	26.10
E80 (A12)			
	Génova – La Spezia	10.80	15.10
	La Spezia – Livorno	7.90	11.60
	Génova – Viareggio	13.50	19.20
	Génova – Livorno	15.80	22.60
	Livorno – Roma	24.70	34.20
E80 (A24)			
	Roma – Téramo	15.20	20.10
E80 (A25)			
	Roma – Pescara	18.50	24.60
E90 (A20)			
	Messina – Palermo	11.20	32.90
E612/E25 (A5)			
	Torino – Aosta	22.50	34.00
E717 (A6)			
	Torino – Savona	11.70	17.30
E842 (A16)			
	Napoli – Bari	18.10	24.80
E843 (A14)			
	Bari – Táranto	4.50	6.20
A13	Bologna – Pádova	6.50	8.90
	Bologna – Ferrara	2.30	3.20
	Ferrara – Pádova	4.20	5.80
A22	Brenner Pass – Modena	22.80	31.30
A27	Venezia – Belluno	7.40	10.20
A30	Caserta – Salerno	5.30	7.50
A31	Vicenza – Trento	9.90	13.60

Bridges and Tunnels		Car	Car towing caravan/ trailer
E25 (A5)	Tunnel Monte Bianco	40.90	54.40
E70 (A32)	Tunnel dél Fréjus	40.90	54.10
	Tunnel Munt La Schera (Livigno)	10.00	20.00
	Tunnel du Grand-St-Bernard	25.00	38.90

Milano congestion charge

€5 weekdays 7.30am-7.30pm

Travel facts: Italy and San Marino

Italian State Tourist Board
1 Princes Street
London W1B 2AY
Tel: 020 7408 1254
www.enit.it

Banking hours
Banks are generally open Monday to Friday 8.30am to 1.30pm. Major banks may open Saturday and have longer weekeday opening hours.

Credit/debit cards
All major credit cards are widely accepted in Italy. Check with your provider. Traveller's cheques can be exchanged at most hotels and shops and at the foreign exchange offices *(cambio)* in main railway stations and at the airports.

Currency
The currency in Italy is the euro (€). Euro coins are issued in denominations of 1, 2, 5, 10, 20 and 50 cents and €1 and €2. Banknotes are issued in denominations of €5, €10, €20, €50, €100, €200 and €500.

Electricity
The power supply is 220 volts AC, 50Hz. Plugs are two-round-pin continental types; UK visitors will require an adaptor.

Health care
Free or reduced-cost medical treatment is available in Italy to European visitors on production of a valid European Health Insurance Card (EHIC). See page 10. Comprehensive travel insurance is still advised and is essential for all other visitors.

Pharmacies
Prescription and other medicines are available from a pharmacy *(una farmacia)*, indicated by a green cross. Pharmacies usually open at the same time as shops Tuesday to Saturday 8am to 1pm and 4pm to 8pm, Monday 4pm to 8pm, and take it in turns to stay open through the afternoon and into late evening.

Post offices
Post offices *(posta)* are usually open Monday to Friday 8.30am to 2pm, Saturday 8.30am to noon or 2pm. Post boxes are red for normal post and blue for priority post *(posta prioritaria)*. Stamps *(francobolli)* can be bought from post offices, bars, and tobacconists showing a 'T' sign.

Safe water
Tap water is safe. So, too, is water from public drinking fountains unless marked '*Acqua Non Potabile*'.

Telephones
Telecom Italia (TI) pay phones are on streets and in bars, tobacconists and restaurants. Most take coins or a phone card *(carta telefonica)*, bought from post offices, shops or bars. Tear the corner off the card before use. When calling within Italy, simply dial the full number. Rome numbers all begin with 06. Dial 12 for operator or directory enquiries. The country code for Italy is 39. To call home from Italy dial the international code (00) followed by the country code. To call the UK from Italy dial 00 44.

Time
Italy is on Central European Time, one hour ahead of Greenwich Mean Time (GMT +1). From late March, when clocks are put forward one hour, until late October, Daylight Saving Time (GMT + 2) operates.

Emergency telephone numbers
General emergencies **113** or **112**
Police **113** or **112**
Fire **115** or **112**
Ambulance **118** or **112**

Driving in Latvia *(Eastern Europe)*

The regulations below should be read in conjunction with the General motoring information on pages 18–21.

Drinking and driving

The maximum permitted level of alcohol in the bloodstream for drivers with more than two years' experience is 0.05 per cent. For drivers with less than two years' experience the maximum permitted level of alcohol in the bloodstream is 0.02 per cent. Penalties are severe if the levels are exceeded. The police can test for alcohol and narcotics.

Driving licence

The minimum age at which a UK licence holder may drive a temporarily imported car and/or motorcycle (over 125cc) is 18.

Fines

The police can issue but not collect fines on the spot; the fines have to be paid or an appeal lodged within 30 days. Police control speeds closely and give fines for even the smallest of speeding offences.

Fuel

Unleaded petrol (95 and 98 octane), diesel and LPG are available. There is no leaded petrol, but petrol with lead substitute is available. Carrying petrol in a can is permitted (duty payable). Visa and MasterCard are accepted at most filling stations; check with your card issuer for usage in Latvia before travel. Cash payments are accepted only in the local currency.

Lights

The use of dipped headlights during the day is compulsory.

Motorcycles

The use of dipped headlights during the day is compulsory. The wearing of crash helmets is compulsory for both driver and passenger.

Motor insurance

Third-party insurance is compulsory.

Passengers/children in cars

A child less than 1.5m (4ft 11in) in height must use either a child-restraint system appropriate to height and weight or the lap strap of an adult seat belt.

Seat belts

It is compulsory for front- and rear-seat occupants to wear seat belts, if fitted.

Speed limits

The standard legal limits, which may be varied by signs, for **private vehicles without trailers** are: in built-up areas 50km/h (31mph), outside built-up areas 90km/h (55mph), dual carriageways 100km/h (62mph). When **towing a trailer or caravan**, the limit outside built-up areas and on dual carriageways is 80km/h (49mph). There are no motorways in Latvia. In some residential areas the speed limit is 20km/h (12mph).

Additional information

- A first-aid kit, fire extinguisher and warning triangle are compulsory. Winter tyres are compulsory from 1 December until 1 March for vehicles up to 3.5 tonnes.
- Spiked tyres are prohibited from 1 May until 1 October.
- It is the responsibility of the driver to carry reflective clothing in case of a forced stop and if leaving the car at night or in poor visibility. This reflective colthing must be worn by anyone who leaves the car.
- It is recommended that visitors carry an assortment of spares for their vehicle, such as a fan belt, replacement bulbs and spark plugs.
- Latvia has very little signposting and very few road markings.
- The use of equipment that interferes with police equipment is prohibited.

Travel facts: Latvia

Latvia Tourism Bureaux
72 Queensborough Terrace
London W2 3SH
Tel: 020 7229 8271
www.latviatourism.lv
www.latviatravel.com

Banking hours
Banks and their retail branches are usually open Monday to Friday 9am to 5 or 6pm; branches at supermarkets close at 8 or 9pm on weekdays. Some banks open 9am to 1pm on Saturday.

Credit/debit cards
Many transactions in Latvia are still dealt with in cash. The most commonly used credit cards accepted in Latvian hotels, larger shops, restaurants, cafés and supermarkets are Eurocard, MasterCard, Visa, JCB, Diners Club, American Express and Eurocheque. ATMs can be found in cities and towns.

Currency
The Latvian national currency is the lat (LVL), 1 lat = 100 santimi. Bank notes are in denominations of LVL500, 100, 50, 20, 10 and 5. Coins are in denominations of LVL2 and 1, and 50, 20, 10, 5, 2 and 1 santimi.

Electricity
The electrical supply in Latvia is 220 volts AC, 50Hz. Sockets take two-round-pin plugs.

Health care
Free or reduced-cost medical treatment is available in Latvia to European visitors on production of a valid European Health Insurance Card (EHIC). See page 10. Comprehensive travel insurance is still advised and is essential for all other visitors.

Pharmacies
There is an extensive network of pharmacies throughout Latvia; some are at hospitals and health centres, shopping malls, stations etc. Opening hours vary; 24-hour pharmacies are denoted with the letter 'A'.

Post offices
Opening hours at post offices *(Pasts)* are Monday to Friday 8am to 5 or 7pm and 8am to 4pm on Saturday. Opening hours for sub-post offices in small villages vary.

Safe water
Drinking water in major towns is generally safe, though you may prefer to buy bottled mineral water.

Telephones
Public phone boxes can be found on the streets and in train and bus stations, shopping malls etc., and contain information about how to make calls within Latvia, international country codes and local telephone books. Public pay phones accept phone cards, credit cards or coins. Phone cards are available from kiosks, shops, post offices and petrol stations where the Lattelekom sign is displayed. The country code for Latvia is 371. To call home from Latvia dial the international code (00) followed by the country code. To call the UK from Latvia dial 00 44.

Time
Latvia is on Eastern European Time. It's two hours ahead of Greenwich Mean Time (GMT + 2), but from late March, when clocks are put forward one hour, to late October, Summer Time (GMT + 3) operates.

Emergency telephone numbers
Police **02** or **112**
Fire **01** or **112**
Ambulance **03** or **112**

Driving in Lithuania *(Eastern Europe)*

The regulations below should be read in conjunction with the General motoring information on pages 18–21.

Drinking and driving

If the level of alcohol in the bloodstream is 0.04 per cent or more, severe penalties include a fine and/or withdrawal of your driving licence for up to 1.5 years. The acceptable level of alcohol in the bloodstream is 0.02 per cent for novice drivers who have held their licence for two years or less.

Driving licence

The minimum age at which a UK licence holder may drive a temporarily imported car and/or motorcycle is 18. UK licences that do not incorporate a photograph must be accompanied by photographic proof of identity e.g. a passport.

Fines

On-the-spot fines can be imposed (some fines may be paid at a local bank depending on the amount/traffic violation). Wheel clamps are in use.

Fuel

Leaded petrol is sold at Statoil petrol stations. Unleaded petrol (95 and 98 octane), diesel and LPG are available. Carrying petrol in a can is permitted (duty payable). Credit cards are accepted at filling stations; check with your card issuer for usage in Lithuania before travel.

Lights

The use of dipped headlights during the day is compulsory; there is a fine for non-compliance.

Motorcycles

The use of dipped headlights during the day is compulsory; a fine can be imposed for non-compliance. The wearing of crash helmets is compulsory for both driver and passenger. A child under 12 cannot travel as a passenger.

Motor insurance

Third-party insurance is compulsory, but fully comprehensive insurance is recommended.

Passengers/children in cars

A child under 12 or under 1.5m (4ft 11in) cannot travel as a front-seat passenger unless using a child restraint appropriate to their age and size. Children under three years must be seated in a child seat appropriate to their age and size on the rear seats. If the car is equipped with a front passenger airbag it is prohibited to place a child in a rear-facing seat.

Seat belts

It is compulsory for front- and rear-seat occupants to wear seat belts, if fitted.

Speed limits

Standard legal limits, which may be varied by signs, for private vehicles without trailers are 50km/h (31mph) in built-up areas, on other roads 70km/h (43mph), outside built-up areas on asphalt roads 90km/h (55mph). For drivers who have held a licence for less than two years the limit is 70km/h (43mph) outside built up areas on asphalt roads. On dual carriageways

1 November to 1 April 100km/h (62mph) and from 1 April to 1 November a limit of 110km/h (68mph) applies. On motorways 1 November to 1 April 110km/h (68mph) and from 1 April to 1 November a limit of 130km/h (80mph) applies between (i) Vilnius–Panevezys and (ii) Kaunas–Klaipeda. When **towing a trailer or caravan** with a combined weight of less than 3.5 tonnes, the limit on all roads outside built-up areas, including motorways, is 90km/h (55mph) year-round. The police control speeds closely and give fines for even the smallest of speeding offences.

Additional information

- A first-aid kit, fire extinguisher and a warning triangle are compulsory.
- A reflective jacket must be worn by the driver exiting a vehicle at night in a breakdown situation. Therefore the jacket/waistcoat must be kept within the passenger compartment of the vehicle.
- Winter tyres are compulsory between 10 November and 1 April. Spiked tyres may also be used during this period.
- It is recommended that visitors carry an assortment of spares for their vehicle, for example, a fan belt, replacement bulbs and spark plugs.
- It is compulsory to call the police to the scene of an accident.

Travel facts: Lithuania

Lithuanian National Tourism Office
86 Gloucester Place
London W1U 6HP
(Not open to the public)
Tel: 020 7034 1222
www.lithuaniatourism.co.uk

Banking hours
Banks are generally open Monday to Friday 9am to 5pm; some banks also open Saturday 9am to 1pm. Currency can be exchanged at banks and bureaux de change. There are ATMs in most cities.

Credit/debit cards
Most major credit and debit cards are accepted in the main hotels, restaurants, shops and in some petrol stations. Check with your credit and debit card company for usage in Lithuania before you travel.

Currency
The official currency of the country is the Lithuania litas (LTL) which is divided into 100 centas. Banknotes come in denominations of LTL500, 200, 100, 50, 20, 10, 5, 2 and 1. Coins are in denominations of LTL5, 2 and 1, and the 50, 20, 10, 5, 2 and 1 centas. The litas is pegged to the euro. Cash payments will be accepted only in litas; however many shopping centres and other service outlets take credit cards.

Electricity
The electricity supply is 220 volts AC, 50Hz. European two-pin plugs are in use.

Health care
Free or reduced-cost medical treatment is available in Lithuania to European visitors on production of a valid European Health Insurance Card (EHIC). See page 10. Comprehensive travel insurance is still advised and is essential for all other visitors.

Pharmacies
Pharmacies in major cities will generally have regular prescription drugs readily available; there is usually at least one that is open 24 hours a day.

Post offices
In major towns, post offices *(pastas)* are open Monday to Friday 8am to 6pm, Saturday 8am to 3pm. Post boxes are yellow.

Safe water
It is advisable to drink bottled or filtered water.

Telephones
All public phones in Lithuania require telephone cards, which are available from the Central Post Office and kiosks. The cards are valid all over Lithuania. The country code for Lithuania is 370. To call home from Lithuania dial the international code (00) followed by the country code. To call the UK from Lithuania dial 00 44.

Time
Lithuania is on Eastern European Time. It's two hours ahead of Greenwich Mean Time (GMT + 2), but from late March, when clocks are put forward one hour, to late October, Summer Time (GMT + 3) operates.

Emergency telephone numbers
Police **02** or **112**
Fire **01** or **112**
Ambulance **03** or **112**

Driving in Luxembourg *(Western Europe)*

The regulations below should be read in conjunction with the General motoring information on pages 18–21.

Drinking and driving

If the level of alcohol in the bloodstream is 0.05 per cent or more, severe penalties can include fines and/or prison. The blood alcohol level for a young driver is 0.019 per cent.

Driving licence

The minimum age at which a UK licence holder may drive a temporarily imported car and/or motorcycle is 18.

Fines

On-the-spot fines can be imposed. Unauthorised and dangerous parking can result in the car being impounded or removed.

Fuel

Unleaded petrol (95 and 98 octane) is available, along with diesel and LPG. It is forbidden to carry petrol in a can. Credit cards are accepted at filling stations, but check with your card issuer before you travel.

Lights

The use of dipped headlights during the day is recommended. Side lights are required when parking where there is no public lighting. When visibility is below 100m (110 yards) due to fog, snow, heavy rain etc., dipped headlights must be used. It is compulsory to flash your headlights at night when overtaking outside built-up areas. In tunnels indicated by a sign, drivers must use their passing lights.

Motorcycles

The use of dipped headlights during the day is compulsory, as is the wearing of crash helmets for both driver and passenger. A child under 12 is not permitted to ride as a passenger.

Motor insurance

Third-party insurance is compulsory.

Passengers/children in cars

Children under three years of age must be seated in an approved restraint system. Children aged three to 18 years and/or under 1.5m (4ft 11in) must be seated in an appropriate restraint system. If they weigh over 36kg a seat belt can be used, but only on the rear seat of the vehicle. Rear-facing child-restraint systems are prohibited on seats with frontal air bags unless the air bag is deactivated.

Seat belts

It is compulsory for front- and rear-seat occupants to wear seat belts, if fitted.

Speed limits

The standard legal limits, which may be varied by signs, for **private vehicles without trailers** are: in built-up areas 50km/h (31mph), outside built-up areas 90km/h (55mph) and motorways 130km/h (80mph) except in rain or snow when the limit is 110km/h (68mph). When **towing a trailer or caravan** the limits are 75km/h (46mph) outside built-up areas and 90km/h

(55mph) on motorways. The speed limit for vehicles with spiked tyres is 70km/h (43mph). 'Zone de rencontre' road sign designates an area where the speed limit is 20km/h (12mph). Within this zone pedestrians have priority and may cross the road whenever they choose.

Winter tyres

From 1 October 2012 motor vehicles (excluding mopeds and motercycles) driving in winter conditions (frost, compacted snow, slush, ice) must be fitted with tyres marked M&S.

Additional information

- It is compulsory for the driver and passengers to wear a reflective waistcoat when exiting a vehicle in a breakdown situation on a motorway or outside built-up areas, at night and in bad visibility.
- A warning triangle is compulsory for all vehicles with four or more wheels.
- All tyres on a car must be of the same type: either winter tyres (marked M&S on the sidewall) or summer tyres.
- The use of spiked tyres is permitted from 1 December until 31 March.
- Use of snow chains permitted, in case of snow or ice.
- Any vehicle immobilised on the motorway must use warning signals, a warning triangle and a flashing light at the rear.
- In built-up areas the use of the horn is prohibited except in case of immediate danger.

Travel facts: Luxembourg

Luxembourg Tourist Office
Sicilian House
Sicilian Avenue
London WC1A 2QR
Tel: 020 7434 2800
www.luxembourg.co.uk

Banking hours
Banks generally open from Monday to Friday 8.30am to 12 noon and 1.30pm to 4.30pm. Some banks open over lunch, and some stay open until 6pm. Some ATMs (e.g. near the Grand Ducal Palace) are open 24 hours.

Credit/debit cards
The use of credit/debit cards is becoming ever more common, but many retailers require a minimum sales amount before accepting them. American Express, Diners Club, MasterCard, Visa and others are all accepted, as well as Eurocheque cards.

Currency
The currency in Luxembourg is the euro (€). Euro coins are issued in denominations of 1, 2, 5, 10, 20 and 50 cents and €1 and €2. Banknotes are issued in denominations of €5, €10, €20, €50, €100, €200 and €500.

Electricity
The power supply in Luxembourg is 220 volts AC, 50Hz. Sockets accept two-round-pin plugs, so an adaptor is needed for most non-continental appliances.

Health care
Free or reduced-cost medical treatment is available in Luxembourg to European visitors on production of a valid European Health Insurance Card (EHIC). See page 10. Comprehensive travel insurance is still advised and is essential for all other visitors.

Pharmacies
Prescription medicines and advice can be obtained from a pharmacy *(pharmacie)* identified by a green cross. Information about the nearest 24-hour facility is posted at all pharmacies.

Post offices
Post offices are open Monday to Friday 9am to 12 noon, and 4.30 or 5pm. The Luxembourg-Ville main office (opposite the railway station) is open Monday to Friday 7am to 7pm, Saturday 6am to 12 noon. Smaller offices may open for only a few hours.

Safe water
Tap water is considered safe to drink and bottled mineral water *(eau minérale)* is widely available.

Telephones
Public telephones are found in most post offices, supermarkets, train or bus stations and close to major public buildings. Phone cards are available from post offices and most newsagents. Most coin-operated public phones have been phased out. The country code for Luxembourg is 352. To call home from Luxembourg dial the international code (00) followed by the country code. To call the UK from Luxembourg dial 00 44.

Time
Luxembourg is on Central European Time, one hour ahead of Greenwich Mean Time (GMT + 1). From late March, when clocks are put forward one hour, until late October, Daylight Saving Time (GMT + 2) operates.

Emergency telephone numbers
General emergencies **112**
Police **112** or **113**
Fire **112**
Ambulance **112**

Driving in Macedonia (Former Yugoslav Republic of Macedonia)

(South East Europe)

The regulations below should be read in conjunction with the General motoring information on pages 18–21.

Drinking and driving

If the level of alcohol in the bloodstream is 0.05 per cent or more, severe penalties, including a fine, imprisonment and/or suspension of driving licence, can be imposed. The limit is 0 per cent for newly qualified drivers.

Driving licence

The minimum age at which a UK licence holder may drive a temporarily imported car and/or motorcycle (exceeding 125cc) is 18.

Fines

On-the-spot fines can be imposed by the police. An official receipt should be obtained. Fines must be paid at a post office or bank. The police can impound a vehicle that is wrongly parked and can detain a vehicle with worn tyres.

Fuel

Unleaded petrol (95 and 98 octane), diesel, Euro diesel and LPG are available. Carrying petrol in a can is permitted. Credit cards are accepted at some filling stations; check with your card issuer before travel. Usually payment can be made only in the local currency.

Lights

Dipped headlights during the day is compulsory. There is an on-the-spot fine for non-compliance.

Motorcycles

The use of dipped headlights during the day is compulsory. The wearing of crash helmets is also compulsory for both driver and passenger.

Motor insurance

Third-party insurance is compulsory; a Green Card is recognised.

Passengers/children in cars

A child under 12 may not travel in the front seat of a vehicle. There are no official regulations but the recommendations are: Children under two can travel in the front seat of a car if they are placed in a child restraint system adapted to their size. If it is a rear-facing seat, the airbag must be deactivated. A child from 5 to 12 years can travel on the back seat using a 3-point seat belt and a booster cushion if necessary.

Seat belts

It is compulsory for front- and rear-seat occupants to wear seat belts, if fitted.

Speed limits

The standard legal limits, which may be varied by signs, for **private vehicles without trailers** are: in built-up areas 50km/h (31mph), outside built-up areas 80km/h (49mph) but 100km/h (62mph) on dual carriageways and 120km/h

(74mph) on motorways. The limit when **towing** is 80km/h (49mph) on all roads outside built-up areas. Special speed limits apply to **newly qualified drivers, for private vehicles without trailers**: outside built up areas 60km/h (37mph), but 80km/h (49mph) on dual carriageways and 100km/h (62mph) on motorways.

Additional information

- It is recommended for visitors to equip their vehicle with a set of replacement bulbs (this does not apply if the vehicle is fitted with xenon, neon or LED lights). It is compulsory for visitors to equip their vehicles with a first-aid kit, fire extinguisher, tow rope and warning triangle; two triangles are required if towing a trailer. A warning triangle is not required for two-wheeled vehicles.
- It is compulsory to carry a reflective jacket, which must be kept within the vehicle (i.e. not in the boot) and worn by the driver before exiting the vehicle in the dark outside of towns and on motorways. It must be compliant with EN471.
- From 15 November to 15 March, all motor vehicles driven outside built-up areas must have winter tyres fitted on all wheels with a minimum tread depth of 4mm. The maximum speed limit if using snow chains is 70km/h (43mph). Four-wheel drive vehicles must have winter tyres with a minimum tread depth of 6mm, or if you carry snow chains the vehicle can be fitted with summer tyres with a minimum tread depth of 6mm.
- A person visibly under the influence of alcohol is not permitted to travel in a vehicle as a front-seat passenger.
- The authorities at the frontier must certify any visible damage to a vehicle entering Macedonia and a certificate obtained; this must be produced when leaving. A certificate must also be obtained if damage occurs while in Macedonia.
- Spiked tyres are prohibited.
- A GPS-based navigation system with maps indicating the location of fixed speed cameras must have the 'fixed speed camera PoI (Points of Interest)' function deactivated.
- The use of radar detectors is prohibited.

Travel facts: Republic of Macedonia

Embassy of the Republic of Macedonia
Suite 2.1/2.2 Buckingham Court
75/83 Buckingham Gate
London SW1E 6PE
Tel: 020 7976 0535
www.exploringmacedonia.com

Banking hours

Banks are generally open Monday to Friday 8am to 7pm, Saturday 8am to noon or 1pm. Banks at airports, railway and bus stations are open longer hours. Money should be exchanged in official exchange offices (banks, post offices, hotels, tourist agencies) according to current exchange rates. When leaving Macedonia visitors can exchange MKDs back into foreign currency (at official places) only after presenting the evidence of exchange for denars when entering the country.

Credit/debit cards

Some major credit cards (Diners, American Express, Visa and MasterCard/EuroCard) and Eurocheques can be used for payment wherever a notice is displayed in hotels, shops, and restaurants, but acceptance throughout the country is limited. Check with your credit card provider. Credit card fraud is widespread in Macedonia so take care when making a purchase using this method. ATMs are widely available in Skopje, less so in other main towns, although the number is increasing, making the withdrawal of local currency much easier. Cash is the common form of payment.

Currency

The local currency is the Macedonian denar (MKD) which is divided into 100 deni. Banknotes come in denominations of Den5,000, 1,000, 500, 100, 50 and 10. Coins are in denominations of Den5, 2 and 1, and 50 deni. Euros are the easiest currency to exchange.
Note: You must declare all foreign currency on arrival.

Electricity

The electrical current is 220 volts AC, 50Hz.
Plugs have two round pins.

Health care

The UK has a reciprocal health-care agreement with Macedonia. If you're visiting Macedonia and need urgent or immediate medical treatment it will be provided at a reduced cost or, in some cases, free. The range of medical services available may be more restricted than under the NHS, therefore it is essential for all visitors to have comprehensive travel insurance. Visit **www.nhs.uk/NHSEngland/Healthcareabroad** for a country-by-country guide.

Pharmacies

You'll find a pharmacy in all bigger towns; service is good and prices moderate.

Post offices

Post offices are generally open Monday to Friday 7am to 7pm, Saturday 7am to 1pm.

Safe water

Mains water is normally chlorinated. Bottled mineral water is available. In rural areas it is recommended that all drinking water is boiled or you buy bottled water.

Telephones

All public telephones in Macedonia are card-operated and have instructions in English. Post offices have telephones where you pay in cash after you finish your call. Telephone cards worth Den150, 250 and 500 are for sale at post offices and kiosks. The country code for Macedonia is 389. To call home from Macedonia dial the international code (00) followed by the country code. To call the UK from Macedonia dial 00 44.

Time

Macedonia is on Central European Time, one hour ahead of GMT (GMT + 1). Daylight Savings Time comes into effect from end March to end October (GMT + 2).

Emergency telephone numbers

Police **192**
Fire **193**
Ambulance **194**
Road assistance **987**

Driving in Malta *(Mediterranean)*

The regulations below should be read in conjunction with the General motoring information on pages 18–21.

Drinking and driving

If the level of alcohol in the bloodstream is 0.08 per cent or more, severe penalties can be imposed, including a fine or imprisonment.

Driving licence

The minimum age at which a UK licence holder may drive a temporarily imported car and/or motorcycle is 18.

Fines

There are no on-the-spot fines, but if a fineable motoring or parking offence is committed, this may be settled prior to departure.

Fuel

Unleaded petrol (95 octane) and diesel are available but not LPG. Carrying petrol in a can is permitted; however, it is forbidden aboard ferries. Credit cards are generally not accepted at filling stations; check with your card issuer for usage in Malta before travel.

Lights

Spot lights are prohibited. Lights should be switched on while travelling through tunnels.

Motorcycles

Helmets are compulsory for driver and passenger.

Motor insurance

Third-party insurance is compulsory; Green Cards are accepted.

Passengers/children in cars

Children under three cannot travel as front- or rear-seat passengers unless using a suitable restraint system. Children between three and 10 or under 1.5m (4ft 11in) in height travelling in front or rear seats must use a restraint system as appropriate, or an adult seat belt if a restraint system is unavailable.

Seat belts

It is compulsory for front- and rear-seat occupants to wear seat belts, if fitted.

Speed limits

The standard legal limits, which may be varied by signs, for **private vehicles with and without trailers** (under 3.5 tonnes combined weight) are: in built-up areas 50km/h (31mph), outside built-up areas 80km/h (49mph).

Additional information

- It is recommended to carry a warning triangle.
- The rule of the road is drive on the left, overtake on the right.
- The use of the horn is prohibited in inhabited areas between 11pm and 6am.
- Parking in Valetta is extremely limited and there is a charge to enter the city.
- There is a park and ride system located on the outskirts of the city offering a free shuttle to the centre.

Travel facts: Malta

Malta Tourist Office
Unit C, Park House
14 Northfields
London SW18 1DD
Tel: 020 7292 4900
www.visitmalta.com
www.gozo.com
www.malta.com

Banking hours
Banks are normally open 8.30am to 12.30pm Monday to Friday and on Saturday up to 11.30am. Some banks work longer hours. Summer and winter opening hours may differ.

Credit/debit cards
Credit cards are accepted in the resorts and ATMs are common. In rural areas it's best to carry cash. Some filling stations, even in built-up areas, accept only cash. Traveller's cheques in sterling are widely accepted. Some establishments, typically those run by ex-pats and with strong links to the UK, will also accept sterling currency, though you may pay a slight premium.

Currency
The currency of Malta is the euro (€). Coins come in denominations of 1, 2, 5, 10, 20 and 50 cents, and €1 and €2. Notes come in denominations of €5, €10, €20, €50, €100, €200 and €500.

Electricity
The power supply is 240 volts AC, 50Hz. Sockets are the three-square-hole type taking square plugs with three square pins. Visitors from continental Europe should bring an adaptor.

Health care
Free or reduced-cost medical treatment is available in Malta to European visitors on production of a valid European Health Insurance Card (EHIC). See page 10. Comprehensive travel insurance is still advised and is essential for all other visitors.

Pharmacies
Pharmacies, usually known as chemists, are recognisable by a neon green cross sign. They sell most international drugs and medicines over the counter or by prescription. They open during normal shop hours, with a Sunday duty roster.

Post offices
Post office opening hours are Monday to Saturday 7.45am to 12.45pm. Closed Sunday. The post office at Castille Place, Valletta **(tel: 21 226224)** is open Monday to Friday 7.30am to 6pm, Saturday 8.15am to 12.30pm. On Gozo the post office at 129 Republic Street, Victoria **(tel: 21 556435)** is open later.

Safe water
Tap water is quite safe, although not very tasty. Water from fountains should be avoided as it may not come directly from the mains supply. Bottled 'table' water is widely available, at a reasonable cost, along with imported mineral water.

Telephones
Malta's public telephone boxes are either green, red or transparent booths. Few phones accept coins, most take a phone card *(telecard)* available for €5 and €10 from most newsagents, post offices and shops. The country code for Malta is 356. To call home from Malta dial the international code (00) followed by the country code. To call the UK from Malta dial 00 44.

Time
Malta is one hour ahead of Greenwich Mean Time (GMT + 1), but from late March, when clocks are put forward one hour, to late October, Summer Time (GMT + 2) operates.

Emergency telephone number
Police, Fire and Ambulance **112**

Driving in Montenegro *(South East Europe)*

The regulations below should be read in conjunction with the General motoring information on pages 18–21.

Drinking and driving

If the level of alcohol in the bloodstream is 0.05 per cent or more or if a medical examination shows that normal bodily functions are impaired, severe penalties can be imposed including a fine, imprisonment and/or suspension of the driving licence.

Driving licence

The minimum age at which a UK licence holder may drive a temporarily imported car and/or motorcycle (exceeding 125cc) is 18. We recommend that you obtain an International Driving Permit to accompany your UK driving licence.

Fines

Officials can issue an on-the-spot fine notice, but cannot collect the payment. Fines vary according to the gravity of the offence. Penalties are higher if the motorist endangers other people or causes an accident.

Fuel

Unleaded petrol (95 and 98 octane), diesel *(dizel)* and LPG are available. You can carry a small amount of petrol in a can. Credit cards are generally accepted; check with your card issuer for usage in Montenegro before travel.

Lights

Dipped headlights are compulsory at all times.

Motorcycles

The use of dipped headlights is compulsory at all times. The wearing of crash helmets is compulsory for both driver and passenger.

Motor insurance

Third-party insurance is compulsory; a Green Card is recognised.

Passengers/children in cars

A person visibly under the influence of alcohol or child under 12 is not permitted to travel in a vehicle as a front-seat passenger.

Seat belts

It is compulsory for front- and rear-seat occupants to wear seat belts, if fitted.

Speed limits

The standard legal limits, which may be varied by signs, for **private vehicles without trailers** are: in built-up areas 50km/h (31mph), outside built-up areas 80km/h (49mph) and 100km/h (62mph) on fast roads.

Additional information

- It is compulsory for visitors to equip their vehicle with a set of replacement bulbs, a first-aid kit (excludes mopeds) and a warning triangle (excluding motorcycles); two triangles are required if towing a trailer.
- It is compulsory to carry a reflective jacket in the passenger compartment of the vehicle. The driver must wear the jacket on exiting the

vehicle in an emergency/breakdown situation.

- The authorities at the frontier must certify any visible damage to a vehicle entering Montenegro and a certificate obtained; this must be produced when leaving, otherwise you may experience serious difficulties. Every car entering the territory of Montenegro will be subject to an ecological tax, approximately €10. The eco tax is to be paid at the border and drivers will get a sticker for their vehicle (valid for one year) as proof of payment.
- It is compulsory for accidents resulting in serious injury or material damage to be reported to the police.
- Spiked tyres are prohibited. In winter, snow chains may be necessary on some roads.
- Vehicles entering a roundabout have right of way.
- Horns must not be used in built-up areas or at night except in cases of imminent danger.
- School buses must not be overtaken or passed when they stop for children to board or alight.

Travel facts: Montenegro

Montenegrin Embassy
Trafalgar House 11
Waterloo Place
London SW1Y 4AU
Tel: 020 7863 8806
http://montenegro.embassyhomepage.com
www.visitmontenegro.org
www.montenegro.org.uk

Banking hours
Banks are generally open Monday to Friday 8am to 7pm, Saturday 8am to 1pm.

Credit/debit cards
The most widely accepted cards are Visa, MasterCard, Maestro and Diners. American Express cards are not accepted in Montenegro. ATMs increasingly accept international bank cards.

Currency
Although not a member of the EU, the currency in Montenegro is the euro (€). Euro coins are issued in denominations of 1, 2, 5, 10, 20 and 50 cents and €1 and €2. Banknotes are issued in denominations of €5, €10, €20, €50, €100, €200 and €500.

Electricity
The power supply is 220 volts AC, 50Hz. Two-round-pin plugs are used.

Health care
Comprehensive travel insurance is essential for all visitors.

Pharmacies
Medicines and basic medical supplies are largely available from private pharmacies. Prescribed medicines must be paid for.

Post offices
Postal services within Montenegro are reasonably good.

Safe water
During the holiday season water shortages can affect quality and the locals will often stop taking ice in drinks. To avoid stomach upsets, drink bottled mineral water and avoid ice in drinks.

Telephones
Public telephones take pre-paid cards, which can be bought in post offices, operators' outlets or tobacco shops/newsagents. The country code for Montenegro is 382. To call home from Montenegro dial the international code (00) followed by the country code. To call the UK from Montenegro dial 00 44.

Time
Montenegro is on Central European Time, one hour ahead of Greenwich Mean Time (GMT + 1). From late March, when clocks are put forward one hour, until late October, Daylight Saving Time (GMT + 2) operates.

Emergency telephone numbers
Police **92** or **112**
Fire Department **93** or **112**
Ambulance **94** or **112**

Toll charges in euros

Bridges and Tunnels	**Car**	**Car towing caravan/ trailer**
Sozina tunnel	2.50	5.00

Driving in the Netherlands

(Western Europe)

The regulations below should be read in conjunction with the General motoring information on pages 18–21.

Drinking and driving

If the level of alcohol in the bloodstream is over 0.05 per cent, severe penalties including a fine, withdrawal of driving licence and imprisonment can be imposed. The lower limit of 0.02 per cent applies to new drivers for the first five years and moped riders up to the age of 24. In some cases a blood test is necessary after a breath test.

Driving licence

The minimum age at which a UK licence holder may drive a temporarily imported car and/or motorcycle is 18.

Fines

On-the-spot fines can be imposed. In the case of illegal parking the police can impose on-the-spot fines or tow the vehicle away. Vehicles can be confiscated in cases of excessive speed and drink driving.

Fuel

Unleaded petrol (95 and 98 octane), diesel and LPG *(Autogas)* are available. There is no leaded petrol (lead-substitute petrol is available as 'super' 98 octane). Carrying petrol in a can is permitted but forbidden aboard ferries and Eurotunnel. Credit cards are accepted at most filling stations; check with your card issuer for use before travel.

Lights

The use of dipped headlights during the day is recommended. At night it is prohibited to drive with only side lights.

Motorcycles

The use of dipped headlights during the day is recommended. The wearing of crash helmets is compulsory on all motorcycles that are capable of exceeding 25km/h (15mph); this also applies to drivers and passengers of open micro cars without seat belts.

Motor insurance

Third-party insurance is compulsory.

Passengers/children in cars

Children up to the age of 18 and less than 1.35m (4ft 5in) in height cannot travel as a front- or rear-seat passenger unless using a suitable restraint system adapted to their size. Suitable child-restraint systems must meet the safety approval of ECE 44/03 or 44/04. If the vehicle is not fitted with rear seat belts, children under three are not permitted to travel in the vehicle. Children under three are permitted to travel in the front seats if using a rear-facing child seat with the air bag deactivated (if fitted). If the vehicle's front seats are not fitted with seat belts, only passengers measuring 1.35m (4ft 5in) or more may travel in the front seat.

Seat belts

It is compulsory for front- and rear-seat occupants to wear seat belts, if fitted.

Speed limits

The standard legal limits, which may be varied by signs, for **private vehicles with and without trailers** (under 3.5 tonnes combined weight) are: in built-up areas 50km/h (31mph), outside built-up areas 80km/h (49mph) or 100km/h (62mph) and motorways 120km/h (74mph). Only vehicles capable of 60km/h (37mph) are permitted on motorways.

Additional information

- A warning triangle or hazard warning lights must be used in case of an accident or breakdown (it is recommended that a warning triangle is always carried).
- Buses have the right of way when leaving bus stops in built-up areas.
- Trams have right of way except when crossing a priority road.
- Beware of large numbers of cyclists and skaters.
- Spiked tyres are prohibited.
- The use of a radar detector is prohibited; if you are caught using such a device by the police the radar detector will be confiscated and you will be fined €250.
- Horns should not be used at night and in moderation during the day. High penalties are incurred for non-compliance.
- Parking discs can be obtained from local stores.

Road signs (a selection of standard and non-standard)

Residential zone

Parking for permit holders only

Disc parking zone

Park and ride

Maximum speed limit

Built-up areas

Travel facts and toll charges: the Netherlands

Netherlands Board of Tourism
PO Box 30783
London WC2B 6DH
Tel: 020 7539 7950
www.holland.com/uk

Banking hours
Most banks are generally open Tuesday to Friday from 9am to 4 or 5pm. On Monday banks open at 1pm. Banks are closed Saturday and Sunday.

Credit/debit cards
The major credit cards are widely accepted, but if in doubt, ask in advance. ATMs for cash advances can be found outside banks in all the major towns.

Currency
The currency in the Netherlands is the euro (€). Euro coins are issued in denominations of 1, 2, 5, 10, 20 and 50 cents and €1 and €2. Banknotes are issued in denominations of €5, €10, €20, €50, €100, €200 and €500.

Electricity
The power supply in the Netherlands is 220 volts AC. Hotels may have a 110-volt or 120-volt outlet for shavers, but travellers are advised to bring a converter and an adapter for two-round-pin plugs.

Health care
Free or reduced-cost medical treatment is available in the Netherlands to European visitors on production of a valid European Health Insurance Card (EHIC). See page 10. Comprehensive travel insurance is still advised and is essential for all other visitors.

Pharmacies
Prescription and non-prescription drugs and other medical products are sold in pharmacies *(apotheeken)*, recognised by a green cross sign. Despite their name, drug stores *(drogerijen)* do not sell medicines, but toiletries and cosmetics. Pharmacies are open Monday to Friday from 8 or 9am to 5:30 or 6pm.

Post offices
Most PTT post offices *(postkaantoren)* are generally open Monday to Friday 9am to 5pm. Larger ones are also open on Saturdays between 9am and 12 noon or 1.30pm.

Safe water
Tap water is safe to drink. Bottled mineral water, often called by the generic name 'spa', after a popular Belgian label, is readily available.

Telephones
There are many types of public phones in the Netherlands, accepting coins or pre-paid or credit cards. As a general principle, the cheapest way to make calls either within the country or abroad is with a pre-paid card (available at tobacconists, supermarkets and bureaux de change); the most expensive method is from a hotel bedroom. The country code for the Netherlands is 31. To call home from the Netherlands dial the international code (00) followed by the country code. To call the UK from the Netherlands dial 00 44.

Time
The Netherlands is on Central European Time (GMT + 1). Dutch Summer Time (GMT+2) operates from lateMarch, when clocks are put forward one hour, until late October.

Emergency telephone numbers
Police **112**
Fire **112**
Ambulance **112**

Toll charges in euros

Bridges and tunnels	**Car**	**Car towing caravan/ trailer**
Westerschelde Tunnel	5.00	7.45
Kil Tunnel	2.00	5.00

Driving in Norway *(Northern Europe)*

The regulations below should be read in conjunction with the General motoring information on pages 18–21.

Drinking and driving

If the level of alcohol in the bloodstream exceeds 0.020 per cent, severe penalties can include heavy fines and/or prison, and the surrender of your driving licence. Random breath test are carried out.

Driving licence

The minimum age at which a UK licence holder may drive a temporarily imported car is 18, for a motorcycle up to 11kw the minimum age is 16, 11–25kw 18, and over 25kw it is 20.

Fines

On-the-spot fines for infringement of traffic regulations can be imposed. Vehicles illegally parked may be towed away.

Fuel

Unleaded petrol (95 and 98 octane) and diesel are available; there is limited LPG. Petrol in a can is permitted but not aboard ferries. Credit cards are accepted at filling stations; check with your card issuer for usage in Norway before travel.

Lights

The use of dipped headlights during the day is compulsory.

Motorcycles

The use of dipped headlights during the day is compulsory. The wearing of crash helmets is compulsory for both driver and passenger.

Motor insurance

Third-party insurance is compulsory.

Passengers/children in cars

A child under four cannot travel as a front- or rear-seat passenger unless seated in a child restraint. Children over four must use a child-restraint system or a seat belt.

Seat belts

It is compulsory for front- and rear-seat passengers to wear seat belts, if fitted.

Speed limits

The standard legal limits, which may be varied by signs, for **private vehicles with and without trailers** are: in built-up areas 50km/h (31mph), outside built-up areas 80km/h (49mph) and up to 90km/h (55mph) or 100km (62mph) on motorways. The speed limit in residential areas can be lowered to 18mph (30km/h).

Congestion charge

There is a congestion charge in Trondheim payable in both directions, double at peak hours.

Additional information

- A warning triangle is compulsory for all vehicles with more than two wheels.
- Reflective jackets are compulsory for residents and recommended for visitors.

We strongly recommended that a reflective jacket is carried in the vehicle and worn if the driver and/or passenger(s) need to exit a vehicle that is immobilised on the carriageway of all motorways and main or busy roads. We recommend that the jacket is carried in the passenger compartment of the vehicle (not the boot). The carriage/use of reflective jackets is compulsory for vehicles registered in Norway.

- Norwegian law does not make snow chains compulsory. However, in snow or icy conditions, winter tyres or tyres with snow chains must be used. You can be fined if using summer tyres on snowy/icy roads. UK vehicles are predominantly fitted with summer tyres. Controls are often in place at border areas to ensure snow chains are carried on board. When used, winter tyres must be fitted to all four wheels, minimum tread depth 3mm.
- We recommended that visitors equip their vehicle with a first-aid kit, fire extinguisher and a set of replacement bulbs.
- In addition to some road, bridge and tunnel tolls, city tolls are payable by motorists entering Bergen, Oslo, Stavanger and Trondheim, see panel opposite. The toll needs to be paid prior to entering the 'zone'. Tolls can be paid at the nearest Esso station.
- Spiked tyres may be used between 1 November and the first Sunday after Easter. Cars with spiked tyres will be charged a fee by the municipalities of Oslo and Bergen. The stickers are available to purchase daily, monthly or yearly. If these tyres are used they must be fitted to all four wheels. In the three northern counties Nordland, Troms and Finnmark spiked tyres are permitted from 15 October to 1 May.

- A vehicle towing a caravan must be equipped with special rear-view mirrors. Trams always have right of way.
- The use of radar detectors is forbidden.
- When hiring a car in Norway, it is the hirer's responsibility to ensure that the vehicle comes complete with the compulsory equipment.

Toll charges in Norwegian kroner

Road		Car	Car towing caravan/ trailer
E6	Trondheim – Stjørdal	15.00-32.00	15.00-64.00
E6	Gardermoen – Dal	14.00	28.00
E6	Skaberud – Kolomoen	17.00	34.00
E6	Dal – Boksrud	15.00	30.00
E6	Boksrud – Minnesund	11.00	22.00
E18	Oslo – Drammen	20.00	40.00
E18	Larvik – Porsgrunn	20.00	40.00
E18	Kristiansaund	10.00	20.00
E18	Kristiansaund fastlandsforbindelse on **E39/RU70**	75.00	255.00

A charge is made on the following ring roads

Oslo	27.00	81.00
Bergen	15.00	30.00
Stavanger	20.00	50.00
Kristiansand	21.00	42.00
Baerum	13.40	40.50
Tunsberg	15.00	30.00
Namsos	18.00	36.00
Nord-Jœren	13.00	26.00

A congestion charge is made on the following road

Trondheim	10.00	22.00

(Peak hours double. Payable in both directions)

Bridges and tunnels	Car	Car towing caravan/ trailer
Askim on **E18**	15.00	30.00
Aust-Agder on **E18**	15.00	30.00
Folgefonntunnelen on **RV551**	72.00	145.00
Moss on **E6**	23.00	46.00
Nordkapp on **E69**	145.00	460.00
Oslofjord Tunnel on **RV23**	60.00	130.00
Oysand-Thamshamn on **E39**	20.00	40.00
Svinesundforbindelsen on **E6**	20.00	100.00
Trekantsambanet on **E39**	85.00	270.00
Vestfold on **E18**	25.00	50.00
Ostfold on **E18** (Eastbound only)	25.00	50.00
Rullerstadjuvet Tunnel	40.00	80.00
Kroppan Bru Bridge (Trondheim)	5.00	10.00
Vestfold Sor on **E18**	30.00	60.00
Listerpakken on **E39**	25.00	50.00
Aust –Agder Nord on **E18**	30.00	60.00

Ferry crossings		Car	Car towing caravan/ trailer
E39	Mortavika – Arsvågen	171.00	588.00
E39	Halhjem – Sandvikåg	203.00	695.00
E39	Lavik – Oppedal	81.00	303.00
E39	Anda – Lote	63.00	247.00
E39	Festøya – Solevågen	75.00	286.00
E39	Molde – Vestnes	116.00	419.00
E39	Halsa – Kanestraum	81.00	303.00
E6	Bognes – Skarberget	92.00	339.00

Travel facts: Norway

Innovation Norway
Charles House
5 Regent Street
London SW1Y 4LR
Tel: 020 7389 8800
www.visitnorway.com

Banking hours
Banks are generally open from 8.15am to 3.30pm. They usually close half an hour earlier from mid-May to mid-August, but stay open until 5pm on Thursday all year. They are closed at weekends.

Credit/debit cards
The use of credits cards is widespread in Norway, and they are accepted almost everywhere. Eurocard/MasterCard, Visa, American Express and Diners Club are the most common. Check with your card provider about acceptability and available services.

Currency
Norway's currency is the krone (NOK), which is divided into 100 øre. The denominatoins of krone banknotes are NOK50, NOK100, NOK200, NOK500 and NOK1,000. There are coins of 50 øre and NOK1, NOK5, NOK10 and NOK20.

Electricity
Norway has a 220-volt AC power supply. Electrical sockets take plugs with two round pins. UK visitors will need an adaptor.

Health care
Free or reduced-cost medical treatment is available in Norway to European visitors on production of a valid European Health Insurance Card (EHIC). See page 10. Comprehensive travel insurance is still advised and is essential for all other visitors.

Pharmacies
A pharmacy *(apotek)* sells prescription medicines; many pharmacists speak English. Pharmacies are generally open Monday to Friday 9am to 4.30pm, Saturday 9am to 2pm. Information about the nearest late-night or 24-hour facility is posted at all pharmacies.

Post offices
Post offices are generally open Monday to Friday 8am to 5pm, Saturday 8am to 1pm; hours for rural post offices may vary. Buy stamps *(frimerker)* at a post office *(posten)*, a news-stand/tobacconist, such as Narvesen or MIX or from a hotel. Post boxes are red.

Safe water
Tap water is safe to drink throughout Norway. Bottled mineral water *(mineralvann)* is widely available.

Telephones
You can use cash or a telephone card *(telekort)* to make a call in Norway. Most phone booths have direct dialling for international calls. Use NOK1, NOK5, NOK10 and NOK20 coins (minimum charge NOK5). Greencard phones accept phone cards NOK40, NOK90 and NOK140, available from Narvesen and MIX kiosks. Some card phones accept credit cards. The country code for Norway is 47. To call home from Norway dial the international code (00) followed by the country code. To call the UK from Norway dial 00 44.

Time
Norway is on Central European Time, one hour ahead of Greenwich Mean Time (GMT + 1). From late March, when clocks are put forward one hour, until late October, Daylight Saving Time (GMT + 2) operates.

Emergency telephone numbers
Police **112**
Fire **110**
Ambulance **113**

Driving in Poland *(Central Europe)*

The regulations below should be read in conjunction with the General motoring information on pages 18–21.

Drinking and driving

The maximum level of alcohol permitted in the bloodstream is 0.02 per cent. If it is between 0.021 per cent and 0.05 per cent a heavy fine can be imposed and your driver's licence suspended. If over 0.05 per cent a fine is determined by a tribunal along with a prison sentence and suspension of the licence.

Driving licence

The minimum age at which a UK licence holder may drive a temporarily imported car and/or motorcycle (over 125cc) is 18. All valid UK driving licences should be accepted in Poland.

Fines

On-the-spot fines can be imposed. An official receipt should be obtained. The police are authorised to request foreign motorists to pay their fines in cash. Wheel clamps are in use. Illegally parked cars causing an obstruction may be towed away and impounded.

Fuel

Unleaded petrol (95 and 98 octane), diesel and LPG are available. There is no leaded petrol, but 95 octane petrol with lead-replacement additive is available. You can carry 10 litres of petrol in a petrol can but not aboard ferries. Credit cards are accepted at most filling stations; check with your card issuer for usage in Poland before travel.

Lights

Dipped headlights or daytime running lights are compulsory for all vehicles at all times. A fine can be imposed for non-compliance.

Motorcycles

Dipped headlights or daytime running lights are compulsory for all vehicles at all times. The wearing of crash helmets is compulsory for both driver and passenger.

Motor insurance

Third-party insurance is compulsory.

Passengers/children in cars

A child under 12 and under 1.5m (4ft 11in) in height cannot travel as front- or rear-seat passenger unless using suitable restraint system adapted to their size. If a car is equipped with front-seat air bags it is prohibited to place a child in a rear-facing seat.

Seat belts

It is compulsory for front- and rear-seat occupants to wear seat belts, if fitted.

Speed limits

The standard legal limits, which may be varied by signs, for **private vehicles without trailers** are: in built-up areas 60km/h (37mph) from 11pm to 5am and 50km/h (31mph) from 5am to

11pm, outside built-up areas 90km/h (55mph), on express roads (2 x 1 lane) 100km/h (62mph) or (2 x 2 lanes) 120km/h (74mph) and 140km/h (80mph) on motorways. The minimum speed on motorways is 40km/h (24mph). Some residential zones have a limit of 20km/h (13mph).

Additional information

- A warning triangle is compulsory for all vehicles with more than two wheels.
- It is recommended that visitors equip their vehicle with a first-aid kit, a set of replacement bulbs and that the vehicle is fitted with M&S tyres. It is also recommended that a fire extinguisher is carried as this is compulsory for Polish-registered vehicles.
- The use of spiked tyres is prohibited. Snow chains may be used only on roads covered with snow.
- It is prohibited to carry and/or use a radar detector.
- The use of the horn is not authorised in built-up areas except to avoid an accident.

Travel facts and toll charges: Poland

Polish National Tourist Office
Westgate House
West Gate
London W5 1YY
Tel: 08700 675 010
www.poland.travel/en/
www.poland.pl

Banking hours
Banks are generally open Monday to Friday 8am to 5 or 7pm and Saturday 8am to 1.30pm. Hours are limited in smaller towns. Withdrawing cash from ATMs is convenient, but not all Polish ATMs take all cards. Inform your bank before you leave home that you intend making withdrawals in Poland.

Credit/debit cards
Card use is on the increase but Poland essentially still has a cash culture. Stickers on the doors and windows of businesses usually indicate which credit cards will be accepted.

Currency
The Polish currency is the zloty (Zl) = 100 groszy. Banknotes come in denominations of Zl10, Zl20, Zl50, Zl100 and Zl200 and coins of Zl1, Zl2 and Zl5 and 1, 2, 5 and 10 groszy. Euros can be used to pay for goods and services at a limited number of shops and hotels but expect exchange rates to be poor.

Electricity
The power supply is 220 volts AC, 50Hz. Sockets take two-round-pin continental-style plugs. Visitors from the UK require an adaptor.

Health care
Free or reduced-cost medical treatment is available in Poland to European visitors on production of a valid European Health Insurance Card (EHIC). See page 10. Comprehensive travel insurance is still advised and is essential for all other visitors.

Pharmacies
Major cities and most towns have several pharmacies *(apteka)*, at least one of which will be open 24 hours. Take adequate supplies of drugs you need on a regular basis as they may not be readily available.

Post offices
Stamps are bought at post offices and at some news kiosks. Post boxes are red and marked with the word *'Poczta'*.

Safe water
Tap water is normally chlorinated and may taste unpleasant. Bottled mineral water is available.

Telephones
There are still many public telephone boxes operated by Telekomunikacja Polska at strategic points in every village, town and city. Telephone cards *(karta telefoniczna)* can be bought at post offices and news kiosks. There are no coin-operated telephones. The country code for Poland is 48. To call home from Poland dial the international code (00) followed by the country code. To call the UK from Poland dial 00 44.

Time
Poland is on Central European Time, one hour ahead of Greenwich Mean Time (GMT + 1). From late March, when clocks are put forward one hour, until late October, Daylight Savings Time (GMT + 2) operates.

Emergency telephone numbers
Police **997**
Fire Brigade **998**
Ambulance **999**

Toll charges in zlotys

Road		**Car**	**Car towing caravan/ trailer**
A1	Rusocin – Nowe Marzy	29.90	71.00
A2	Nowl Tomysl – Konin	42.00	81.00
A2	Konin – Strykow	9.90	
A4	Katowice – Kraków	9.00	15.00

Driving in Portugal *(South West Europe)*

The regulations below should be read in conjunction with the General motoring information on pages 18–21.

Drinking and driving

If the level of alcohol in the bloodstream is between 0.05 per cent and 0.08 per cent, a fine and withdrawal of the driving licence for a minimum of one month to a maximum of one year can be imposed; if more than 0.08 per cent, there is a fine and withdrawal of the driving licence for a minimum of two months up to a maximum of two years. The police are also empowered to test drivers for narcotics.

Driving licence

The minimum age at which UK licence holders may drive a temporarily imported car and/or motorcycle (over 50cc) is 17; however visitors under the age of 18 years may encounter problems even though they hold a valid UK licence. All valid UK driving licences should be accepted in Portugal. This includes the older all-green-style UK licences (in Northern Ireland older paper-style with photographic counterpart) although the EC appreciates that these may be more difficult to understand and that drivers may wish to update them voluntarily before travelling abroad, if time permits. Alternatively, older licences may be accompanied by an International Driving Permit (IDP).

Fines

On-the-spot and must be paid in euros. Most traffic police materials are equipped with portable ATM machines for immediate payment of the fines. An official receipt showing the maximum amount of the fine should be obtained. **Note:** Foreign motorists refusing to pay an on-the-spot fine will be asked for a deposit to cover the maximum fine for the offence committed. If a motorist refuses to do this, the police can take the driving licence, registration document or, failing that, they can confiscate the vehicle. Wheel clamping and towing operate for illegally parked vehicles.

Fuel

Unleaded petrol (95 and 98 octane), diesel and LPG are available. There is no leaded petrol (lead replacement petrol is available as 98 octane). Carrying petrol in a can is permitted. Credit cards are accepted at most filling stations; check with your card issuer for use in Portugal before travel. **Note:** a tax of €0.50 is added to credit card transactions.

Lights

Dipped headlights must be used in poor daytime visibility and in tunnels.

Motorcycles

The use of dipped headlights during the day is compulsory. The wearing of crash helmets is compulsory. A child under seven is not permitted to ride as a passenger.

Motor insurance

Third-party insurance is compulsory.

Motorways

See Spain/Portugal motorway map on page 152.

Passengers/children in cars

Children under 12 and less than 1.5m (4ft 11in) in height cannot travel as front-seat passengers. They must travel in the rear in a special restraint system adapted to their size, unless the vehicle has only two seats, or is not fitted with seat belts. Children under three can be seated in the front passenger seat if using a suitable child restraint; however, the air bag must be switched off if using a rear-facing child-restraint system.

Seat belts

It is compulsory for front- and rear-seat occupants to wear seat belts, if fitted.

Speed limits

The standard legal limits, which may be varied by signs, for **private vehicles without trailers** are: in built-up areas 50km/h (31mph), outside built-up areas 90km/h (55mph) or 100km/h (62mph) and on motorways 120km/h (74mph). The minimum speed on motorways is 50km/h (31mph). Motorists who have held a driving licence for less than one year must not exceed 90km/h (55mph) or any lower speed limit.

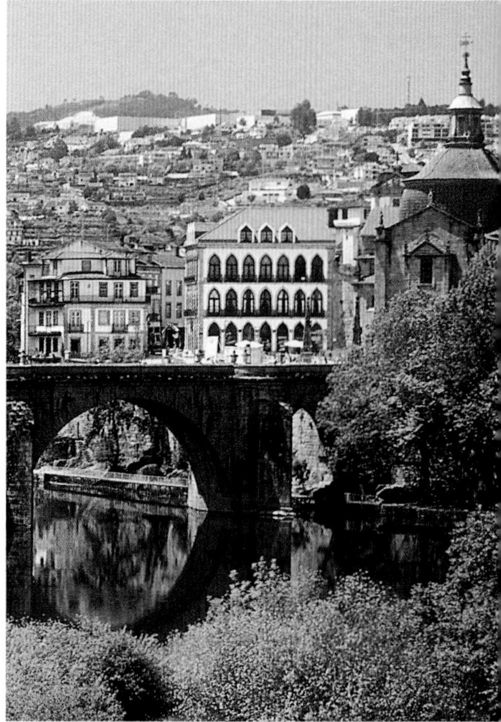

Additional information

- It is a legal requirement to carry photographic proof of identity at all times.
- It is compulsory for residents to carry reflective jackets in their cars; this regulation is recommended for visitors. The wearing of reflective jacket/waistcoat is recommended if the driver and/or passenger(s) exits an immobilised vehicle on the carriageway on all motorways and main or busy roads. We recommend that the jacket is carried in the passenger area of the vehicle (not the boot).
- Depending on the roads to be travelled, tolls are payable via a preloaded Toll Card, a prepaid Toll Service ticket with unlimited use for a fixed period or using Easy Toll, an automatic system where a credit card is linked to the registration of the vehicle.
- A warning triangle is recommended as the use of hazard warning lights or a warning triangle is compulsory in an accident/breakdown situation.
- It is prohibited to carry and/or use a radar detector.
- Spiked tyres and winter tyres are prohibited. Snow chains may be used, where the weather conditions require.
- It is illegal to carry bicycles on the back of a passenger car.
- In built-up areas the use of the horn is prohibited during the hours of darkness except in the case of immediate danger.

Toll charges in euros

Road		Car	Car towing caravan/ trailer
E1 (A1)	Lisboa – Porto	21.25	21.25
E1 (A2)	Lisboa – VLA (Algarve)	20.20	20.20
E1 (A3)	Porto – Valença do Minho (Spain/Vigo)	10.00	10.00
E82 (A4)	Porto – Amarante	7.15	7.15
A5	Lisboa – Cascais	1.35	1.35
E90 (A6)	**E1/E90** Marateca – Badajoz (Spanish border)	13.30	13.30
A7	Vila do Conde – **A24**	7.85	7.85
A7	Vila Nova de Farmilicao-Guimaraes	9.30	9.30
A8	Lisboa – Leiria	9.90	9.90
A9	Alverca – Oeiras	3.20	3.20
A10	A9 – Arruda dos Vinhos – **E1 (A13)**	1.80	1.80
A11	Braga **(A3)** – Guimaraes **(A7)** – **A4**	8.15	8.15
A12	Setúbal – Ponte Vasco de Gama	2.10	2.10
A13	Santo Estevao – Marateca (**A2/A6**)	14.35	14.35
A14	Figueira da Foz – Coimbra (Nord)	2.50	2.50
A15	Caldas – Santarem (**E1**)	3.80	3.80

Road		Car	Car towing caravan/ trailer
A16	Cascais (A5) – Belas (A9)	2.20	2.20
A17	Mirinha Grande – Aveiro	10.55	10.55
A19	Var Batalha-Azoia	1.15	1.15
A21	Malveria (**A8**) – Ericeira	2.10	2.10
A22	Castro Marim – Bensafrim	10.05	10.05
A23	Torres Novas-Guarda	16.75	16.75
A24	Viseu – V.V. da Raia	14.20	14.20
A25	Aveiro – Vilar Formoso	14.90	14.90
A28	Porto – V.N. de C'erveira	3.70	3.70
A29	Angeja – Porto	2.75	2.75
A32	Oliv. Azemeis – A1	3.05	3.05
A33	Charneca – Belverde	1.70	1.70
A41	Freixieiro – Espinho	4.75	4.75
A42	A41/A42 – A11	1.60	1.60
A43	Porto – Aguiar de Sousa	1.00	1.00

Bridges and tunnels

	Car	Car towing caravan/ trailer
25th April Bridge (Ponte 25 de Abril) on **A2**	1.60	1.60
(tolls are payable in one direction only, when travelling north into Lisbon)		
Vasco da Gama Bridge (Ponte Vasco da Gama) on **A12**	2.60	2.60
(payable in one direction only, when travelling north)		

Travel facts: Portugal

Portuguese National Tourist Office,
11 Belgrave Square
London SW1X 8PP
Tel: 0845 355 1212
www.visitportugal.com
www.portugal.org

Banking hours

Banks are open Monday to Friday from 8.30am to 3pm. The national network of ATMs is identified by the symbol MB (Multibanco), from which you can withdraw cash 24 hours a day.

Credit/debit cards

Major credit cards are accepted in most resorts. In rural areas it is advisable to have small denomination notes to hand.

Currency

The currency in Portugal is the euro (€). Euro coins are issued in denominations of 1, 2, 5, 10, 20 and 50 cents and €1 and €2. Banknotes are issued in denominations of €5, €10, €20, €50, €100, €200 and €500. **Note:** €200 and €500 notes are not issued in Portugal, but those issued elsewhere are valid.

Electricity

The native power supply is 220 volts AC, 50Hz. Sockets take two-round-pin continental-style plugs. Visitors from the UK require an adaptor.

Health care

Free or reduced-cost medical treatment is available in Portugal to European visitors on production of a valid European Health Insurance Card (EHIC). See page 10. Comprehensive travel insurance is still advised and is essential for all other visitors.

Pharmacies

Chemists *(farmâcia)* are open Monday to Friday 9am to 1pm and 2.30 to 7pm and Saturday 9am to 12.30pm. Some open through lunch and the late-night duty chemist is posted in pharmacy windows. Pharmacists are highly trained and can sell some drugs that require prescriptions in other countries. However, take adequate supplies of any drugs you take regularly as they may not be available.

Post offices

There is at least one post office *(correio)* in every town and reasonably large village. They sell stamps *(selos)* as do many places with *correios* signs. Opening hours are Monday to Friday 8.30am to 6pm, Saturday 9am to noon at main branches in cities, shorter hours in provincial areas.

Safe water

Tap water is generally safe but not too pleasant. Anywhere, but especially outside the main cities, towns and resorts, it is advisable to drink bottled water *(água mineral)*, either still *(sem gás)* or carbonated *(com gás)*.

Telephones

Most public telephones now accept coins and credit cards or phone cards. Phone cards are available from post offices, kiosks and shops displaying the PT (Portugal Telecom) logo and can be used for international calls. International calls are cheaper between 9pm and 9am and at weekends. The country code for Portugal is 351. To call home from Portugal dial the international code (00) followed by the country code. To call the UK from Portugal dial 00 44.

Time

Portugal is on Greenwich Mean Time (GMT), the same as the UK, and one hour behind most of continental Europe. During the summer, from the last Sunday in March to the last Sunday in October, the time in Portugal is GMT plus one hour (GMT + 1).

Emergency telephone numbers

Police **112**
Fire **112**
Ambulance **112**

Driving in Romania *(South East Europe)*

The regulations below should be read in conjunction with the General motoring information on pages 18–21.

Drinking and driving

Drinking and driving is strictly forbidden. Nil percentage of alcohol is allowed in the driver's blood. The driving licence can be suspended for a maximum of 90 days or a prison sentence imposed for offenders.

Driving licence

The minimum age at which a UK licence holder may drive a temporarily imported car and/or motorcycle (for up to 90 days) is 18. Driving licences issued in the UK that do not incorporate a photograph must be accompanied by an International Driving Permit (IDP).

Fines

Police can impose fines on the spot; they must be paid at local post offices. A vehicle that is illegally parked may be clamped and removed. If a fine is paid within 48 hours the amount is halved.

Fuel

Lead replacement petrol (95 and 98 octane), unleaded petrol, diesel and LPG are available. Carrying petrol in a can is permitted (must be empty when leaving Romania). Tax is payable on petrol and diesel in the vehicle tank when leaving Romania. Credit cards are accepted at many stations; check with your card issuer for usage in Romania before travel. Payment is usually made in local currency.

Lights

It is forbidden to drive at night if the vehicle lighting is faulty. Additional headlamps are prohibited. Dipped headlights must be used outside built-up areas during the day.

Motorcycles

The use of dipped headlights during the day is compulsory. The wearing of crash helmets is compulsory for the driver and passenger of machines of 50cc and above.

Motor insurance

A Green Card/third-party insurance is compulsory. Drivers of vehicles registered abroad who are not in possession of a valid Green Card must take out short-term insurance at the frontier.

Passengers/children in cars

A child under 12 cannot travel as a front-seat passenger.

Seat belts

It is compulsory for front- and rear-seat occupants to wear seat belts, if fitted.

Speed limits

The standard legal limits, which may be varied by signs, for **private vehicles without trailers** are: in built-up areas 50km/h (31mph), outside built-up areas 90km/h (55mph), 100km/h (62mph) on dual carriageways and 130km/h (80mph) on motorways. There is no minimum speed on motorways. **If towing** a 10km/h (6mph) reduction of the standard speed limit applies. A driver who has held a licence for less than one year is restricted to a speed limit of 20km/h (12mph) below the indicated speed. The speed limit for mopeds is 45km/h (28mph) inside and outside built-up areas.

Additional information

- A fire extinguisher, first-aid kit and a red warning triangle are compulsory (warning triangle not required for two-wheeled vehicles).
- All persons exiting a vehicle to walk on the road when in a breakdown or emergency situation must wear a reflective jacket.
- Winter tyres should be used from the 1st November to 31st March if there is snow or ice covering. Alternatively tyres marked M&S are permitted.
- It is against the law to drive a dirty car.
- If a temporarily imported vehicle is damaged before arrival in Romania, the importer must ask a Romanian customs or police officer to write a report on the damage so that the vehicle can be exported without problems. If any damage occurs inside the country a report must be obtained at the scene of the accident. Damaged vehicles may be taken out of the country only on production of this evidence.
- The use of the horn is prohibited between 10pm and 6am in built-up areas. *'Claxonarea interzisa'* – use of horn prohibited.
- Spiked tyres are prohibited.
- The use of snow chains is recommended for winter journeys to the mountains and may be compulsory in case of heavy snow.
- Road tax stickers *(rovinieta)* have been replaced by a system of electronic tax. This is payable at the National Road Administration offices at border crossing points, from post office branches in Romania and some petrol stations. The driver must give details of the vehicle, driver identity and place of residence. You must advise of the number of days in Romania and pay the tax accordingly. This information is then entered into a database at the Road Information Centre. Cameras are situated along roads. This enables the traffic police to check your vehicle number plate against the database. The cost depends on the weight of the vehicle and period of use in Romania. Fines for non-compliance or expired road tax are between €50 and €900.

Travel facts: Romania

Romanian National Tourist Office
22 New Cavendish Street
London W1G 8TT
Tel: 020 7224 3692
www.romaniatourism.com
www.romaniatravel.com

Banking hours
Banks are generally open Monday to Friday 9am to 2pm.

Credit/debit cards
Romania is largely a cash-only economy. American Express, Diners Club, MasterCard and Visa are accepted by an increasing number of hotels and some restaurants and shops, but you are advised to use cash due to the risk of credit card fraud. There are an increasing number of ATMs *(bancomat)* throughout the major cities. Do not expect to find ATMs in remote areas or villages.

Currency
The monetary unit of Romania is the lei (RON), divided into 100 bani. Notes are in denominations of Lei500, 100, 50, 10, 5 and 1. Coins are in denominations of bani 50, 10, 5 and 1. Foreign currencies may be exchanged at banks or authorised exchange offices *(casa de schimb* or *birou de schimb valutar)*. International airports and larger hotels also offer currency exchange services. It is illegal to change money on the black market.

Electricity
The electrical supply is 220 volts AC, 50Hz. Plugs are of the two-pin type.

Health care
Free or reduced-cost medical treatment is available in Romania to European visitors on production of a valid European Health Insurance Card (EHIC). See page 10. Comprehensive travel insurance is still advised and is essential for all other visitors.

Pharmacies
Pharmacies *(farmacie)* in Bucharest are well stocked and pharmacists may be able to suggest a medication for certain complaints. Some pharmacies in the city are open 24 hours a day.

Post offices
Post offices are generally open Monday to Friday 8am to 7pm, Saturday 8am to 2pm. Bucharest main post office is open 7.30am to 8pm. Airmail to Western Europe takes one week.

Safe water
Mains water is normally chlorinated, and while relatively safe, may cause abdominal upsets. You are advised to drink bottled mineral water, which is widely available.

Telephones
Public telephones are widely available and can be used for direct international calls; most require a phone card. Hotels often impose a high service charge for long-distance calls. The country code for Romania is 40. To call home from Romania dial the international code (00) followed by the country code. To call the UK from Romania dial 00 44.

Time
Romania is on Eastern European Time, which is two hours ahead of Greenwich Mean Time (GMT + 2), but from the last Sunday in March to the last Sunday in October, when clocks are put forward one hour, Summer Time (GMT + 3) operates.

Emergency telephone numbers
Police **955** or **112** Fire **981** or **112** Ambulance **961** or **112**

Charges in leu

General	Car	Car towing caravan/trailer
7-day *vignette (rovinieta)*	12.97	25.93
1-month *vignette (rovinieta)*	30.26	69.61
90 days *vignette (rovinieta)*	56.19	155.61
1 year *vignette (rovinieta)*	121.03	414.95

Driving in the Russian Federation

(Eastern Europe)

The regulations below should be read in conjunction with the General motoring information on pages 18–21.

Drinking and driving

No amount of alcohol is permitted in a driver's blood and a policy of zero tolerance is applied. Driving under the influence of narcotics is strictly prohibited.

Driving licence

An International Driving Permit (IDP) is compulsory for the holder of any type of UK driving licence. The minimum age at which a visitor may drive a temporarily imported car and/or motorcycle is 17.

Fines

On-the-spot fines can be imposed. Fines should be paid through a bank according to the ticket given by the policeman. It is illegal to pay cash. Police can clamp or remove illegally parked vehicles.

Fuel

Leaded petrol is available, but it may be in short supply and low octane. Unleaded petrol (82, 92 and 95 octane) is available, but it is advisable to keep your tank topped up whenever possible. It is not permitted to import fuel in a can, but once in the country it is advisable to carry spare fuel. Diesel *(solyarka)* and limited supplies of LPG are available. Credit cards are not widely accepted at filling stations; check with your card issuer for usage in the Russian Federation before travel.

Lights

The use of passing lights during the day is compulsory outside built-up areas; a fine is imposed for non-compliance.

Motorcycles

The wearing of crash helmets is compulsory when riding a scooter or motorcycle. A child under 12 is not permitted as a passenger. Motorcycles must use dipped headlights at all times.

Motor Insurance

Third-party insurance is compulsory and fully comprehensive insurance is recommended. Additional insurance can be purchased at the border and Green Cards are recognised. If a motorist travels to Russia with a Green Card, they must ensure the code RUS is included on the document.

Passengers/children in cars

Children under 12 cannot travel as a front-seat passenger unless using a restraint system appropriate to their size.

Seat belts

It is compulsory for front- and rear-seat occupants to wear seat belts, if fitted.

Speed limits

Speed limits must be strictly adhered to.
The standard legal limits, which may be varied by signs, for **private vehicles without trailers** are: in built-up areas 60km/h (37mph), outside built-up areas 90km/h (55mph) but 110km/h (68mph) on expressways. Motorists who have held a driving licence for less than two years must not exceed 70km/h (43mph). In some residential zones the speed limit is 20km/h (13mph) as signposted.

Additional information

- It is compulsory to carry a first-aid kit, fire extinguisher, warning triangle and a set of replacement bulbs.
- A road tax is payable at the frontier.
- In addition to the original vehicle registration document it is recommended that you carry an International Certificate for Motor Vehicles
- State Traffic Inspectorate officials will stop vehicles to check documents, especially if vehicles are displaying foreign plates.
- We recommend that visitors carry an assortment of spares for their vehicle such as a fan belt and spark plugs.
- It is against the law to drive a dirty car, where the registration plate isn't legible.
- Use of the horn in towns is prohibited.
- It is forbidden to pick up hitch-hikers.
- Anti-radar equipment that interferes with specific radio frequencies to jam police signals is prohibited.
- It is necessary to pre-plan itineraries and book accommodation before departure.
- A visitor whose vehicle is involved in an accident or breakdown must contact the Militia; the police must always be called to the scene of an accident.
- Avoid driving at night if possible.

Travel facts: The Russian Federation

Russian National Tourist Office
70 Piccadilly
London W1J 8HP
Tel: 0207 495 7570
www.visitrussia.org.uk

Banking hours
Local banking hours are from Monday to Friday 9am to 5pm. Major banks are open Monday to Friday 9am to 8pm.

Credit/debit cards
Most hotels, restaurants and larger shops accept credit and debit cards, including Visa and MasterCard, but cash (in roubles) is often preferred. Smaller shops do not accept cards. You'll find ATMs in most major cities. Traveller's cheques are not widely accepted.

Currency
The official currency in Russia is the rouble with 100 kopeks in 1 rouble. Banknotes come in denominations of 10, 50, 100, 500, 1,000 and 5,000 roubles; coins in denominations of 1, 2, 5 and 10 roubles and 1, 2, 10, 50 kopecks. It is advisable to take US dollars or euros (all notes should be in good condition) that can be exchanged at banks, hotels and recognised exchange kiosks. It is an offence to change money from street traders. It is illegal to pay directly with dollars or euros.

Electricity
The power supply throughout Russia is 220 volts AC, 50Hz. The plug is two-pin European standard. Bring your own converter as most places in Russia do not have them.

Health care
The UK has a reciprocal health care agreement with Russia. If you're visiting Russia and need urgent or immediate medical treatment it will be provided at a reduced cost or, in some cases, free. The range of medical services available may be more restricted than under the NHS, therefore it is essential for all visitors to have comprehensive travel insurance. Visit **www.nhs.uk/NHSEngland/Healthcareabroad** for a country-by-country guide.

Pharmacies
It is advisable to take a supply of medicines that are likely to be required during your stay in Russia (check first that they may be imported legally). Pharmacies can be identified by a large green cross.

Post offices
Post offices are generally open Monday to Friday 8am to 6pm. Some also open on Saturday morning.

Safe water
Water quality varies throughout Russia. Do not drink tap water – buy bottled water.

Telephones
Public telephones accept telephone tokens and cards that can be purchased from news-stands, some stores and many kiosks. The country code for Russia is 7. To call home from Russia dial the international code (00) followed by the country code. To call the UK dial 00 44.

Time
Both Moscow and St Petersburg are three hours ahead of Greenwich Mean Time (GMT + 3). From late March to late October they are three hours ahead of Greenwich Mean Time (GMT + 3).

Emergency telephone numbers
Police **02**
Fire **01**
Ambulance **03**

Toll charges in rubles

The following toll roads are under construction:
St Petersburg ring road
M4 Moscow – Novorossiysk
Moscow – St Petersburg

Driving in Serbia *(South East Europe)*

The regulations below should be read in conjunction with the General motoring information on pages 18–21.

Drinking and driving

If the level of alcohol in the bloodstream is 0.03 per cent or more, or if a medical examination shows that normal bodily functions are impaired, severe penalties including a fine, imprisonment and/or suspension of the driving licence can be imposed. Nil percentage of alcohol is permitted in the driver's blood for motorcyclists, novice and professional drivers. Police can carry out random breath tests. All drivers involved in an accident will be tested for alcohol and narcotics. Drivers who refuse a test will be automatically imprisoned.

Driving licence

The minimum age at which a UK licence holder may drive a temporarily imported car and/or motorcycle (exceeding 125cc) is 18. We recommend that you obtain an International Driving Permit (IDP) to accompany your UK driving licence.

Fines

Fines are no longer payable on the spot. A ticket will be issued by the policeman and the fine must be paid at a post office or bank within 8 days. Fines vary according to the gravity of the offence. Penalties are higher if the motorist endangers other people or causes an accident.

Fuel

Diesel *(dizel)*, LPG and unleaded petrol (95 octane) are available. Carrying petrol in a can is permitted (duty payable). Credit cards are generally accepted; check with your card issuer for usage in Serbia before travel.

Lights

It is compulsory to use daytime running lights or dipped headlights during the day. A fine will be imposed for non-compliance.

Motorcycles

The wearing of crash helmets is compulsory for both driver and passenger on a motorcycle, moped, motorised tricycle or quadricycle. Passengers on motorcycles are not permitted to travel under the influence of alcohol. A child aged 12 or under is not permitted as a passenger.

Motor insurance

Third-party insurance is compulsory. Although recognised, a Green Card is no longer needed. UK drivers may enter Serbia with their valid compulsory motor insurance policy (without having to pay border insurance). Check with your motor insurer prior to travel, to confirm cover in Serbia.

Passengers/children in cars

A person visibly under the influence of alcohol is not permitted to travel in a vehicle as a front-seat passenger. Children up to the age of three years old can travel in the front of a car on the condition that they are placed in a rear-facing child restraint adapted to their size and the air bag is deactivated.

Seat belts

It is compulsory for front/rear-seat occupants to wear seat belts, if fitted.

Speed limits

The standard legal limits, which may be varied by signs, for **private vehicles without trailers** are: in built-up areas 50km/h (31mph), outside built-up areas 80km/h (49mph) but 100km/h (62mph) on dual carriageways and 120km/h (74mph) on motorways. The speed limit in school areas is 30km/h (18mph). When **towing a trailer or caravan** the speed limit on all roads outside built-up areas, including dual carriage-ways and motorways, is 80km/h (49mph). Drivers who have held their licence for one year or less can drive at 90% of the limits above.

Additional information

- It is compulsory to carry a first-aid kit (type A for motorcycles and type B for other vehicles; excludes mopeds); a spare bulb set (excludes two-wheeled motor vehicles and vehicles fitted with LED, Halogen or Xenon headlights; a warning triangle – two if towing a trailer (not required for two-wheeled vehicles); a spare wheel (which must be of the same dimensions and load of those fitted); and a tow rope/tow bar (minimum 3m).
- From 1st November to 1st April, winter tyres (marked M&S) will have to be fitted on the drive wheels of all motor vehicles up to 3.5 tonnes and must have a minimum of 4mm tread. Snow chains must be carried all the time in the vehicle as their use may become compulsory if the International 'snow chains' sign is displayed.
- It is compulsory to carry reflective jackets. Any person exiting a vehicle to walk on the road must wear the reflective jacket; therefore the jackets should be kept in the passenger compartment of the vehicle.
- A European Accident claim form must be completed if an accident involves a Serbian registered vehicle. Therefore it is recommended that a European Accident claim form be carried.
- The use or carriage of radar detectors is prohibited.
- Tolls are payable on most sections of motorway. See page 141.
- The authorities at the frontier must certify any visible damage to a vehicle entering Serbia and a certificate obtained; this must be produced when leaving, otherwise you may experience serious difficulties on leaving the country.
- Spiked tyres are prohibited.
- Vehicles entering a roundabout have right of way.
- It is forbidden to use a vehicle that has tinted front and rear windscreens. The side windscreens can only be tinted to a maximum of 25%.
- Use of the horn is prohibited in built-up areas and at night except in cases of imminent danger.
- Do not overtake school buses that have stopped for children to board or alight.

Travel facts and toll charges: Serbia

Embassy of the Republic of Serbia
28 Belgrave Square
London SW1X 8QB
Tel: 020 7235 9049
www.serbianembassy.org.uk
www.serbia-tourism.org

Banking hours
Most banks are open Monday to Friday from 8am to 7pm and Saturday from 8am to 3pm. On Sunday a designated bank is usually open.

Credit/debit cards
Major credit cards such as Visa, MasterCard and Diners Club are accepted in most shops, hotels and restaurants in Serbia. Very few ATMs accept international bank cards. There are several money exchange machines in Belgrade (including one at the airport), which accept pounds Sterling, US dollars and euros, giving back dinars. Scottish and Northern Irish pound Sterling banknotes are not accepted.

Currency
The official currency in Serbia is the dinar (CSD) which is divided into 100 paras. Bank notes are in denominations of CSD5,000, 1,000, 200, 100, 50, 20 and 10 and coins in denominations of CSD20, 10, 5, 2 and 1 and 50 paras. Money should be exchanged through official exchange offices only.

Electricity
The electric current in Serbia 220 volts AC, 50Hz. Two-round-pin plugs are used.

Health care
Comprehensive travel insurance is essential for all visitors.

Pharmacies
Pharmacies are open Monday to Friday from 8am to 3pm and on Saturdays from 8am to 1pm. Each city has a pharmacy that is open on Sundays and throughout the night.

Post offices
Most post offices are open Monday to Friday from 8am to 7pm and on Saturday from 8am to 3pm. On Sunday there is usually a designated post office that maintains services.

Safe water
Mains water is normally chlorinated and, while relatively safe, may cause mild abdominal upsets. Bottled water is available.

Telephones
The country code for Serbia is 381. To call home from Serbia dial the international code (00) followed by the country code. To call the UK from Serbia dial 00 44.

Time
Serbia observes Central European Time (CET), which is one hour ahead of Greenwich Mean Time (GMT + 1), until late March to late October, when clocks are put forward one hour (GMT + 2).

Emergency telephone numbers
Police **92**
Fire **93**
Medical emergency **94**
Help on the road **987**
General information (hospitals, chemists on duty etc.) **9812**

Contact the Serbian Embassy for details of specific entry/exit requirements.

Toll charge in dinars

Road		**Car**	**Car towing caravan/ trailer**
E70	Beograd – Sid	340.00	520.00
E75	Beograd – Novi Sad	240.00	350.00
E75	Novi Sad – Feketic	330.00	500.00
E75	Beograd – Nis	730.00	1,100.00
E75	Nis – Leskovac	190.00	280.00

Driving in Slovakia *(Central Europe)*

The regulations below should be read in conjunction with the General motoring information on pages 18–21.

Drinking and driving

Drinking and driving is strictly forbidden. Nil percentage of alcohol is allowed in the driver's blood. Penalties include a fine, withdrawal of licence and imprisonment. The driver may be breath tested and, according to the result of the test, may then be obliged to give a blood sample.

Driving licence

The minimum age at which a UK licence holder may drive a temporarily imported car is 18, for a motorcycle (exceeding 50cc) it is 17.

Fines

On-the-spot fines can be imposed; an official receipt should be obtained. Wheel clamps are in use and vehicles may be towed away.

Fuel

Unleaded petrol (95 octane), diesel *(nafta)* and LPG are available. There is no leaded petrol. Carrying petrol in a can is permitted. LPG can be used for road vehicles only on the condition that a safety certificate covers the equipment for its combustion. Credit cards are accepted at filling stations; check with your card issuer for usage in Slovakia before travel.

Lights

The use of dipped headlights during the day is compulsory. Any vehicle warning lights, other than those supplied with the vehicle as original equipment, must be made inoperative.

Motorcycles

The use of dipped headlights during the day is compulsory. The wearing of a crash helmet is compulsory when riding a machine over 50cc. It is forbidden for motorcyclists to smoke while riding their machine.

Motor insurance

Third-party insurance is compulsory.

Passengers/children in cars

No person under 1.5m (4ft 11in) in height or a child under 12 years may travel in a vehicle as a front-seat passenger. The use of child seats is compulsory for all children under 12 years of age or under 1.5m (4ft 11in). Specially adapted child restraint/seats must be used for children weighing less than 36kg.

Seat belts

It is compulsory for all occupants to wear seat belts, if fitted.

Speed limits

The standard legal limits, which may be varied by signs, for **private vehicles without trailers**, are: on motorways and expressways outside built-up areas 130km/h (80mph), motorways and expressways in built-up areas 90km/h (55mph). Other roads outside built-up areas 90km/h (55mph), other roads in built-up areas 50km/h (31mph). Drivers must not exceed a speed of 30km/h (18mph), 30m before a level crossing and while crossing over it. The minimum speed on motorways is 80km/h (49mph), 65km/h (40mph) on urban motorways.

Additional information

- A first-aid kit is compulsory.
- A warning triangle is compulsory (not required for two-wheeled vehicles).
- Winter tyres (M&S type) with a minimum tread depth of 3mm are compulsory when compacted snow or ice is on the road.
- Drivers are also obliged to clear their vehicles of ice and snow prior to moving to avoid endangering other road users.
- Reflective jackets are compulsory for two- and four-wheeled vehicles on all roads outside built-up areas. Any person getting out of the vehicle as a result of a breakdown, puncture or accident must wear a reflective jacket. A fine of up to €150 will be imposed for non-compliance. Reflective jackets must comply with EU standard EN471.
- For vehicles under 3.5 tonnes a motorway tax (see page 144) is payable to travel on certain highways and motorways. A sticker must be displayed on the right-hand side of the windscreen of all vehicles (except motorcycles) as evidence of payment. Stickers may be purchased at border crossings and from selected filling stations and post offices for periods of one year, one month or 10 days. Fines are imposed for non-display. It is compulsory to remove stickers that are no longer valid.
- A mobile home exceeding 3.5 tonnes can be considered as a private vehicle if the registration certificate shows that it has a maximum of 9 seats (including the driver). In this case the driver can purchase the vignette/sticker as if for a private car.
- Radar detection equipment is strictly prohibited in Slovakia.
- The authorities at the frontier must certify any visible damage to a vehicle entering Slovakia.
- If any damage occurs inside the country with an estimated cost over €4,000 or where injury or fatality occurs, a police report must be obtained at the scene of the accident. Damaged vehicles may be taken out of the country only on production of this evidence.
- Drivers are advised by the Slovak police to be wary of people approaching their vehicle at border crossings and petrol stations near the border who may cause damage to tyres and then offer their assistance further along your route when the tyre becomes deflated.
- Spiked tyres are prohibited and snow chains may be used only where there is enough snow to protect the road surface.
- All foreign visitors are required to show proof of medical insurance cover on entry.
- Horns may be used only to warn of danger or to signify intention to overtake.
- A GPS device must not be placed in the middle of the windscreen; the drivers view must not be impeded.
- All road users must give way to trams.

Travel facts: Slovakia

Slovakian Tourist Board
Slovak Tourist Centre
16 Frognal Parade
Finchley Road
London NW3 5HG
Tel: 020 7794 3263 or **0800 026 79432**
www.slovakia.travel/

Banking hours
Banks are usually open Monday to Friday from 8am to 4.30pm. In the largest shopping centres, the bank services are also available during weekends and holidays to 8pm.

Credit/debit cards
Major credit cards (American Express, Diners Club, MasterCard and Visa) and debit cards (Maestro and Visa Electron) are widely accepted in Slovakia

Currency
The euro (€) is the official currency of Slovakia. Coins are issued in denominations of 1, 2, 5, 10, 20 and 50 cents and €1 and €2. Notes are issued in denominations of €5, €10, €20, €50, €100, €200 and €500.

Electricity
The power supply in Slovakia is 220 volts AC, 50Hz. Sockets take two-round-pin plugs.

Health care
Free or reduced-cost medical treatment is available in Slovakia to European visitors on production of a valid European Health Insurance Card (EHIC). See page 10. Comprehensive travel insurance is essential for all visitors. All visitors must show proof of medical insurance cover on entry.

Pharmacies
Pharmacies *(apothéka)* are the only places to sell over-the-counter medicines. They also dispense many drugs *(leky)* normally available on prescription in other Western countries. Pharmacies are usually open from 7.30am to 4pm.

Post offices
Post offices are usually open Monday to Friday from 8am to 6pm and on Saturday to 1pm. Main post offices in larger towns or shopping malls are open daily to 8pm. Stamps *(známky)* for postcards and letters are available from post offices and some newspaper stands

Safe water
The tap water is normally be safe to drink in Slovakia. If in doubt, bottled mineral water is widely available.

Telephones
There is a network of public pay phones; most take phone cards (which can be purchased at most news-stands); some are coin operated. Some phones do not allow outgoing calls to international and mobile numbers (marked by an orange sticker with Slovak and English text). If you have any problems, dial 149 and ask for an English-speaking operator. The country code for Slovakia is 421. To call home from Slovakia dial the international code (00) followed by the country code. To call the UK from Slovakia dial 00 44.

Time
Slovakia is on Central European time (GMT + 1). Daylight Saving Time comes into effect on the last Sunday in March and ends on the last Sunday in October (GMT + 2).

Emergency telephone numbers
Police **112**
Fire **112**
Ambulance **112**

Charges in euros

General	Car
7-day *vignette*	7.00
1-month *vignette*	14.00
1-year *vignette*	50.00

Driving in Slovenia *(Central Europe)*

The regulations below should be read in conjunction with the General motoring information on pages 18–21.

Drinking and driving
If the level of alcohol in the bloodstream is 0.05 per cent or more, severe penalties including a fine or suspension of the driving licence can be imposed. Nil percentage of alcohol is permitted in the driver's blood if the licence has been held for less than two years, the person is under 21 or employed as a professional driver. The driver can still be fined for levels under 0.05 per cent if unable to drive safely. These rules also apply to narcotics.

Driving licence
The minimum age at which a UK licence holder may drive a temporarily imported car and/or motorcycle exceeding 125cc is 18. An Internatioinal Driving Permit (IDP) is compulsory for holders of driving licences not incorporating a photograph.

Fines
On-the-spot fines must be paid in local currency. Refusal to pay could result in your passport being held. Illegally parked vehicles will be towed away or clamped.

Fuel
Unleaded petrol (95 and 100 octane), diesel and LPG are available. There is no leaded petrol (a lead-substitute additive is available). Carrying petrol in a can is permitted. Credit cards are accepted at filling stations; check with your card issuer for usage in Slovenia before travel.

Lights
The use of dipped headlights during the day is compulsory.

Motorcycles
The use of dipped headlights during the day is compulsory. The wearing of crash helmets is also compulsory for both driver and passenger. A child under 12 is not permitted as a passenger.

Motor insurance
Third party insurance is compulsory.

Passengers/children in cars
Children under 1.5m (4ft 11in) must use a restraint system suitable for their size. Children taller than 1.5m may wear normal seat belts. If a child is transported on the front seat in a rear facing child restraint, the airbag must be de-activated. A child under 3 years of age must not be transported in a vehicle if a child restraint can not be fitted.

Seat belts
It is compulsory for front- and rear-seat occupants to wear seat belts, if fitted.

Speed limits
The standard legal limits, which may be varied by signs, for **private vehicles without trailers** are: in built-up areas 50km/h (31mph), outside built-up areas 90km/h (55mph) but 110km/h (68mph) on 'fast roads' (dual carriageways)

and 130km/h (80mph) on motorways. There are areas with a restricted speed limit of 30km/h (18mph). The minimum speed on motorways is 60km/h (37mph). When **towing a trailer or caravan** with a combined weight less than 3.5 tonnes, the limit on all roads outside built-up areas is 80km/h (49mph). Vehicles with snow chains must not exceed 50km/h (31mph). In bad weather and when visibility is reduced to less than 50m due to bad weather the maximum speed limit is 50km/h (31mph).

Additional information

- A reflective jacket is compulsory (not required for motorcycles). The reflective jacket(s)/ waistcoat(s) should be kept in the vehicle and not in the boot as each person must wear one as soon as they leave their vehicle in an accident/breakdown situation. There is a fine for non-compliance.
- A warning triangle is compulsory (not required for two-wheeled vehicles); two are necessary if towing a trailer.
- A first aid kit is compulsory.
- Snow chains must be carried between 15 November and 15 March (and at other times in winter weather conditions) by private cars and vehicles up to 3.5 tonnes unless the vehicle fitted with four winter tyres marked M&S. The minimum tyre tread depth is 3mm at times when snow chains/winter tyres are required.
- Warning triangle and/or hazard warning lights must be used in an accident/breakdown situation. At night if hazard lights fail, in addition to a warning triangle a yellow flashing light or position lights must mark the vehicle.
- A fire extinguisher and set of replacement bulbs are recommended. Replacement bulbs are compulsory for residents.
- Foreign drivers involved in an accident must call the police and obtain a written report. Keep this report as customs officials will ask to see it to allow exit.
- It is prohibited to overtake a bus transporting children when passengers are getting on/off.
- Use of the horn is prohibited in built-up areas or at night, except in cases of danger, injury or illness.
- A *vignette* system has been introduced that replaces tolls (see page 147). The *vignette* will have to be displayed when travelling on motorways and expressways and will be available to purchase from filling stations in Slovenia and in neighbouring countries. Vignettes (for vehicles up to 3.5 tonnes) are available for periods of one year, one month and seven days. The 1-year *vignette* is valid from 1 December to 31 January the following year. The minimum fine for non-display is €300. Visit **www.dars.si** for information.
- The use of spiked tyres is prohibited.
- Hazard warning lights must be used when reversing.

Travel facts: Slovenia

Slovenian Embassy
10 Little College Street,
London SW1P 3SJ
Tel: 020 7222 5400
www.london.embassy.si

Banking hours
Banks are open Monday to Friday 9am to 12 noon and 2 to 5pm, some banks open on Saturday from 8.30am to 11/12. Money can also be exchanged in exchange offices, at hotel reception desks, tourist agencies, petrol stations and larger supermarkets.

Credit/debit cards
Major cards accepted for payment are MasterCard, Visa, American Express and Diners. ATMs are located across the country.

Currency
The Euro (€) is the official currency of Slovenia. Coins are issued in denominations of 1, 2, 5, 10, 20 and 50 cents and €1 and €2. Notes are issued in denominations of €5, €10, €20, €50, €100, €200 and €500.

Electricity
The power supply is 220 volts AC, 50Hz. Sockets take round plugs with two round pins.

Health care
Free or reduced-cost medical treatment is available in Slovenia to European visitors on production of a valid European Health Insurance Card (EHIC). See page 10. Comprehensive travel insurance is still advised and is essential for all other visitors.

Pharmacies
Prescription and over-the-counter medicines are sold in pharmacies. A 24-hour service is available in large towns.

Post offices
Post offices are generally open Monday to Friday 8am to 6pm, Saturday 8am to 12 noon. Stamps can be bought at bookstalls.

Safe water
Mains water is considered safe to drink. However, bottled mineral water is available and is advised for the first few weeks of the stay.

Telephones
Calls can be made with phone cards, which are sold at post offices, newspaper kiosks and tobacco shops. The country code for Slovenia is 386. To call home from Slovenia dial the international code (00) followed by the country code. To call the UK from Slovenia dial 00 44.

Time
Slovenia is on Central European time (GMT +1), Daylight Saving Time comes into effect on the last Sunday in March and ends on the last Sunday in October (GMT + 2).

Emergency telephone numbers
Police **113** or **112**
Fire **112**
Ambulance **112**

Charges in euros

General	Vehicles up to 3.5 tonnes
7-day *vignette*	15.00
1-month *vignette*	30.00
1-year *vignette*	95.00

Bridges and tunnels

Road		Car	Car towing caravan/ trailer
A2	Karawanken Tunnel	6.50	6.50

Driving in Spain *(South West Europe)*

The regulations below should be read in conjunction with the General motoring information on pages 18–21.

Drinking and driving

If the level of alcohol in the bloodstream is 0.05 per cent or more, severe penalties can include a fine and withdrawal of the visitor's driving licence. The level for drivers with less than two years' experience is 0.03 per cent. Severe penalties include imprisonment for non-compliance

Driving licence

The minimum age at which a UK licence holder may drive a temporarily imported car is 18, for motorcycles up to 125cc it is 16 years, and over 125cc 18 years. All valid UK driving licences should be accepted in Spain. This includes the older all-green-style UK licences (in Northern Ireland the older paper-style with photographic counterpart) although the EC appreciates that these may be more difficult to understand and that drivers may wish to update them voluntarily before travelling abroad, if time permits. Alternatively, older licences may be accompanied by an International Driving Permit.

Fines

On-the-spot fines can be imposed. An official receipt should be obtained. Illegally parked vehicles can be towed away. Wheel clamps are also in use.

Fuel

Unleaded petrol (95 and 98 octane) is available. There is no leaded petrol. Carrying petrol in a can is permitted. Diesel (*Gasoleo 'A'* or *Gas-oil*) is available. **Note:** *Gasoleo 'B'* is heating oil only. LPG is available under the name of *Autogas*, but there are only a few sales outlets at present. For locations visit **www.repsolypf.com** or **www.spainautogas.com**. Credit cards are accepted at most filling stations; check with your card issuer for usage in Spain before travel.

Lights

The use of full headlights in built-up areas is prohibited; use side lights or dipped headlights depending on how well lit the roads are. Dipped headlights must be used in tunnels.

Motorcycles

The use of dipped headlights during the day is compulsory. The wearing of crash helmets is compulsory; this includes trikes and quads unless they are equipped with seat belts. A child between seven and eleven years old may be a passenger on a motorcycle driven by his mother, father or authorised person. The child must wear a suitable helmet. Moped drivers under the age of 18 cannot transport passengers. A child under the age of seven cannot be transported at all.

Motor insurance

Third-party insurance is compulsory.

Motorways

On Spanish motorways tolls can be paid in cash (euros), credit card or electronic toll collection (ETC). Visit **www.aseta.es** for details of ETC

and other information. Manual lanes, with toll collectors, accept cash and most major credit cards. Other lanes *(VIAS AUTOMATICAS)* are exclusively for motorists paying by credit card. See motorway map and tolls on pages 152–153.

Passengers/children in cars

Children up to the age of 12 and under 1.35m (4ft 5in) must be in a child-restraint system adapted to their size and weight, except when travelling in a taxi in an urban area. Children over 1.35m (4ft 5in) may use adult seat belt.

Seat belts

It is compulsory for front- and rear-seat occupants to wear seat belts, if fitted.

Speed limits

The standard legal limits, which may be varied by signs, for **private vehicles without trailers** are: in built-up areas 50km/h (31mph), outside built-up areas 90km/h (55mph) on 2nd category roads, 100km/h (62mph) on 1st category roads and 120km/h (74mph) on motorways. On motorways and dual carriage ways in built-up areas 80km/h (49mph). The minimum speed on motorways is 60km/h (37mph). The limit in some residential zones is 20km/h (13mph). When **towing**, and the combined weight exceeds 750kg, the limits are 70km/h (43mph) on conventional roads outside built-up areas, and 80km/h (49mph) on all major roads, including motorways and single carriageways with a hard shoulder wider than 1.5m.

Additional information

- It is compulsory for visitors to equip their vehicle with a spare tyre, or tyre-repair kit, and the equipment to change the tyre; a warning triangle (one warning triangle is compulsory for foreign-registered vehicles but carrying two is recommended as, in an accident/breakdown situation, local officials may impose a fine if only one is produced). A warning triangle is not required for two-wheeled vehicles.

- The wearing of reflective jacket/waistcoat is compulsory if the driver and/or passenger(s) exits a vehicle that is immobilised on the carriageway of all motorways and main or busy roads. However, it is not mandatory to carry a reflective jacket in the vehicle and Spanish police cannot fine a foreign motorist who does not carry one. Car-hire companies are not under legal obligation to supply them to persons hiring vehicles, so often don't.
- It is recommended that drivers who wear glasses carry a spare pair with them if this is noted on the driving licence.
- Apparatus with a screen that can distract a driver (such as television, video, DVD equipment) should be positioned where the driver is unable to see it. This excludes GPS systems. It is prohibited for the driver to touch or program the device unless parked in a safe place.
- The use of radar detectors is prohibited.
- In urban areas it is prohibited to sound the horn except in an emergency. Lights may be flashed instead of using the horn.
- The use of snow chains is recommended in snow conditions; police can stop vehicles not fitted with snow chains. Maximum speed when using snow chains is 50km/h. The winter period is usually November to March.
- The use of spiked tyres is prohibited.
- In the case of a car towing a caravan/trailer exceeding 12m, there must be two yellow reflectors at the rear of the towed caravan or trailer.
- A load may exceed the length of a private vehicle at the rear by up to 10 per cent of its length. The load must be indicated by a panel with diagonal red and white stripes. If you wish to carry bicycles on the rear of your vehicle you will need a 50 x 50cm reflectorised panel.
- In some cities with one-way streets, vehicles must be parked on the side of the road where houses bear uneven numbers on uneven days of the month, and on the side of even numbers on even days.
- Only fully hands-free phone systems are permitted. The use of earpieces or headphones while driving is banned. Failure to comply carries a fine of €200.
- Motorists should be aware of contrived incidents. Foreign registered vehicles, especially those towing caravans, and hire cars, are often targeted in service areas or tricked into stopping on the hard shoulder. Lock all doors and keep bags out of sight. The number of thefts by bogus policemen has increased in Madrid and Catalonia.

Road signs (a selection of standard and non-standard)

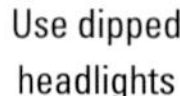

Use dipped headlights

Motorway

Dual carriageway

Turning permitted

Limited parking zone

Water

Viewpoint

Travel facts: Spain

Spanish Tourist Office
22–23 Manchester Square
London W1M 5AP
Tel: 020 7486 8077
www.tourspain.co.uk

Banking hours
Banks are generally open Monday to Friday 8.30 or 9am to 1pm. Some banks open Saturday (October to May only) 8.30am to 1pm.

Credit/debit cards
All major credit cards are accepted in shops, restaurants and hotels throughout Spain. The most popular are Visa, MasterCard, American Express, Eurocheque, and to a lesser extent Diners.

Currency
The euro (€) is the official currency of Spain. Coins are issued in denominations of 1, 2, 5, 10, 20 and 50 cents and €1 and €2. Notes are issued in denominations of €5, €10, €20, €50, €100, €200 and €500.

Electricity
The power supply is 220 volts AC (in some bathrooms and older buildings it is 110/125 volts). Round two-hole sockets take two-round-pin plugs. British visitors will need an adaptor.

Health care
Free or reduced-cost medical treatment is available in Spain to European visitors on production of a valid European Health Insurance Card (EHIC). See page 10. Comprehensive travel insurance is still advised and is essential for all other visitors.

Pharmacies
Prescription and non-prescription drugs and medicines are available from pharmacies *(farmacias)* distinguished by a large green cross. They are able to dispense many over-the-counter drugs that would be available only on prescription in other countries.

Post offices
Post offices *(correos)* are generally open 8.30am to 2.30pm (1pm Saturday). In main centres they may open extended hours. Stamps *(sellos)* can also be bought at tobacconists *(estancos)*. Post boxes are yellow.

Safe water
Tap water is chlorinated and generally safe to drink; however, unfamiliar water may cause mild abdominal upsets. Bottled mineral water *(agua mineral)* is cheap and widely available. It is sold still *(sin gas)* and carbonated *(con gas)*.

Telephones
All telephone numbers throughout Spain consist of nine digits, and no matter where you call from, you must always dial all nine digits. Many public telephones *(teléfono)* take phone cards *(credifone)*, which are available from post offices and some shops for €6 or €12. The country code for Spain is 34. To call home from Spain dial the international code (00) followed by the country code. To call the UK from Spain dial 00 44.

Time
Spain is on Central European Time (GMT + 1); Daylight Saving Time comes into effect on the last Sunday in March and ends on the last Sunday in October (GMT + 2).

Emergency telephone numbers
Police **092** or **112**
Guardia Civil **062** or **112**
Fire **080** or **112**
Ambulance **061** or **112**

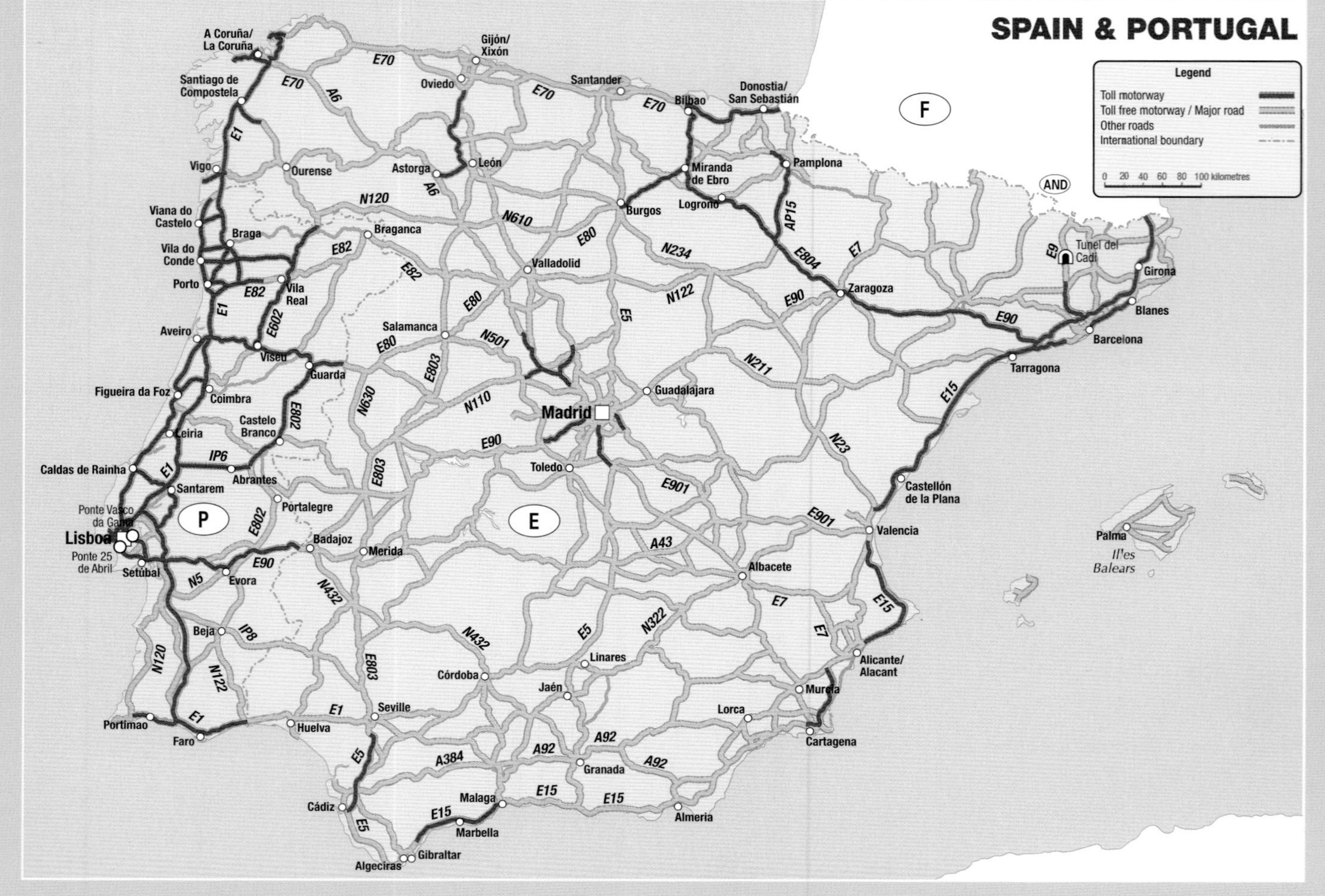
SPAIN & PORTUGAL
Legend
Toll motorway
Toll free motorway / Major road
Other roads
International boundary
0 20 40 60 80 100 kilometres
F
AND
P
E
A Coruña/ La Coruña
Gijón/ Xixón
Santander
Donostia/ San Sebastián
Bilbao
Oviedo
Santiago de Compostela
Vigo
Ourense
Astorga
León
Miranda de Ebro
Pamplona
Burgos
Logroño
Viana do Castelo
Braga
Vila do Conde
Porto
Vila Real
Braganca
Valladolid
Zaragoza
Tunel del Cadi
Girona
Blanes
Barcelona
Tarragona
Aveiro
Viseu
Guarda
Salamanca
Figueira da Foz
Coimbra
Castelo Branco
Leiria
Madrid
Guadalajara
Caldas de Rainha
Abrantes
Santarem
Toledo
Castellón de la Plana
Ponte Vasco da Gama
Lisboa
Ponte 25 de Abril
Setúbal
Portalegre
Badajoz
Merida
Evora
Valencia
Albacete
Palma
Il'es Balears
Beja
Linares
Córdoba
Jaén
Alicante/ Alacant
Murcia
Lorca
Cartagena
Portimao
Faro
Huelva
Seville
Granada
Cádiz
Malaga
Marbella
Almeria
Algeciras
Gibraltar
E70
E1
A6
N120
N610
E80
E82
N234
E7
E804
AP15
E90
N122
E5
E602
E803
N501
N211
N630
N110
E802
IP6
N23
E15
E901
A43
N5
N432
IP8
N322
E9
A384
A92

Toll charges in euros

Road		Car	Car towing caravan/ trailer
E1 (A9)	Santiago de Compostela – Vigo	8.65	8.65
E1 (A9)	La Coruna – Santiago de Compostela	6.05	6.05
E1 (A9)	Ferrol – La Coruña	4.25	4.25
E5 (A4)	Cádiz – Dos Hermanas (Sevilla)	6.95	6.95
E5 (A4) (R4)	Madrid – Ocaña	5.25	5.25
E5/E80 (A1)	Burgos – **E804 (A68)** (Miranda de Ebro)	10.30	10.30
E9 (C16)	Barclelona (Puigcerda) – Túnel del Cadí (Baga)	20.50	20.50
E15 (A7)	Barcelona – Tarragona	9.91	9.91
	Tarragona – València	26.40	26.40
	La Jonquera (French border) – Barcelona	14.67	14.67
	Málaga – Gibraltar	15.15	15.15
	València – Alacante	16.40	16.40
E70 (A8)	Bilbao – Irun (French border)	9.13	9.13
E90 (A2)	Zaragoza – Tarragona	20.55	20.55
E90 (R2)	Madrid – Guadalajara	3.60	3.60
E90 (R5)	Madrid – Navalcarnero	4.00	4.00
E804 (A68)	Zaragoza – Miranda de Ebro	20.70	20.70
E805 (A68)	Miranda de Ebro – Bilbao	10.40	10.40
E901 (R3)	Madrid – Arganda del Rey	2.70	2.70
M12	Madrid (Barajas) Airport – **E5 (A1)** Alcobendas	1.90	1.90
A6	Madrid – Valladolid	11.65	11.65
A7	Cartagena – Alicante	3.40	3.40
A12	León – Astorga	4.80	4.80
A15/A68	Pamplona – Irurtzun	2.05	2.05
	Pamplona – Tudela	12.85	12.85
A41	Madrid – Toledo	4.05	4.05
A51	Madrid – Ávila	9.70	9.70
A55	La Coruña – Carballo	2.35	2.35
A57	Vigo – Baiona	1.60	1.60
A61	Madrid – Segovia	7.90	7.90
A66	León – Oviado	11.50	11.50
AP53	Santiago de Compostela – Ourense	5.65	5.65
C32	Barcelona – Tarragona	13.31	13.31

Bridges and tunnels

E9 (C16)	Túnel del Cadí (French border)	12.57	12.57
	Tunels de Vallvidrera (Barcelona)	4.07	4.07

Driving in Sweden *(Northern Europe)*

The regulations below should be read in conjunction with the General motoring information on pages 18–21.

Drinking and driving

If the level of alcohol in the bloodstream is 0.02 per cent or more, severe penalties including fines, withdrawal of licence and/or prison can be imposed.

Driving licence

The minimum age at which a UK licence holder may drive a temporarily imported car is 18. **Note:** UK driving licences that do not incorporate a photograph will not be recognised unless accompanied by photographic proof of identity e.g. a passport.

Fines

Police can impose but not collect fines on the spot for minor traffic offences. Fines must be paid at a bank within 2 to 3 weeks. However, as a non-resident you may be asked to pay cash on the spot. Illegally parked vehicles may be towed away; the release charge is up to SEK1,400.

Fuel

Unleaded *(Blyfri)* petrol (95 and 98 octane) and diesel are available. There is very limited LPG. Carrying petrol in a can is permitted. Credit cards are accepted at filling stations; check with your card issuer for usage in Sweden before travel.

Lights

The use of dipped headlights during the day is compulsory. Fines will be imposed for inadequate lighting.

Motorcycles

The use of dipped headlights during the day is compulsory. The wearing of crash helmets is also compulsory.

Motor insurance

Third-party insurance is compulsory.

Passengers/children in cars

Children aged under 15 or under 1.35m (4ft 5in) must use an appropriate child restraint. There is only one exception in that they are permitted to travel unrestrained in the rear of a taxi if the correct child restraint is not available. A child aged 15 and over or 1.35m in height may use an adult seat belt. A child less than 1.40m may travel in the front seat of any vehicle if the passenger seat airbag is deactivated. Rear-facing baby seats may only be used if the airbag has been deactivated. Children weighing up to 13kg must use a baby restraint facing backwards placed on the front or back seats. It is only permitted to have the seat forward facing once the child weighs more than 18kg.

Seat belts

It is compulsory for front- and rear-seat occupants to wear seat belts, if fitted.

Speed limits

Speed limits are no longer based on the type of road, but on the quality and safety of the actual road itself. Speed limits may subsequently vary along the same road. It is therefore recommended that you pay particular attention to road signs. The lowest speed limits, which may be varied by signs, for **private vehicles without trailers** are in built-up areas: 30km/h (18mph), outside built-up areas 70km/h (43mph), motorways 90km/h (55mph). When **towing** the limit is 80km/h (49mph) on dual carriageways and motorways.

Additional information

- From 1 December to 31 March it is compulsory to use winter tyres (marked M&S) with a minimum tread depth of 3mm. This period varies according to weather conditions. Winter road conditions include snow, ice or a wet road surface combined with temperatures around or below 0 degrees. The police are authorised to make the final decision on whether winter conditions affect a specific road. If there are no winter road conditions, summer tyres are allowed, even between 1 December and 31 March. As weather conditions can not be predicted it is strongly advised to use winter tyres.
- It is compulsory to carry a shovel, to clear snow and to have antifreeze in the vehicle windscreen fluid.
- A warning triangle, first-aid kit, tow rope, jump leads, reflective jackets and fire extinguisher are recommended.
- Beware game (moose, deer, elk, etc. – a yellow warning triangle with a red border, see below, depicts animals most common on a particular stretch of road), as animals constitute a very real danger on many roads.
- Spiked tyres (which must be fitted on all wheels) may be used from 1 October to 15 April. However, local authorities have the power to ban spiked/studded tyres on their roads. Snow chains may also be used if the weather or road conditions require.
- Congestion charges in Stockholm do not apply to foreign-registered vehicles.
- The use of radar detectors is strictly forbidden.
- In some towns and suburban areas, parking restrictions are regulated by the date 'Datumparkering'. On odd days, parking is not permitted on the side of the road with odd numbers. On even days, parking is not permitted on the side of the road with even numbers.

Road signs (a selection of standard and non-standard)

Elks

Additional stop sign

Slow lane

End of lane

Travel facts and toll charges: Sweden

Swedish Travel and Tourism Council (administration)
11 Montagu Place
London W1H 2AL
Tel: 020 7108 6168
www.visitsweden.com

Banking hours
Banks are generally open Monday to Friday 9.30am to 3pm (in some cities until 6pm), Saturday 8am to noon or 1pm. Banks are also open on Thursday until 4 to 5.30pm.

Credit/debit cards
Major credit cards are widely accepted at banks, hotels, stores and restaurants. Most shops and restaurants require an identity card when paying with a credit card. You can get cash with your Visa, MasterCard, Maestro or Cirrus card at any *'Bankomat'* or *'Minuten'* ATM.

Currency
Sweden's currency is the krona (SEK, SKr or Kr; plural kronor), which is divided into 100 öre. Bank notes are issued in values of SEK20, 50, 100, 500 and 1,000; coins 50 öre, 1SEK, 5 and 10.

Electricity
Sweden has a 220 volts AC, 50Hz power supply. Electrical sockets take two-round-pin plugs.

Health care
Free or reduced-cost medical treatment is available in Sweden to European visitors on production of a valid European Health Insurance Card (EHIC). See page 10. Comprehensive travel insurance is still advised and is essential for all other visitors.

Pharmacies
Prescription and non-prescription medicines are available from a pharmacy *(apotek)*. A 24-hour service is available in most cities.

Post offices
You'll find post offices in various shops, stores, kiosks and petrol stations. The opening hours differ according to the specific establishment. Buy stamps *(frimarken)* at a post office *(postkontoret)*, supermarket, news-stand *(nyhetsbyra)*, or kiosk displaying a blue-and-yellow post sign. Hours for rural post offices may vary. There are two different types of post boxes – the blue box is for local deliveries, the yellow box for national and international deliveries.

Safe water
Tap water is safe to drink, and bottled mineral water *(mineralvatten)* is widely available.

Telephones
You can use pre-paid phone cards or credit cards to make a call from a public phone *(telefon)* in Sweden. A telephone card *(telefonkort)* can be bought from news-stands, shops, hotels or magazine kiosks. Post offices do not have telephone facilities. The country code for Sweden is 46. To call home from Sweden dial the international code (00) followed by the country code. To call the UK from Sweden dial 00 44.

Time
Sweden is on Central European Time, which is one hour ahead of Greenwich Mean Time (GMT + 1). Daylight Saving Time (GMT + 2) is in effect from the last weekend in March to the last weekend in October.

Emergency telephone numbers
Police **112**
Fire **112**
Ambulance **112**

General
Stockholm congestion charge 60.00 Mon-Fri 06.30-18.30
Foreign registered cars exempt

Toll charges in Swedish krona

Bridges and tunnels	**Car**	**Car towing caravan/ trailer**
Öresund Bridge (one way)	385.00	770.00
Svinesund Bridge	23.00	115.00
Roads		
Gothenburg Congestion Charge	18.00	18.00

Driving in Switzerland and Liechtenstein *(Central Europe)*

The regulations below should be read in conjunction with the General motoring information on pages 18–21.

Drinking and driving

If the level of alcohol in the bloodstream is 0.05 per cent or more, severe penalties include a fine or prison. The police may request any driver to undergo a breath test or drugs test. Visiting motorists may be forbidden from driving in Switzerland for a minimum of one month.

Driving licence

The minimum age at which a UK licence holder may drive a temporarily imported car is 18, for a motorcycle (up to 50cc) it is 16, for a motorcycle (50cc or over) 18.

Fines

On-the-spot fines can be imposed in certain cases. Vehicle clamps are not used in Switzerland but vehicles causing an obstruction can be removed. Speeding fines are severe.

Fuel

Unleaded petrol (95 and 98 octane) and diesel *(gasoil)* are available. There is no leaded petrol (a lead-substitute additive is available). There is limited LPG availability (only eight outlets). Carrying petrol in a can is permitted. Credit card acceptance is variable, especially at night due to automatic pumps not recognising UK chip-and-PIN cards; check with your card issuer for usage in Switzerland and Liechtenstein before travel. Some automatic pumps accept banknotes.

Lights

The use of dipped headlights during the day is recommended for all vehicles. They are compulsory when passing through tunnels even if they are well lit. A fine will be imposed for non-compliance.

Motorcycles

The wearing of crash helmets is compulsory. The use of dipped headlights during the day is recommended.

Motor insurance

Third-party insurance is compulsory.

Passengers/children in cars

The national requirement is that children up to 12 years of age or up to 1.5m have to be placed in a child restraint approved to UN ECE regulation 44.03. This also applies to hire cars.

Seat belts

It is compulsory for front- and rear-seat occupants to wear seat belts, if fitted.

Speed limits

The standard legal limits, which may be varied by signs, for **private vehicles without trailers** are: in built-up areas 50km/h (31mph), outside built-up areas 80km/h (49mph), semi-motorways 100km/h (62mph) and 120km/h (74mph) on motorways. The maximum speed **with a trailer** on semi-motorways and motorways is 80km/h (49mph). The minimum speed on motorways is 80km/h (49mph). **Note:** Towing a car on the motorway is permitted only up to next exit at a maximum speed of 40km/h (24mph).

Additional information

- Snow chains are compulsory in areas indicated by the appropriate sign and they must be fitted on at least two drive wheels.
- Each motor vehicle must be equipped with a warning triangle, which must be kept within easy reach (not in the boot). This must be used in any breakdown/emergency situation (excludes motorcycles).
- Hitch-hiking is prohibited on motorways and semi-motorways.
- The Swiss authorities levy an annual motorway tax and a vehicle sticker (costing CHF40 for vehicles up to 3.5 tonnes maximum total weight and known locally as a *'vignette'*) must be displayed in the prescribed manner by each vehicle (including motorcycles, trailers and caravans) using Swiss motorways and semi-motorways. The fine for non-display of the *vignette(s)* is the cost of *vignette(s)* plus CHF100. Motorists may purchase the stickers in the UK (telephone the Swiss Centre on **free-phone 00800 100 20030** for information) or in Switzerland from customs offices at the frontier or service stations and garages throughout the country.
- Vehicles over 3.5 tonnes maximum total weight are taxed on all roads; coaches and caravans pay a fixed tax for periods of one day, 10 days, one month or one year but lorries are taxed on weight and distance travelled.
- A GPS-based navigation system that has maps indicating the location of fixed speed cameras must have the 'fixed speed camera PoI (Points of Interest)' function deactivated.
- Radar detectors are prohibited even if not switched on.
- All vehicles with spiked tyres are prohibited on motorways and semi-motorways except for certain parts of the A13 and A2.
- Snow tyres are not compulsory; however vehicles that are not equipped to travel through snow and which impede traffic are liable to a fine.
- Drivers who are involved in an accident who do not call the police must complete a European Accident Claim Form (available from some motor insurers).
- During daylight hours outside built-up areas drivers must sound their horns before sharp bends where visibility is limited; after dark this warning must be given by flashing headlights.
- In Switzerland, pedestrians generally have right of way. Some pedestrians may just step into the road when on crosswalks (crossings) and will expect your vehicle to stop.
- Blue-zone parking discs are available from many petrol stations, garages, kiosks, restaurants and police stations.

Travel facts and toll charges: Switzerland

Switzerland Tourism
30 Bedford Street
London WC2E 9ED
Tel: 020 7420 4900
www.MySwitzerland.com

Banking hours
Banks are generally open Monday to Friday from 8.30am to 4.30pm. Once a week they extend their hours. Check locally. They are closed Saturday, Sunday and public holidays. Many banks have ATMs, check with your local bank that your bank card is valid in Switzerland.

Credit/debit cards
The cards most used are Visa, MasterCard and American Express. Many Swiss banks have ATMs for cash advances with your credit card.

Currency
Switzerland's currency is the Swiss franc (CHF) issued in CHF1,000, CHF200, CHF100, CHF50, CHF20 and CHF10 notes, and 5CHF, 2CHF and 1CHF coins. There are 100 centimes in a franc and 20, 10 and 5 centime coins. Many prices are indicated in euros to aid comparing prices. Merchants may accept euros but are not obliged to do so. Change will likely be in Swiss francs.

Electricity
The power supply in Switzerland is 220 volts AC, 50Hz. Most power sockets take three-round-pin-plugs. The standard continental plug with two round pins may be used without a problem.

Health care
Free or reduced-cost medical treatment is available in Switzerland to European visitors on production of a valid European Health Insurance Card (EHIC). See page 10. Comprehensive travel insurance is still advised and is essential for all other visitors.

Pharmacies
Many prescription and non-prescription medicines are available from pharmacists.

Post offices
Post offices are usually open Monday to Friday from 7.30am to 12 noon and 1.45 to 6pm. Branches in shopping centres are usually open the same hours as the shopping centres. On Saturday, post offices in large cities are open from 7.30 to 11am.

Safe water
The tap water is safe to drink.

Telephones
Public payphones take the Swiss phone card, *Taxcard*, on sale for CHF5, CHF10 and CHF20 at post offices, newsagents, railway stations, etc. The country code for Swizerland is 41. To call home from Swizerland dial the international code (00) followed by the country code. To call the UK from Swizerland dial 00 44.

Time
Switzerland is on Central European Time, which is one hour ahead of Greenwich Mean Time (GMT + 1), until late March to late October, when clocks are put forward one hour (GMT + 2).

Emergency telephone numbers
Police **117** Fire **118**
Ambulance (not all areas) **144**

Toll charges in Swiss Francs
For details of where to buy the motorway tax *(vignette)* see page 158.

General	Car	Car towing caravan/ trailer
Annual *vignette* (includes use of Gotthard Tunnel and San Bernardino Tunnel)	40.00	40.00
Bridges and tunnels		
Munt La Schera Tunnel	15.00	20.00
Grand St Bern'ard Tunnel	25.00	38.90
Lötschberg Tunnel	22.00	22.00

Driving in Turkey *(South East Europe)*

The regulations below should be read in conjunction with the General motoring information on pages 18–21.

Drinking and driving

If the level of alcohol in the bloodstream is 0.05 per cent or more, severe penalties can be imposed. For drivers of cars with caravans or trailers the alcohol level in the bloodstream is nil.

Driving licence

The minimum age at which a UK licence holder may drive a temporarily imported car and/or motorcycle is 18. A UK driving licence is valid for 90 days; licences that do not incorporate a photograph must be accompanied by an International Driving Permit (IDP).

Fines

On-the-spot fines can be imposed. Vehicles may be towed away if causing an obstruction.

Fuel

Leaded (95 octane), unleaded petrol (95 and 97 octane) and diesel are available. LPG is available in large centres. Carrying petrol in a can (fireproof container) is permitted. Credit cards are accepted at many filling stations; check with your card issuer for usage in Turkey before travel.

Lights

Dipped headlights should be used in poor daytime visibility, and also after sunset in built-up areas.

Motorcycles

The wearing of crash helmets is compulsory.

Motor insurance

Third-party insurance is compulsory. Foreign insurance, e.g. UK insurance, is recognised in the European part of Turkey, if the policy covers Turkey. Visiting motorists driving vehicles registered in the UK may use a valid Green Card when driving in Turkey. The Green Card must cover the whole of Turkey, i.e. both the European Part and the Asian part (Anatolia). Visiting motorists who are not in possession of a valid Green Card or who are not in possession of a valid UK insurance policy (validated for the whole of Turkey) must take out short-term insurance at the border or TTOK offices.

Passengers/children in cars

Children under 1.5m and lighter than 36kg must use suitable child seats/restraint. However, children taller than 1.36m may sit without a child restraint in the rear seats. Children under three years old can not be carried in a car without a child restraint system. If they are travelling on the front seat of a vehicle in a rear facing seat, the airbag must be deactivated. Children under 10 cannot travel in the front seat.

Seat belts

It is compulsory for front and rear-seat occupants to wear seat belts, if fitted.

Speed limits

The standard legal limits, which may be varied by signs, for **private vehicles without trailers** are: in built-up areas 50km/h (31mph), outside built-up areas 90km/h (55mph) for cars, 70km/h (43mph) for motorcycles; motorways 120km/h (74mph) for cars and 80km/h (49mph) for motorcycles. The minimum speed on motorways is 40km/h (24mph). Speed limits are 10km/h (6mph) **less if the car is towing a trailer**.

Additional information

- It is compulsory to carry a first-aid kit and a fire extinguisher – these are not required for two-wheeled vehicles.
- It is compulsory for all vehicles to carry two warning triangles.
- The use of the horn is generally prohibited in towns from 10pm until sunrise.
- The use of spiked tyres is prohibited. Snow chains can be used if necessary.
- It is recommended that winter tyres are used in snowy areas and snow chains are carried.
- In the event of an accident it is compulsory to call the police and obtain a report.

Travel facts and toll charges: Turkey

Turkish Tourist Office
29–30 St James's Street, 4th Floor
London SW1A 1HB
Tel: 020 7839 7778; www.gototurkey.co.uk

Banking hours
Banks are generally open Monday to Friday 8.30am to 12 noon and 1.30 to 5pm. Some banks open weekends in tourist areas.

Credit/debit cards
Credit cards are widely accepted in hotels, restaurants and shops. However, it is advisable to carry cash for the smaller shops and cafés, particularly in rural areas. ATMs are found in convenient locations in cities, towns, resorts and the arrivals halls at most airports.

Currency
Turkey's currency is the Turkish lira (TL) divided into 100 kurus (Kr). Banknotes are issued in denominations of 1, 5, 10, 20, 50 and 100TL. Coins in 1, 5, 10, 25 and 50Kr and 1TL. Many shops and restaurants in the coastal resorts and big cities accept payment in foreign currency.

Electricity
The power supply in Turkey is 220 volts AC. Sockets take two-round-pin plugs but there are two sizes in use. Bring your own adaptor. Power cuts are frequent in rural areas but usually short lived.

Health care
Comprehensive travel insurance is essential for all visitors.

Pharmacies
Prescription and non-prescription drugs and medicines are available from pharmacies *(eczane)*.

Post offices
Post offices (PTT) have a black-on-yellow logo. In major resorts and towns the main PTT will stay open for phone calls until midnight. Post offices are open Monday to Friday from 8am to 7 or 8pm and Saturday mornings. You can normally buy stamps with your postcards.

Safe water
Tap water is generally safe to drink, though it can be heavily chlorinated and taste unpleasant. Bottled mineral water is inexpensive and is sold either sparkling *(maden suyu)* or still *(memba suyu)*.

Telephones
There are pay phones on many streets, and at PTT offices. Phone cards are sold at post offices and newsagents. Most phones also accept credit cards. The country code for Turkey is 90. To call home from Turkey dial the international code (00) followed by the country code. To call the UK from Turkey dial 00 44.

Time
Turkey is on Eastern European Time, which is two hours ahead of Greenwich Mean Time (GMT + 2), but from the last Sunday in March to the last Sunday in October, when clocks are put forward one hour, Summer Time (GMT + 3) operates.

Emergency telephone numbers
Police **155** Fire **110**
Emergency (including ambulance) **112**

Toll charges in Turkish Lira

Road		Car	Car towing caravan/ trailer
E80 (O-3)	Edirne – Istanbul	6.50	15.25
E80/89 (O-4)	Istanbul – Ankara	13.50	30.50
E87 (O31)	Izmir – Aydin	2.75	6.50
E881 (O32)	Izmir – Cesme	2.00	5.00
E90 (O-21)	Pozanti – Tarus	2.00	6.50
E91 (O-53)	Ceyhan – Iskenderun	2.75	7.00
E51 (O-52)	Adana – Mersin	2.75	7.75

Bridges and tunnels

Bosphorus and Fatih Sultan Mehmet Bridge (Istanbul) on **E80** Eastbound only		4.25	26.00

Driving in Ukraine *(Eastern Europe)*

The regulations below should be read in conjunction with the General motoring information on pages 18–21.

Drinking and driving
Drinking and driving is strictly forbidden, although a 0.02 per cent tolerance has been established in order to allow for some medications and mouthwashes that may contain alcohol. Fines for driving under the influence of alcohol can be very high. The driving licence can be confiscated for a repeat offence.

Driving licence
An International Driving Permit (IDP) is compulsory for the holder of any type of UK driving licence. The minimum age at which a visitor may drive a temporarily imported car and/or motorcycle is 18.

Fines
At present, the police are not permitted to collect money for fines on the spot from a visitor. If a visitor has not paid a penalty imposed before his departure or within 15 days, the offender's vehicle can be detained. The authorities can clamp or remove a vehicle that is parked illegally.

Fuel
Unleaded petrol (95 and 98 octane), diesel *(solyarka)* and LPG are available. Carrying petrol in a can is permitted. It is advisable to carry petrol in spare cans when undertaking a long journey. Credit cards are accepted at filling stations; check with your card issuer for usage in Ukraine before travel. Fuel is usually paid for in local currency.

Lights
Dipped headlights should be used in poor daytime visibility.

Motorcycles
The wearing of crash helmets is compulsory for both driver and passenger. Children under 12 and less than 1.45m (4ft 9in) in height are not permitted to travel as a passenger.

Motor insurance
Third party insurance is compulsory. Green Cards are accepted.

Passengers/children in cars
Children under 12 and less than 1.45m (4ft 9in) cannot travel as front-seat passengers.

Seat belts
It is compulsory for front-seat occupants to wear seat belts.

Speed limits
Signed speed limits must be strictly adhered to. The standard legal limits, which may be varied by signs, for **private vehicles without trailers** are: in built-up areas 60km/h (37mph), outside built-up areas 90km/h (55mph), major roads 110km/h (68mph), motorways 130km/h (80mph). In some residential zones the limit is 20km/h (13mph). Motorists who have held a driving licence for less than two years must not exceed 70km/h (43mph). When **towing a caravan or trailer** with a combined weight less

than 3.5 tonnes, the limit on all roads outside built-up areas is 90km/h (55mph).

Additional information

- It is compulsory to carry a first-aid kit, a fire extinguisher and a warning triangle.
- Winter tyres are compulsory on all four wheels during snowy weather conditions (November to April), minimum tread 6mm.
- A person temporarily taking a vehicle into the Ukraine must pay an ecological tax at the border. The amount varies according to the engine power.
- In addition to the original vehicle registration document, it is recommended that an International Certificate for Motor Vehicles also be carried if visiting any Russian speaking areas. State Traffic Inspectorate officials will stop vehicles to check documents, especially if they are displaying foreign plates.
- We recommend that visitors carry an assortment of spares such as fan belt, replacement bulbs and spark plugs.
- It is necessary to pre-plan itineraries and book accommodation before departure.
- During cold winters it is highly recommended that you use spiked tyres or snow chains.
- If a foreign-registered vehicle is involved in an accident it is compulsory to call the police and to obtain an accident document. This will be required at the border.

Travel facts: Ukraine

Ukrainian Embassy
60 Holland Park
London W11 3SJ
Tel: 020 7727 6312
http://ukraine.embassyhomepage.com

Banking hours
Banks are usually open Monday to Friday 9am to 6pm. Some banks open on Saturday.

Credit/debit cards
Some credit/debit cards, including MasterCard and Visa, are accepted in large cities, but don't rely solely on cards or traveller's checks. ATMs *(Bankomat)* are located in public places such as shopping malls, hotels, inside or next to banks, inside travel agencies or ticket offices. Make sure your card logo is on the ATM machine. Usually ATMs offer hryvnias. Instructions are in Russian, Ukrainian or English.

Currency
The official currency of Ukraine is the hryvnia (Hrn), also known as hryvnia or grivna. There are 100 Kopiyka in a Hryvnia. There are banknotes for Hrn1, 2, 5, 10, 20, 50, 100, 200 and 500. There are coins for Hrn1, 2, and 5 and 1, 2, 5, 10, 25, and 50 kopiykas. US dollars and euros are preferred foreign currency; they can be exchanged at hotels, banks and airports. Make sure your foreign banknotes are new-looking and crisp or they may not be exchanged. Avoid changing money with private individuals. The use of foreign currency is officially forbidden in shops, bars and restaurants.

Electricity
The power supply is 220 volts AC, 50Hz in Ukraine. Plugs and wall sockets are mostly the European two-pin style or can be the old Soviet type which have narrower pins.

Health care
The UK has a reciprocal healthcare agreement with Ukraine. If you're visiting Ukraine and need urgent or immediate medical treatment it will be provided at a reduced cost or, in some cases, free. The range of medical services available may be more restricted than under the NHS, therefore it is essential for all visitors to have comprehensive travel insurance. Visit **www.nhs.uk/NHSEngland/Healthcareabroad** for a country-by-country guide.

Pharmacies
Take a supply of medicines that you are likely to need during your stay as they may be difficult to obtain locally. Check first that they may be legally imported. In Kiev the pharmacy at Shevchenko Boulevard 36a, opposite the University metro stop. is open seven days a week from 8am to 9pm; English is spoken.

Post offices
Post offices are generally open 9am to 6pm. The main post office in Kiev is located at Khreshchatik 22 and is open 24 hours. You can make telephone calls and send faxes here.

Safe water
Mains water is not considered safe to drink. You are advised to buy bottled mineral water from supermarkets. Be aware that some bottled water from the smaller kiosks can be counterfeit.

Telephones
You can buy telephone cards for public pay phones in post offices. The country code for the Ukraine is 380. To call home from Ukraine dial the international code (00) followed by the code. To call the UK from Ukraine dial 00 44.

Time
Ukraine is in the Eastern European Time Zone (EET) and is two hours ahead of Greenwich Mean Time (GMT + 2). From the last Sunday in March to the last Sunday in October it is three hours ahead of Greenwich Mean Time (GMT + 3).

Emergency telephone numbers
Police **102**
Fire **101**
Ambulance **103**

Historischer Sta
Schwerdtners Ka
Kleiner Hafen & G
Am Mühlenwehr
Strubels Stübche

Useful words and phrases

Dutch: words and phrases

For clarity we have put the English phrase in light type, foreign language terms in dark type and their phonetic pronunciation in light italic.

Asking for directions

Excuse me, could I ask you something?
Pardon, mag ik u iets vragen?
Pardon, makh ik oo eets frakhen?

I've lost my way
Ik ben de weg kwijt
Ik ben de vekh kwayet

Is there a...around here?
Weet u een...in de buurt?
Vayt oo an...in de boo-ert

Is this the way to...?
Is dit de weg naar...?
Is dit de vekh naar...?

Could you tell me how to get to... by car/on foot?
Kunt u me zeggen hoe ik naar... moet rijden/lopen?
Kunt-oo me zekhen hoo ik naar... moot rayeden/loapen?

What's the quickest way to...?
Hoe kom ik het snelst in...?
Hoo kom ik het snel-ste in...?

How many kilometres is it to...?
Hoeveel kilometer is het nog naar...?
Hoofayl keelomayter is het nokh naar...?

Could you point it out on the map?
Kunt u het op de kaart aanwijzen?
Kunt oo het op de kaart aan-wayezen?

☞ Ask the speaker to point to what they are saying

Ik weet het niet, ik ben hier niet bekend
I don't know, I don't know these parts

U zit verkeerd
You're going the wrong way

U moet terug naar...
You have to go back to...

Daar wijzen de borden u verder
From there on just follow the signs

Daar moet u het opnieuw vragen
When you get there, ask again

Useful words

rechtdoor
straight on
linksaf
turn left
rechtsaf
turn right
afslaan
turn
volgen
follow
oversteken
cross
de kruising
intersection
de straat
the street
het verkeerslicht
the traffic light
de tunnel
the tunnel/ underpass
het verkeersbord 'voorrangskruis-ing'
the 'give-way' sign
het gebouw
the building
op de hoek
at the corner
de rivier
the river
het viaduct
the fly-over
de brug
the bridge
de spoorwegovergang/ de spoorbomen
the level crossing/the crossing barriers
het bord richting...
the sign pointing to...
de pijl
the arrow

Road traffic signs

afrit
exit

alle richtingen
all directions

andere richtingen
other directions

centrum
town centre

doodlopende weg
dead end (cul-de-sac)

doorgaand verkeer gestremd
road closed

doorgaand verkeer
through traffic

eenrichtingsverkeer
one-way traffic

einde snelheidsbeperking
end of speed limit

fabrieksuitgang
works exit

fietsers
cyclists

fietspad
cycle path

gevaar
danger

gevaarlijke bochten
dangerous bends

helling
incline

ijzel
black ice

inrijden verboden
no entry

kruising
junction

langzaam
slow

links houden
keep left

maximum snelheid
maximum speed

ondergrondse parkeergarage
underground car park

ontsteek uw lichten
switch on lights

oversteekplaats voetgangers
pedestrian crossing

overweg
level crossing

parkeerplaats
parking/layby (out of town)

parkeerzone (parkeerschijf verplicht)
zone parking (disc must be shown)

rechts houden
keep right

rijbaan voor bus
bus lane

slecht wegdek
irregular road surface

slipgevaar
slippery road

snelheid verminderen
reduce speed

snelweg
motorway

stapvoets
drive at walking pace

steenslag
loose chippings

tegenliggers
oncoming traffic

uitgang
exit/way out

uitrit
exit

uitrit vrijlaten
keep exit free

verboden in te halen
no overtaking

verboden linksaf te slaan
no left turn

verboden rechtsaf te slaan
no right turn

verminder snelheid
reduce speed

verplichte rijrichting
compulsory route

voetgangers
pedestrians

voorangsweg
major road

voorrang verlenen
give way

voorsorteren
get in lane

wachtverbod
no waiting

weg afgesloten
road closed

wegomlegging
diversion

wegversmalling
road narrows

werk in uitvoering
roadworks

zachte berm
soft verge

ziekenhuis
hospital

French: words and phrases

For clarity we have put the English phrase in light type, foreign language terms in dark type and their phonetic pronunciation in light italic.

Asking for directions

Excuse me, could I ask you something?
Pardon, puis-je vous demander quelque chose?
pahrdawn, pwee jhuh voo duhmohnday kehlkuh shoaz?

I've lost my way
Je me suis égaré(e)
jhuh muh swee zaygahray

Is there an... around here?
Connaissez-vous un...dans les environs?
konehssay voo zuhn... dohn lay zohnveerawn?

Is this the way to...?
Est-ce la route vers...?
ehs lah root vehr...?

Could you tell me how to get to...?
Pouvez-vous me dire comment aller à...?
poovay voo muh deer komohn tahlay ah...?

What's the quickest way to...?
Comment puis-je arriver le plus vite possible à...?
komohn pwee jhuh ahreevay luh plew veet pohseebl ah...?

How many kilometres is it to...?
Il y a encore combien de kilomètres jusqu'à...?
eel ee yah ohnkor kohnbyahn duh keeloamehtr jhewskah...?

Could you point it out on the map?
Pouvez-vous me l'indiquer sur la carte?
poovay voo muh lahndeekay sewr lah kahrt?

☞ Ask the speaker to point to what they are saying

Je ne sais pas, je ne suis pas d'ici
I don't know, I don't know my way around here

Vous vous êtes trompé
You're going the wrong way

Vous devez retourner à...
You have to go back to...
Là-bas les panneaux vous indiqueront la route
From there on just follow the signs

Là-bas vous demanderez à nouveau votre route
When you get there, ask again

Useful words

tout droit
straight ahead
à gauche
left
à droite
right
tourner
turn
suivre
follow
traverser
cross
le carrefour
the intersection
la rue
the street
le feu (de signalisation)
the traffic light
le tunnel
the tunnel
le panneau 'cédez lapriorité'
the 'give-way' sign
l'immeuble
the building
à l'angle, au coin
at the corner
la rivière, le fleuve
the river
l'autopont
the fly-over
le pont
the bridge
le passage à niveau
the level crossing
la barrière
boom
le panneau direction...
the sign pointing to...
la flèche
the arrow

Road traffic signs

carrefour dangereux
dangerous crossing
chaussée à gravillons
loose chippings
chaussée déformée
uneven road surface
chaussée glissante
slippery road
circulation alternée
alternate priority
danger
danger
danger priorité à droite
priority to vehicles from right
descente dangereuse
steep hill
déviation
diversion
fin d'allumage des feux
end of need for lights
fin de...
end of...
fin de chantier
end of roadworks
interdiction de dépasser
no overtaking
interdiction de klaxonner
no horns
interdiction de stationner
no parking
interdiction sauf riverains
access only
limite de vitesse
speed limit
passage à niveau
level crossing
passage d'animaux
animals crossing
passage pour piétons
pedestrian crossing
péage
toll
poids lourds
heavy goods vehicles
rappel
reminder
remorques et semi-remorques
lorries and articulated lorries
sens unique
one-way traffic
serrez à droite
keep right
sortie
exit
sortie de camions
factory/works exit
taxis
taxi rank
travaux (sur...km)
roadworks ahead
véhicules lents
slow traffic
véhicules transportant des matières dangereuses
vehicles transporting dangerous substances
verglas fréquent
ice on road
virages sur...km
bends for...km
vitesse limite
maximum speed
zone bleue
parking disc required
zone piétonne
pedestrian zone

German: words and phrases

For clarity we have put the English phrase in light type, foreign language terms in dark type and their phonetic pronunciation in light italic.

Asking for directions

Excuse me, could I ask you something?
Verzeihung, dürfte ich Sie etwas fragen?
fair tsaioong, duerfter ikh zee etvass frargen?

I've lost my way
Ich habe mich verlaufen/(with car) mich verfahren
ikh harber mikh fairlowfen/mikh fairfahren

Is there a(n)... around here?
Wissen Sie, wo hier in der Nähe ein(e)...ist?
vissen zee, vo heer in dayr nayher ain(er)...ist?

Is this the way to...?
Ist dies die Strasse nach...?
ist dees dee shtrasser nakh...?

Could you tell me how to get to the... (name of place) by car/on foot?
Können Sie mir sagen, wie ich nach... (name of the place) fahren/gehen muss?
koenen zee meer zargen, vee ikh nakh ... fahren/gayhen muss?

What's the quickest way to...?
Wie komme ich am schnellsten nach...?
vee kommer ikh am shnellsten nakh...?

How many kilometres is it to...?
Wieviel Kilometer sind es noch bis...?
veefeel kilomayter zint ez nokh biss...?

Could you point it out on the map?
Können Sie es mir auf der Karte zeigen?
koennen zee ez meer owf dayr karter tsaigen?

☞ Ask the speaker to point to what they are saying

Ich weiss nicht, ich kenne mich hier nicht aus
I don't know, I don't know my way around here

Da sind Sie hier nicht richtig
You're going the wrong way

Sie müssen zurück nach...
You have to go back to...

Sie fahren über die...Strasse
You take...Street

Sie fahren über die...Strasse drüber
You cross over...Street

Da sehen Sie schon die Schilder
From there on you will see the signs

Da müssen Sie noch mal fragen
When you get there, you will have to ask again

Useful words

geradeaus
straight
nach links/links abbiegen
left/turn left
nach rechts/ rechts abbiegen
right/turn right
abbiegen
turn
folgen
follow
überqueren
cross
die Kreuzung
the intersection
die Strasse
the street
die (Verkehrs)ampel
the traffic light
das Gebäude
the building
an der Ecke
at the corner
der Fluss
the river
die Brücke
the bridge
die (Bahn)schranken
the level crossing/the boomgates
das Schild Richtung...
the sign pointing to...
der Pfeil
the arrow

Road traffic signs

abbiegen
turn

Anlieger frei
residents only

Auffahrt
slip road/approach to house

Auflieger schwenkt aus
trailer may swing out

Ausfahrt
exit

Autobahndreieck
motorway merging point

Baustelle
roadworks ahead

bei Nässe/Glätte
in wet/icy conditions

Durchgangsverkehr (verboten)
(no) throughway

Einbahnstrasse
one-way street

Einfahrt
entry/access

Ende der Autobahn
end of motorway

Frostaufbrüche
frost damage

Gefahr
danger

gefährlich
dangerous

Gegenverkehr
oncoming traffic

gesperrt (für alle Fahrzeuge)
closed (for all vehicles)

Glatteis
ice on road

Kurve(nreiche Strecke)
bend/dangerous bends

Licht einschalten/ ausschalten
switch on lights/end needs for lights

LKW
heavy goods vehicle

Naturschutzgebiet
nature reserve

Nebel
beware fog

Parkscheibe
parking disk

PKW
motorcar

Radfahrer kreuzen
cyclists crossing

Rasthof-stätte
services

Rastplatz bitte sauberhalten
please keep picnic area tidy

Rollsplit
loose chippings

Schleudergefahr
danger of skidding

Seitenstreifen nicht befahrbar
soft verges

Seitenwind
cross wind

Spurrillen
irregular road surface

Standstreifen
hard shoulder

Starkes Gefälle
steep hill

Stau
traffic jam

Stauwarnanlage
hazard lights

Steinschlag
falling stones

Talbrücke
bridge over a valley

Überholverbot
no overtaking

Umleitung
diversion

Unbeschränkter Bahnübergang
unguarded level crossing/ dangerous crossing

Verengte Fahrbahn
narrow lane

Vorfahrt beachten
give way

Vorfahrtsstrasse
major road

Wasserschutzgebiet
protected reservoir area

zurückschalten
to change back

Greek: words and phrases

For clarity we have put the English phrase in light type, foreign language terms in dark type and their phonetic pronunciation in light italic.

Asking for directions

Excuse me, could I ask you something?
Συγγνώμη, μπορώ να σας ρωτήσω κάτι;
sighnómi, boró na sas rotíso káti?

I've lost my way
'Εχασα το δρόμο
échasa to dhrómo

Is there a(n)...around here?
Ξέρετε κανένα...εδώ κοντά
xérete kanéna...edhó kondá?

Is this the way to...?
Αυτός είναι ο δρόμος για...;
aftós íne o dhrómos ya...?

Could you tell me how to get to... (name of place)
Μπορείτε να μου πείτε πώς μπορώ να πάώ σε...;
boríte na moo píte pos boró na páo se...?

What's the quickest way to...?
Ποιός είναι ο πιο σύντομος δρόμος για...;
pyos íne o pyo síndomos dhrómos ya ...?

How many kilometres is it to...?
Πόσα χιλιόμετρα είναι ακόμα ως...;
pósa hilyómetra íne akóma os...?

Could you point it out on the map?
Μπορείτε να το δείξετε στο χάρτη;
boríte na to dhíxete sto chartí?

☞ Ask the speaker to point to what they are saying

Δεν ξέρω, δεν είμαι από δω
I don't know, I don't know my way around here

Πήρατε λάθος δρόμο
You're going the wrong way

Πρέπει να γυρίσετε σε...
You have to go back to...

Εκεί θ' ακολουθήσετε τις πινακίδες
From there on just follow the signs

Εκεί θα ξαναρωτήσετε
When you get there, ask again-

Useful words

ίσια
straight ahead
αριστερά
left
δεξιά
right
στρίβω
turn
ακολουθώ
follow
περνάω το δρόμο
cross the road
η διασταύρωση
the intersection
ο δρόμος/η οδός
the street
το φανάρι
the traffic light
το τούνελ
the tunnel
η πινακίδα διασταύρωση προτεραιότητας
the `give way' sign
το κτίριο
the building
στη γωνιά
at the corner
το ποτάμι
the river
η ανισόπεδη διασταύρωση
the fly-over

Road traffic signs

ΑΠΑΓΟΡΕΥΕΤΑΙ Η ΠΡΟΣΠΕΡΑΣΗ
no overtaking
ΑΠΑΓΟΡΕΥΕΤΑΙ Η ΣΤΑΘΜΕΥΣΗ
no parking
ΑΡΓΑ
slow
ΑΥΤΟΚΙΝΗΤΟΔΡΟΜΟΣ
road suitable for cars
ΑΦΥΛΑΚΤΗ ΔΙΑΒΑΣΗ
unmanned crossing
ΔΕΥΤΕΡΕΥΩΝ ΔΡΟΜΟΣ
minor road
ΔΙΑΧΩΡΙΣΜΟΣ
road divides
ΔΙΟΔΙΑ
toll
ΔΩΣΕΤΕ ΠΡΟΤΕΡΑΙΟΤΗΤΑ
give way
ΕΘΝΙΚΗ ΟΔΟΣ (ΜΕ ΔΙΟΔΙΑ)
motorway (with toll)
ΕΙΣΟΔΟΣ
entrance
ΕΛΑΤΤΩΣΑΤΕ ΤΑΧΥΤΗΤΑ
reduce speed
ΕΛΕΥΘΕΡΗ ΚΥΚΛΟΦΟΡΙΑ
clearway
ΕΠΑΡΧΙΑΚΗ ΟΔΟΣ
minor road
ΕΠΙΚΙΝΔΥΝΗ ΔΙΑΣΤΑΥΡΩΣΗ
dangerous junction
ΕΠΙΚΙΝΔΥΝΗ ΚΑΤΩΦΕΡΕΙΑ
steep hill
ΕΠΙΚΙΝΔΥΝΗ ΣΤΡΟΦΗ
dangerous bend
ΕΞΟΔΟΣ
exit
ΕΞΟΔΟΣ ΟΧΗΜΑΤΩΝ
exit for heavy goods vehicles
Η ΤΑΧΥΤΗΤΑ ΕΛΕΓΧΕΤΑΙ ΜΕ ΡΑΝΤΑΡ
radar speed checks
ΚΑΤΟΛΙΣΘΗΣΕΙΣ
loose chippings
ΚΕΝΤΡΟ
centre
ΚΙΝΔΥΝΟΣ
danger
ΚΛΕΙΣΤΗ ΟΔΟΣ
road closed
ΚΥΚΛΟΦΟΡΙΑ ΑΠΟ ΑΝΤΙΘΕΤΗ ΚΑΤΕΥΘΥΝΣΗ
oncoming traffic
ΜΟΝΟΔΡΟΜΟΣ
one-way street
ΝΟΣΟΚΟΜΕΙΟ
hospital
ΟΔΟΣ ΠΡΟΤΕΡΑΙΟΤΗΤΑΣ
road with priority over vehicles entering from side roads
ΠΑΡΑΚΑΜΠΤΗΡΙΟΣ
diversion
ΠΕΖΟΔΡΟΜΟΣ
pavement
ΠΕΡΙΜΕΝΕΤΕ
wait
ΠΡΟΣΟΧΗ
look out!
ΠΡΟΣ ΠΑΡΑΛΙΑ
to the beach
ΣΤΑΘΜΟΣ ΠΡΩΤΩΝ ΒΟΗΘΕΙΩΝ
first-aid post
ΣΤΕΝΩΜΑ ΟΔΟΣΤΡΩΜΑΤΟΣ
road narrows
ΣΤΡΟΦΕΣ
bends
ΤΕΛΟΣ ΑΝΑΓΟΡΕΥΜΕΝΗΣ ΖΩΝΗΕ
end of forbidden zone
ΥΨΟΣ ΠΕΡΙΟΡΙΣΜΕΝΟ
restricted height
ΧΩΜΑΤΟΔΡΟΜΟΣ
packed-earth road

Italian: words and phrases

For clarity we have put the English phrase in light type, foreign language terms in dark type and their phonetic pronunciation in light italic.

Asking for directions

Excuse me, could I ask you something?
Mi scusi, potrei chiederLe una cosa?
Mee skoozee potray keeaydayrlay oonah kozah?

I've lost my way
Mi sono perso/a
Mee sono payrso/ah

Is there a(n)...around here?
Sa se c'è un/una... da queste parti?
Sah say chay oon/oonah...dah kwaystay pahrtee?

Is this the way to...?
E' questa la strada per...?
Ay kwaystah lah strahdah payr...

Could you tell me how to get to....?
Mi può indicare la strada per...?
Mee pwo eendeekahray lah strahdah payr...?

What's the quickest way to...?
Qual'è la strada più diretta per...?
Kwahlay ay lah strahdah peeoo deerayttah payr...?

How many kilometres is it to...?
A quanti chilometri è...?
Ah qwahntee keelomaytreeay....?

Could you point it out on the map?
Me lo può indicare sulla mappa?
May lo pwo eendeekahray soollah mahppah?

☞ Ask the speaker to point to what they are saying

Non lo so, non sono di questa città/regione
I don't know, I don't know my way around here

Ha sbagliato strada
You're going the wrong way

Deve ritornare a...
You have to go back to...

Là, deve seguire le indicazioni
From there on just follow the signs

Là, chieda di nuovo
When you get there, ask again

Useful words

Vada dritto
Go straight ahead
Giri a sinistra
Turn left
Giri a destra
Turn right
Volti a destra/ sinistra
Turn right/left
Segua
Follow
Attraversi
Cross
l'incrocio
the intersection/ crossroads
la strada
the road/street
il semaforo
the traffic light
la galleria
the tunnel
il cartello/segnale stradale di 'dare la precedenza'
the 'give way' sign
il palazzo
the building
all'angolo
at the corner
il fiume
the river
il viadotto
the flyover
il ponte
the bridge
il passaggio a livello
the level crossing
le indicazioni per...
the signs pointing to....
la freccia
the arrow

Road traffic signs

accendere i fari (in galleria)
switch on headlights (in the tunnel)

alt
stop

altezza limitata a...
maximum headroom...

area/stazione di servizio
service station

attenzione
beware

autocarri
heavy goods vehicles

banchina non transitabile
impassable verge

caduta massi
beware, falling rocks

cambiare corsia
change lanes

chiuso al traffico
road closed

corsia di emergenza
emergency lane

curve
bends

deviazione
detour

diritto di precedenza a fine strada
right of way at end of road

disco orario (obbligatorio)
parking disk (compulsory)

divieto di accesso
no entry

divieto di sorpasso/di sosta
no overtaking/no parking

galleria
tunnel

incrocio
intersection/crossroads

(isola/zona) pedonale
traffic island/ pedestrian precinct

lasciare libero il passo/ passaggio
do not obstruct

lavori in corso
roadworks

pagamento/ pedaggio
toll payment

parcheggio a pagamento/ riservato a...
paying car park/parking reserved for...

parcheggio custodito
supervised car park

passaggio a livello
level crossing

passo carrabile
driveway

pericolo(so)
danger(ous)

pioggia o gelo per km....
rain or ice for...kms

precedenza
right of way

rallentare
slow down

senso unico
one way

senso vietato
no entry

soccorso stradale
road assistance (breakdown service)

sosta limitata
parking for a limited period

strada deformata/ in dissesto
broken/uneven surface

strada interrotta
road closed

strettoia
narrowing in the road

tenere la destra/sinistra
keep right/left

traffico interrotto
road blocked

transito con catene
snow chains required

uscita
exit

velocità massima
maximum speed

vietato l'accesso/ai pedoni
no access/no pedestrian access

vietato l'autostop
no hitch-hiking

vietato svoltare a destra/ sinistra
no right/left turn

zona disco
disk zone

zona rimozione (ambo i lati)
tow-away area (both sides of the road)

Portuguese: words and phrases

For clarity we have put the English phrase in light type, foreign language terms in dark type and their phonetic pronunciation in light italic.

Asking for directions

Excuse me, could I ask you something?
Desculpe, posso-lhe fazer uma pergunta?
deshcoolp possoo lher fazair ooma pergoonta?

I've lost my way
Perdi-me
perdee muh

Is there a...around here?
Conhece um...perto daqui?
coonyes oom...pairtoo dakee?

Is this the way to...?
É este o caminho para...?
eh esht oo cameenyoo parra...?

Could you tell me how to get to the... (name of place) by car/on foot?
Poderia dizer-me como devo fazer para ir para...a pé/de carro?
pooderia dizair muh como dayvoo fazair parra eer parra...ah peh/duh cahroo?

What's the quickest way to...?
Como é que chego o mais depressa possível a...?
como eh kuh chaygoo oo mysh depressa posseevel ah...?

How many kilometres is it to...?
Quantos quilómetros faltam ainda para chegar a...?
cuarntoosh keelometroosh faltam ayeenda parra sheggar ah...?

Could you point it out on the map?
Poderia indicar-me aqui no mapa?
pooderiah eendiccar muh akee noo mappa?

☞ Ask the speaker to point to what they are saying

Não sei, não conheço isto aqui
I don't know, I don't know my way around here

Está enganado
You're going the wrong way

Tem de voltar a...
You have to go back to...

Aí as placas indicam-lhe o caminho a seguir
From there on just follow the signs

Aí deve perguntar de novo
When you get there, ask again

Useful words

em frente
straight ahead

à esquerda
left

à direita
right

cortar
turn

seguir
follow

atravessar
cross

cruzamento
intersection

estrada
street

semáforo
traffic light

placa de trânsito `cruzamento com prioridade'
`give-way' sign

rio
river

passagem de nível; cancelas
level crossing

placa indicando o caminho à...
sign pointing to...

ponte
bridge

seta
arrow

Road traffic signs

aberto
open

animais cruzando
animals crossing

auto-estrada (com portagem)
motorway (with tolls)

bermas baixas
low hard shoulder

bifurcação
road fork

centro da cidade
city centre

circule pela direita
keep right

circule pela esquerda
keep left

cruzamento perigoso
dangerous crossroads

cuidado
caution

curva a...quilómetros
road bends in... km

curva perigosa
dangerous bend

dê passegem
give way

desvio
diversion

devagar
slow down

espere
wait

estacionamento
parking

estacionamento proibido
no parking

estrada em mau estado
irregular road surface

estrada interrompida
no through road

estrada nacional
main road

excepto
except

fechado
closed

fim de...
end of...

fim de obras
end of roadworks

gelo
ice on road

neve
snow

nevoeiro
fog

obras
roadworks

passagem de nivel (sem guarda)
level crossing (unmanned)

perigo
danger

portagem
toll

posto de primeiros socorros
first-aid post

saída
exit

sentido único
one-way street

vedado ao trânsito
road closed

veículos pesados
heavy vehicles

velocidade máxima
maximum speed

via de acesso
access only

Russian: words and phrases

For clarity we have put the English phrase in light type, foreign language terms in dark type and their phonetic pronunciation in light italic.

Asking for directions

Excuse me, could I ask you something?
Извините, можно вас спросить?
Eezvineetyeh, morzhna vuss sprusseet?

I've lost my way
Я заблудился (заблудилась)
Ya zubloodeelsya (zubloodeelas)

Is there a(n)... around here?
Вы не знаете, здесь поблизости...?
Vy nyeh znah-yetyeh, zdyess publeezusti...?

Is this the way to...?
Это дорога в...? *Eto durrorga v...?*

Could you tell me how to get to the... (name of place) by car/on foot?
Вы не подскажете, как доехать/дойти до...?
Vy nyeh pudskarzhityeh, kukk duh-yekhat/duytee dor...?

What's the quickest way to...?
Как можно быстрее доехать до...?
Kukk morzhna bystrayeh duh-yekhat dor...?

How many kilometres is it to...?
Сколько километров до...?
Skorlka keelumyetruff dor...?

Could you point it out on the map?
Покажите на карте, пожалуйста
Pukkuzheetyeh nah kartyeh, puzharlooysta

☞ Ask the speaker to point to what they are saying

Я не знаю, я не отсюда
I don't know, I don't know my way around here

Вы едете в неправильном направлении
You're going the wrong way

Вам нужно вернуться в...
You have to go back to...

Вы увидите, там будет написано
From there on just follow the signs

Там вам придётся снова спросить
When you get there, ask again

Useful words

прямо
straight ahead
налево
left
направо
right
повернуть
turn
последовать
follow
перейти
cross
перекрёсток
the intersection
улица
the street
светофор
the traffic lights
туннель
the tunnel
знак "уступите дорогу"
the 'give-way' sign
здание
the building
на углу
at the corner
река
the river
путепровод
the fly-over
мост
the bridge
железнодорожный переезд/шлагбаум
level crossing/barrier
указатель направления...
the sign pointing to...
стрелка
the arrow

Road traffic signs

Russia uses international traffic signs, but there are two special forms:

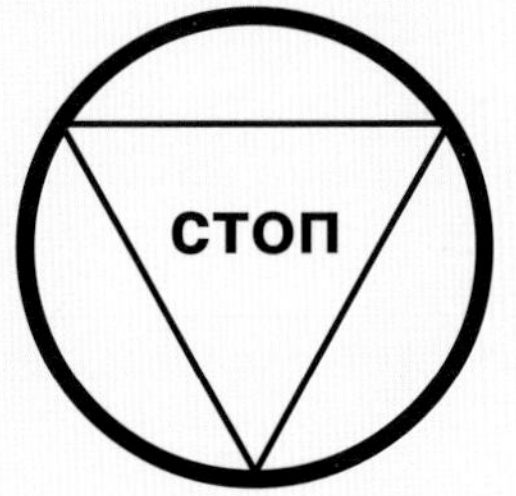

means STOP

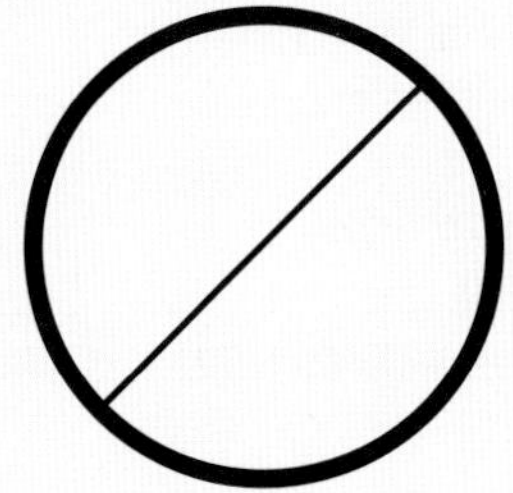

means END OF RESTRICTION

Берегитесь автомобиля!
watch out for cars
велосипедисты
cyclists
внимание, впереди ведутся работы
road works ahead
(внимание) пешеходы
watch out for pedestrians
встречное движение
oncoming traffic
въезд запрещён
no entry
ГАИ
traffic police
движение в один ряд
single-file traffic
держитесь правой стороны
keep to the right
камнепад
falling rocks
обгон запрещён
no overtaking
обочина
kerb
объезд
diversion
ограничение скорости
speed limit
одностороннее движение
one-way traffic
опасно
dangerous
опасный поворот
dangerous bend
остановка автобуса
bus stop
остановка запрещена
no stopping
переход
crossing
плохая дорога
bad surface
светофор через сто метров
lights ahead 100 metres
стоп
stop
стоянка запрещена
no parking
сужение дороги
road narrows
такси
taxi
таможня
customs

Spanish: words and phrases

For clarity we have put the English phrase in light type, foreign language terms in dark type and their phonetic pronunciation in light italic.

Asking for directions

Excuse me, could I ask you something?
Perdone, ¿podría preguntarle algo?
pehrdohneh, pohdreeah prehgoontahrleh ahlgoh?

I've lost my way
Me he perdido
meh eh pehrdeedoh

Is there a(n)...around here?
¿Sabe dónde hay un(a)...por aquí?
sahbeh dohndeh ay oon(ah)...pohr ahkee?

Is this the way to...?
¿Se va por aquí a...?
seh bah pohr ahkee ah...?

Could you tell me how to get to the... (name of place) by car/on foot?
¿Podría decirme cómo llegar a... (en coche/a pie)?
pohdreeah dehtheermeh kohmoh lyehgahr ah... (ehn kohcheh/ah pyeh)?

What's the quickest way to...?
¿Cómo hago para llegar lo antes posible a...?
kohmoh ahgoh pahrah lyehgahr loh ahntehs pohseebleh ah...?

How many kilometres is it to...?
¿Cuántos kilómetros faltan para llegar a...?
kwahntohs keelohmehtrohs fahltahn pahrah lyehgahr ah...?

Could you point it out on the map?
¿Podría señalarlo en el mapa?
pohdreeah sehnyahlahrloh ehn ehl mahpah?

☞ Ask the speaker to point to what they are saying

No sé, no soy de aquí
I don't know, I don't know my way around here

Por aquí no es
You're going the wrong way

Tiene que volver a...
You have to go back to...

Allí los carteles le indicarán
From there on just follow the signs

Vuelva a preguntar allí
When you get there, ask again

Useful words

todo recto
straight ahead
a la izquierda
left
a la derecha
right
doblar
turn
seguir
follow
cruzar
cross
el cruce
the intersection
la calle
the street
el semáforo
the traffic light
el túnel
the tunnel
el stop
the `give-way' sign
el edificio
the building
en la esquina
at the corner
el río
the river
el viaducto
the fly-over
el puente
the bridge
el paso a nivel/las barreras
the level crossing/ the boom gates
el cartel en dirección de...
the sign pointing to...
la flecha
the arrow

Road traffic signs

a la derecha
right

a la izquierda
left

abierto
open

altura máxima
maximum height

arcenes sin afirmar
soft verges

žatención, peligro!
danger

autopista de peaje
toll road

autovía
motorway

bajada peligrosa
steep hill

calzada resbaladiza
slippery road

cambio de sentido
change of direction

cañada
animals crossing

carretera comarcal
secondary road

carretera cortada
road closed

carretera en mal estado
irregular road surface

carretera nacional
main road

ceda el paso
give way

cerrado
closed

cruce peligroso
dangerous crossing

curvas en...km
bends for...km

despacio
drive slowly

desprendimientos
loose rocks

desvío
diversion

dirección prohibida
no entry

dirección única
one-way traffic

encender las luces
switch on lights

espere
wait

estacionamiento reglamentado
limited parking zone

excepto...
except for...

fin de...
end of...

hielo
ice on road

niebla
beware fog

obras
roadworks ahead

paso a nivel (sin barreras)
level crossing (no gates)

paso de ganado
cattle crossing

peaje
toll

peatones
pedestrian crossing

precaución
caution

prohibido adelantar
no overtaking

prohibido aparcar
no parking

puesto de socorro
first aid

salida
exit

salida de camiones
factory/works exit

substancias peligrosas
dangerous substances

travesía peligrosa
dangerous crossing

zona peatonal
pedestrian zone

Turkish: words and phrases

For clarity we have put the English phrase in light type, foreign language terms in dark type and their phonetic pronunciation in light italic.

Asking for directions

Excuse me, could I ask you something?
Özür dilerim, size bir şey sorabilir miyim?
urzewR dileRim, sizeh biR shey soRabiliR miyim?

I've lost my way
Yolumu kaybettim
yoloomoo kíbet-tim

Is there a(n)...around here?
Bu civarda bir...var mı?
boo jivaRda biR...vaR muh?

Is this the way to...?
...giden yol bu mu?
...giden yol boo moo?

Could you tell me how to get to the... (name of place) by car/on foot?
Bana...arabayla/yaya nasıl gidebileceğimi söyleyebilir misiniz?
bana...aRabíla/ya-ya nasuhl gidebileje:imi suhyleyebiliR misiniz?

What's the quickest way to...?
...en çabuk nasıl gidebilirim?
...en chabook nasuhl gidebiliRim?

How many kilometres is it to...?
...kaç kilometre kaldı?
...kach kilometReh kalduh?

Could you point it out on the map?
Haritada gösterebilir misiniz?
haRitada gursteRebiliR misiniz?

☞ Ask the speaker to point to what they are saying

Bilmiyorum, buralı değilim
I don't know, I don't know my way around here

Yanlış yoldasınız
You're going the wrong way

...geri dönmelisiniz
You have to go back to...

Oradan levhaları takip ediniz
From there on just follow the signs

Oraya varınca tekrar sorun
When you get there, ask again

Useful words

doğru
straight ahead
sola
left
sağa
right
dönmek
turn
takip etmek
follow
karşıya geçmek
cross
kavşak
the intersection
sokak
the street
trafik ışıkları
the traffic lights
tünel
the tunnel
'yol ver' işareti
the 'give-way' sign
bina
the building
köşede
at the corner
ırmak/nehir
the river
bağlantı yolu
the fly-over
köprü
the bridge
hemzemin geçit
the level crossing/the boom gates
...giden yolu gösteren levha
the sign pointing to...

Road traffic signs

Beklemek yasaktır
no waiting

Bozuk yol
poor road surface

D (durak)
D (bus stop)

Dikkat
caution

Dur
stop

Gümrük
customs

H (hastane)
H (hospital)

Havaalanı
airport

Jandarma
gendarmarie

Park etmek yasaktır
no parking

Polis
police

Şehir merkezi
city centre

Tamirat
roadworks

Tek yön
one way

Tünel
tunnel

Viraj
bend

Yangın tehlikesi
danger of fire

Yavaş
slow

Useful information

Channel Tunnel maps

The Eurotunnel shuttle service for cars, cars towing caravans and trailers, motorcycles, coaches and HGV vehicles runs between terminals at Folkestone in Kent and Calais/ Coquelles in France.

It takes just over one hour to travel from the M20 motorway in Kent, via the Channel Tunnel, to the A16 autoroute in France. The service runs 24 hours a day, every day of the year.

Liquefied petroleum gas (LPG)

An LPG-fuelled car will not be allowed through the Eurotunnel, even if you can prove the tank has been disconnected or emptied. If you are travelling by ferry, check with the operator before you book.

Travel information

For the latest ticket and travel information call the Eurotunnel Call Centre (**tel: 08443 353535**) or visit **www.eurotunnel.com**

There are up to three departures per hour at peak times, with the journey in the tunnel from platform to platform taking just 35 minutes. Travellers pass through British and French frontier controls on departure, saving time on the other side of the Channel.

Each terminal has plenty of parking, ATMs, bureaux de change, restaurants, toilet facilities, a 24-hour information point and a variety of shops. In Calais/Coquelles, the Cité de l'Europe contains numerous shops, restaurants and a hypermarket.

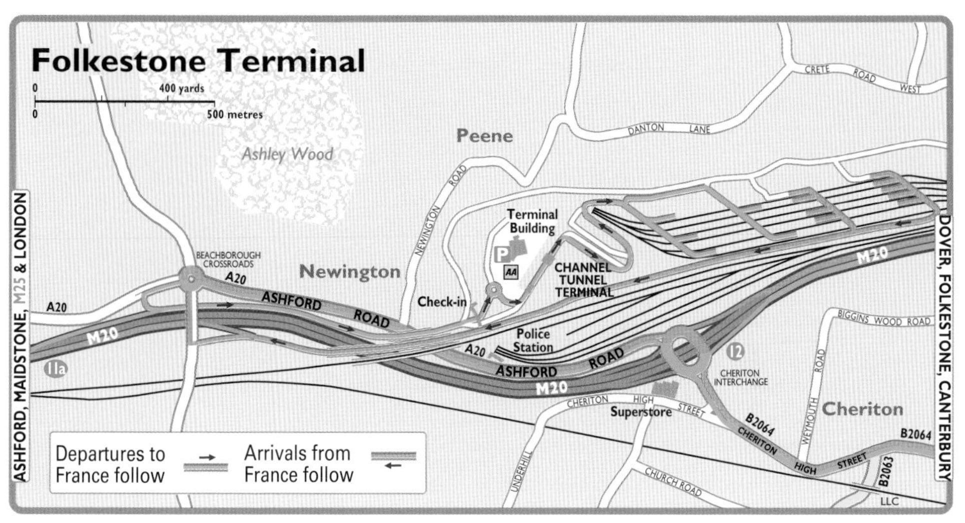
Folkestone Terminal
0 400 yards
0 500 metres
Ashley Wood
Peene
Newington
Cheriton
Terminal Building
CHANNEL TUNNEL TERMINAL
Check-in
Police Station
Superstore
BEACHBOROUGH CROSSROADS
CHERITON INTERCHANGE
ASHFORD ROAD
A20
M20
B2064
B2063
CRETE ROAD WEST
DANTON LANE
NEWINGTON ROAD
BIGGINS WOOD ROAD
WEYMOUTH ROAD
CHERITON HIGH STREET
CHURCH ROAD
UNDERHILL
ASHFORD, MAIDSTONE, M25 & LONDON
DOVER, FOLKESTONE, CANTERBURY
Departures to France follow
Arrivals from France follow
LLC

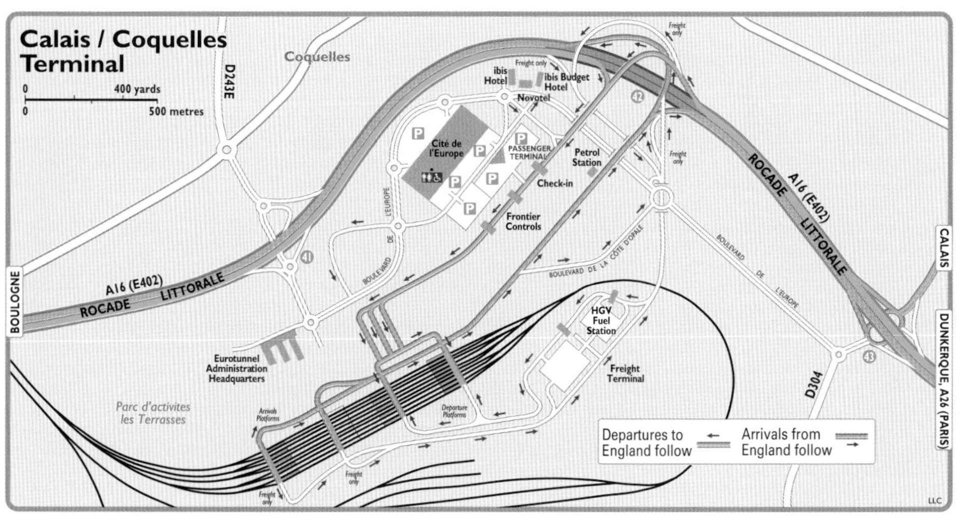
Calais / Coquelles Terminal
0 400 yards
0 500 metres
Coquelles
D243E
ibis Hotel
ibis Budget Hotel
Novotel
Cité de l'Europe
PASSENGER TERMINAL
Petrol Station
Check-in
Frontier Controls
BOULEVARD DE L'EUROPE
BOULEVARD DE LA CÔTE D'OPALE
A16 (E402) ROCADE LITTORALE
HGV Fuel Station
Freight Terminal
Eurotunnel Administration Headquarters
Parc d'activites les Terrasses
D304
BOULOGNE
CALAIS
DUNKERQUE, A26 (PARIS)
Departures to England follow
Arrivals from England follow
LLC

Road distance chart

Frankfurt am Main–Ljubljana = 804 km

Amsterdam	Athina	Barcelona	Belfast	Beograd	Berlin	Bern	Birmingham	Bordeaux	Bratislava	Brussel/Bruxelles	București	Budapest	Dublin	Edinburgh	Frankfurt am Main	Genève	Göteborg	Hamburg	Helsinki/Helsingfors	Istanbul	København	Köln	Kyïv	Lisboa	Ljubljana	London	Luxembourg	Madrid
2760																												
1557	2520																											
1312	3520	2265																										
1718	1044	1981	2816																									
655	2288	1863	1868	1247																								
838	1971	944	1725	1363	922																							
738	3285	1691	582	2244	1295	1152																						
1091	3049	552	1815	2007	1634	852	1241																					
1225	1618	1866	2324	577	671	938	1750	1879																				
206	2568	1355	1148	1673	763	637	574	883	1181																			
2181	1106	2597	3279	619	1646	1893	2706	2613	977	2136																		
1398	1429	1897	2497	388	864	1111	1923	2053	194	1353	788																	
1088	3455	2041	164	2594	1644	1502	358	1585	2101	925	3057	2274																
1190	3557	2143	305	2695	1746	1603	460	1686	2203	1026	3159	2376	468															
445	2323	1323	1545	1281	565	423	971	1150	788	400	1744	961	1321	1422														
908	2372	778	1683	1331	1072	165	1109	687	1088	706	1946	1261	1457	1561	573													
1178	3131	2479	2412	2090	823	1637	1839	2185	1514	1307	2490	1708	2187	2290	1214	1787												
463	2602	1763	1696	1561	294	910	1123	1470	985	591	1961	1178	1471	1574	487	1059	728											
2580	3590	3788	3792	2641	1959	2847	3220	3551	2208	2687	2483	2252	3567	3670	2489	2996	982	2192										
2649	1092	2913	3748	935	2179	2294	3175	2929	1509	2605	681	1320	3522	3626	2213	2261	3022	2493	3164									
920	2873	2220	2153	1832	564	1378	1580	1927	1255	1048	2231	1449	1928	2031	955	1528	269	469	1123	2764								
265	2506	1342	1352	1464	575	585	778	1062	972	208	1928	1145	1126	1230	192	735	1141	425	2500	2396	882							
2016	1994	3093	3228	1322	1398	2190	2655	2988	1251	2123	888	1123	3003	3106	1884	2340	2211	1681	1595	1569	1952	1935						
2296	3787	1237	3019	3188	2838	2150	2446	1202	3090	2095	3804	3103	2793	2897	2355	1989	3397	2681	4764	4119	3138	2273	4199					
1241	1572	1455	2294	530	999	836	1721	1471	435	1153	1146	443	2069	2173	804	803	1916	1203	2623	1462	1656	987	1565	2661				
533	2910	1486	766	2039	1090	947	193	1030	1546	370	2502	1719	541	645	766	905	1634	918	3015	2970	1375	574	2450	2243	1537			
386	2355	1149	1355	1469	762	431	782	946	1010	213	1965	1183	1129	1233	240	500	1326	610	2687	2401	1066	188	2081	2159	956	582		
1800	3145	614	2523	2573	2343	1535	1950	706	2458	1599	3189	2489	2298	2402	1859	1374	2901	2185	4268	3505	2642	1778	3684	619	2046	1750	1662	
868	3415	1821	461	2374	1425	1282	138	1365	1881	705	2837	2054	310	339	1101	1240	1969	1253	3350	3305	1710	909	2785	2578	1872	323	911	2082
1236	2567	505	2003	1526	1541	623	1429	654	1419	1034	2141	1441	1778	1881	1003	422	2158	1442	3467	2457	1899	1025	2564	1711	999	1230	832	1096
1077	1218	977	1963	1026	1033	350	1390	985	919	876	1642	942	1737	1841	662	317	1833	1120	2959	1958	1574	823	2064	2182	499	1190	669	1568
1742	2448	2878	2955	1513	1124	1938	2381	2714	1178	1850	1341	1125	2729	2833	1620	2088	1938	1408	1183	2023	1678	1662	557	3927	1593	2181	1817	3432
2449	2864	3584	3661	2084	1830	2644	3088	3420	1885	2556	1758	1831	3435	3539	2326	2794	2643	2114	1116	2440	2385	2368	871	4364	2300	2888	2523	4138
827	1990	1370	1880	949	585	442	1297	1278	466	739	1421	639	1655	1759	390	591	1502	789	2511	1880	1242	573	1718	2576	435	1107	521	1961
1859	597	1555	2746	1483	1693	1132	2173	1704	1376	1658	2099	1399	2521	2624	1444	1085	2586	1874	3563	2415	2327	1606	2521	2761	956	1973	1476	2146
1490	3443	2790	2723	2402	1134	1949	2150	2497	1826	1618	2801	2019	2498	2601	1525	2098	315	1039	1030	3333	580	1446	2522	3710	2248	1950	1636	3214
525	2465	1039	1248	1800	1068	592	659	583	1340	324	2295	1513	1023	1126	604	529	1626	910	2993	2732	1367	502	2428	1796	1287	475	407	1300
2094	4028	1076	2818	2986	2637	1948	2244	1000	2889	1893	3602	2902	2592	2696	2153	1788	3196	2480	4563	3918	2936	2072	3997	300	2459	2044	1956	531
891	1946	1709	2045	904	341	769	1471	1601	328	902	1304	522	1820	1923	510	919	1186	657	2178	1836	927	693	1389	2814	664	1272	731	2300
1618	2807	2825	2830	1766	996	1885	2257	2590	1333	1725	1676	1378	2604	2708	1527	2035	1760	1230	962	2357	1501	1537	1029	3803	1748	2057	1724	3307
1658	1190	1354	2545	1282	1493	932	1972	1503	1175	1457	1898	1198	2320	2423	1243	884	2386	1673	3363	2214	2126	1405	2321	2560	755	1772	1275	1945
2180	3190	3388	3393	2241	1558	2447	2819	3152	1809	2288	2084	1853	3167	3271	2089	2597	2284	1793	387	2765	2063	2099	1196	4365	2223	2619	2286	3869
1727	1121	1990	2826	303	1389	1372	2252	2007	707	1682	824	539	2600	2704	1290	1339	2402	1644	2791	1113	2143	1474	1601	3196	539	2052	1478	2581
2277	3998	998	3000	2957	2838	1919	2427	1183	2842	2076	3573	2873	2775	2878	2299	1759	3378	2662	4763	3889	3119	2255	4068	403	2430	2227	2128	510
2139	654	2402	3237	424	1668	1783	2664	2418	998	2094	598	809	3012	3115	1702	1750	2512	1982	3061	781	2253	1885	1485	3608	951	2464	1890	2993
2095	735	2358	3193	380	1624	1739	2620	2375	954	2050	372	765	2968	3071	1658	1707	2468	1938	2854	555	2209	1841	1259	3564	907	2420	1846	2949
1534	3488	2835	2768	2446	1175	1993	2195	2541	1870	1663	2846	2064	2543	2646	1570	2143	481	1084	505	3378	624	1497	2566	3755	2293	1995	1681	3259
1920	3105	3127	3132	2063	1298	2187	2559	2892	1631	2027	1973	1675	2907	3011	1829	2337	2062	1533	90	2654	1803	1839	1326	4105	2046	2359	2026	3609
2333	454	2597	3432	619	1862	1978	2858	2613	1193	2288	656	1004	3207	3310	1896	1945	2707	2177	3139	642	2447	2080	1543	3802	1145	2658	2085	3188
2103	735	2366	3201	606	1765	1748	2628	2383	1083	2058	886	915	2976	3163	1666	1715	2778	2020	3167	1069	2518	1849	1773	3572	915	2428	1854	2957
3071	4692	4371	4304	3743	2715	3529	3731	4078	3311	3199	3586	3355	4114	4182	3106	3679	1949	2620	1360	4267	2160	3033	2698	5291	3829	3531	3217	4795
1897	3363	363	2603	2322	2202	1283	2030	803	2206	1695	2937	2237	2378	2482	1663	1123	2819	2103	4128	3253	2560	1686	3433	894	1795	1830	1492	342
1636	2550	2776	2849	1509	1018	1836	2275	2608	1077	1744	1384	1121	2623	2727	1518	1986	1733	1203	1142	2066	1474	1555	738	3821	1492	2075	1715	3325
1202	2097	2342	2414	1056	584	1402	1841	2174	643	1309	1240	668	2189	2293	1084	1552	1397	868	1566	1922	1138	1121	815	3387	1057	1641	1281	2891
1148	1664	1789	2246	622	629	861	1673	1802	66	1103	1022	240	2021	2125	711	1010	1473	943	2246	1554	1214	895	1319	3016	378	1473	933	2380
1326	1435	1586	2424	394	988	968	1852	1603	417	1281	1009	347	2199	2302	889	936	2001	1243	2604	1325	1741	1073	1470	2793	135	1647	1074	2177

Distances (in kilometres) are calculated by the shortest or quickest route and should be considered to be approximate.
The calculation includes any part of the journey taken by car ferry.

	Milano	Minsk	Moskva	München	Napoli	Oslo	Paris	Porto	Praha	Rīga	Roma	Sankt-Peterburg	Sarajevo	Sevilla	Skopje	Sofiya	Stockholm	Tallinn	Thessaloniki	Tiranë	Tromsø	València	Vilnius	Warszawa	Wien
Minsk	2048																								
Moskva	2755	704																							
München	502	1524	2231																						
Napoli	779	2534	3240	1109																					
Oslo	2144	2248	2954	1813	2898																				
Paris	874	2154	2861	852	1643	1937																			
Porto	1981	3724	4430	2375	2559	3506	1589																		
Praha	859	1149	1855	375	1483	1498	1031	2611																	
Rīga	1996	472	931	1548	2655	2072	2016	3601	1260																
Roma	578	2333	3040	908	237	2697	1417	2358	1281	2456															
Sankt-Peterburg	2558	784	716	2110	3164	2325	2574	4164	1778	562	2963														
Sarajevo	1034	1664	2370	958	1492	2713	1779	2995	1046	1917	1291	2392													
Sevilla	1952	3853	4559	2346	2530	3690	1771	650	2684	3802	2329	4364	2968												
Skopje	1446	1934	2356	1370	1903	2823	2191	3406	1324	2187	936	2662	470	3377											
Sofiya	1402	1713	2130	1326	1859	2779	2147	3363	1281	2047	1317	2455	558	3333	227										
Stockholm	2189	2293	2656	1858	2943	537	1964	3551	1541	910	2743	906	2756	3736	2867	2823									
Tallinn	2298	770	1043	1850	2957	2374	2314	3903	1562	302	2757	357	2214	4103	2484	2344	595								
Thessaloniki	1641	1997	2414	1565	2098	3018	2385	3601	1519	2381	1164	2740	698	3572	228	284	3062	2678							
Tiranë	1410	2040	2644	1334	640	3089	2155	3371	1422	2293	816	2768	385	3342	288	514	3133	2660	393						
Tromsø	3725	2286	2219	3394	4479	1616	3500	5089	3077	2064	4279	1502	3894	5272	4164	3957	1605	1859	4242	4346					
València	1316	3217	3924	1710	1895	3130	1375	879	2048	3166	1694	3728	2328	644	2743	2699	3175	3538	2936	2706	4744				
Vilnius	1947	181	863	1424	2432	2044	2030	3620	1046	291	2231	743	1660	3752	1929	1756	2089	658	2040	2111	2245	3116			
Warszawa	1513	541	1247	990	1998	1709	1596	3185	612	692	1797	1167	1207	3317	1476	1433	1753	1059	1671	1659	2669	2682	435		
Wien	861	1216	1923	388	1318	1784	1233	2814	285	1371	1117	1847	758	2765	1043	999	1829	1739	1237	1225	3398	2179	1115	681	
Zagreb	632	1472	2178	554	1089	2312	1406	2591	645	1730	887	2205	400	2562	815	771	2356	2097	1008	862	3926	1926	1473	1039	359

Mountain passes

It is best not to attempt to cross mountain passes at night, and daily schedules should make allowances for the comparatively slow speeds inevitable in mountainous areas.

Gravel surfaces (such as dirt and stone chips) vary considerably; they are dusty when dry, slippery when wet. Where known to exist, this type of surface has been noted. Road repairs can be carried out only during the summer, and may interrupt traffic. Precipitous road sides are rarely, if ever, totally unguarded; on the older roads, stone pillars are placed at close intervals. Gradient figures take the mean figure on hairpin bends, and may be steeper on the inside of the curves, particularly on the older roads.

Gradients conversion table

All steep hill signs show the grade in percentage terms. The following conversion table may be used as a guide:

30% = 1 in 3	**14% = 1 in 7**
25% = 1 in 4	**12% = 1 in 8**
20% = 1 in 5	**11% = 1 in 9**
16% = 1 in 6	**10% = 1 in 10**

Before attempting late-evening or early-morning journeys across frontier passes, check the times of opening of the frontier controls. A number close at night; for example, the Timmelsjoch border is closed between 8pm and 7am and during the winter.

Always engage a low gear before either ascending or descending steep gradients, and keep well to the right-hand side of the road and avoid cutting corners. Avoid excessive use of brakes. If the engine overheats, pull off the road, making sure that you do not cause an obstruction, leave the engine idling, and put the heater controls (including the fan) into the maximum heat position. Under no circumstances should you remove the radiator cap until the engine has cooled down. Do not fill the coolant system of a hot engine with cold water.

Always engage a lower gear before taking a hairpin bend, give priority to vehicles ascending and remember that as your altitude increases, so your engine power decreases. Always give priority to postal coaches travelling in either direction. Their route is usually signposted.

Caravans

Passes suitable for caravans are indicated in the table on the following pages. Those shown to be negotiable by caravans are best used only by experienced drivers in cars with ample power;

the rest are probably best avoided. A correct power-to-load ratio is always essential.

Winter conditions

Mountain passes – key to abbreviations:
Winter conditions are given in italics in the last column of the table on pages 194–203.
UO means 'usually open', although a severe fall of snow may temporarily obstruct the road for 24 to 48 hours, and wheel chains are often necessary; OC means 'occasionally closed'; UC, usually closed, between the dates stated. Dates for opening and closing of passes are approximate only. Warning notices are usually posted at the foot of a pass if it is closed, or if indicating that chains or snow tyres should or must be used.

Wheel chains may be needed early and late in the season, and between short spells (a few hours) of obstruction. At these times, conditions are usually more difficult for caravans on the passes.

In fair weather, wheel chains or snow tyres are necessary only on the higher passes, but in severe weather you will probably need to use them (as a rough guide) at altitudes exceeding 610 metres (2,000ft).

Mountain passes

Pass name, height and country	From and to	Distances from summit and max gradient	Min width of road	Conditions (see page 193 for key to abbreviations)
***Albula** 2312 metres (7585ft) Switzerland	Tiefencastel 851 metres (2792ft) La Punt 1687 metres (5535ft)	30km 1 in 10 18.6 miles 9km 1 in 10 5.6 miles	3.5 metres 11ft 6in	UC Nov–early Jun. An inferior alternative to the Julier; tar and gravel, fine scenery. Alternative rail tunnel.
Allos 2250 metres (7382ft) France	Barcelonnette 1132 metres (3714ft) Colmars 1235 metres (4052ft)	20km 1 in 10 12.4 miles 24km 1 in 12 14.9 miles	4 metres 13ft 1n	UC early Nov–early Jun. Very winding, narrow mostly unguarded but not difficult otherwise; passing bays on southern slope, poor surface (maximum width vehicles 1.8 metres, 5ft 11in).
Aprica 1176 metres (3858ft) Italy	Tresenda 375 metres(1230ft) Edolo 699 metres (2293ft)	14km 1 in 11 8.7 miles 15km 1 in 16 9.3 miles	4 metres 13ft 1in	UO Fine scenery, good surface, well graded; suitable for caravans.
Aravis 1498 metres (4915ft) France	La Clusaz 1040 metres (3412ft) Flumet 917 metres (3009ft)	8km 1 in 11 5.0 miles 12km 1 in 11 7.4 miles	4 metres 13ft 1in	OC Dec–Mar. Outstanding scenery, and a fairly easy road.
Arlberg 1802 metres (5912ft) Austria	Bludenz 581 metres (1905ft) Landeck 816 metres (2677ft)	35km 1 in 8 21.7 miles 32km 1 in 7.5 20 miles	6 metres 19ft 8in	OC Dec–Apr. Modern road; short, steep stretch from west easing towards the summit; heavy traffic; parallel toll road tunnel. Suitable for caravans; using tunnel. Pass road closed to vehicles towing trailers.
Aubisque 1710 metres (5610ft) France	Eaux Bonnes 750 metres (2461ft) Argelés-Gazost 463 metres (1519ft)	12km 1 in 10 7 miles 30km 1 in 10 19 miles	3.5 metres 11ft 6in	UC mid Oct–Jun. A very winding road; continuous but easy ascent; the descent incorporates the Col de Soulor (1450 metres, 4757ft); 8km (5 miles) of very narrow, rough unguarded road, with a steep drop.
Ballon d'Alsace 1178 metres (3865ft) France	Giromagny 476metres (1562ft) St-Maurice-sur-Moselle 549 metres (1801ft)	17km 1 in 9 10.6 miles 9km 1 in 9 5.6 miles	4 metres 13ft 1in	OC Dec–Mar. A fairly straightforward ascent and descent, but numerous bends; negotiable by caravans.
Bayard 1248 metres (4094ft) France	Chauffayer 911 metres (2989ft) Gap 733 metres (2405ft)	18km 1 in 12 11.2 miles 8km 1 in 7 5.0 miles	6 metres 19ft 8in	UO Part of the Route Napoléon. Fairly easy, steepest on the southern side with several hairpin bends; negotiable by caravans from north to south.
***Bernina** 2330 metres (7644ft) Switzerland	Pontresina 1805 metres (5922ft) Poschiavo 1019 metres (3343ft)	15.5km 1 in 10 10.5 miles 18.5km 1 in 8 11.5 miles	5 metres 16ft 5in	OC Dec–Mar. A good road on both sides; negotiable by caravans.
Bonaigua 2072 metres (6797ft) Spain	Viella 974 metres (3195ft) Esterri d'Aneu 957 metres (3140ft)	23km 1 in 12 14 miles 23km 1 in 12 14 miles	4.3 metres 14ft 1in	UC Nov–Apr. A sinuous and narrow road with many hairpin bends and some precipitous drops; the alternative route to Lleida (Lérida) through the Viella tunnel is open in winter.
Bracco 613 metres (2011ft) Italy	Riva Trigoso 43 metres (141ft) Borghetto di Vara 104metres (341ft)	15km 1 in 7 9.3 miles 18km 1 in 7 11.2 miles	5 metres 16ft 5in	UO A two-lane road with continuous bends; passing usually difficult; negotiable by caravans; alternative toll motorway available.

* Permitted maximum width of vehicles 7ft 6in + Permitted maximum width of vehicles 8ft 2.5in ++ Maximum length of vehicle 30ft

Pass name, height and country	From and to	Distances from summit and max gradient	Min width of road	Conditions (see page 193 for key to abbreviations)
Brenner 1374 metres (4508ft) Austria–Italy	Innsbruck 574 metres (1883ft) Vipiteno 948 metres (3110ft)	36km 1 in 12 22miles 15km 1 in 7 9.3 miles	6 metres 19ft 8in	UO Parallel toll motorway open; heavy traffic; suitable for caravans using toll motorway. Pass road closed to vehicles towing trailers.
+Brünig 1007 metres (3304ft) Switzerland	Brienzwiler Station 575 metres (1886ft) Giswil 485 metres (1591ft)	6km 1 in 12 3.7 miles 13km 1 in 12 8.1 miles	6 metres 19ft 8in	UO An easy but winding road, heavy traffic at weekends; suitable for caravans.
Bussang 721 metres (2365ft) France	Thann 340 metres (1115ft) St Maurice-sur-Moselle 549 metres (1801ft)	24km 1 in 14 15 miles 8km 1 in 14 5.0 miles	4 metres 13ft 1in	UO A very easy road over the Vosges; beautiful scenery; suitable for caravans.
Cabre 1180 metres (3871ft) France	Luc-en-Diois 580 metres (1903ft) Aspres sur Buëch 764 metres (2507ft)	24km 1 in 11 15 miles 17km 1 in 14 10.6 miles	5.5 metres 18ft	UO An easy, pleasant road; suitable for caravans.
Campolongo 1875 metres (6152ft) Italy	Corvara in Badia 1568 metres (5144ft) Arabba 1602 metres (5256ft)	6km 1 in 8 3.7 miles 4km 1 in 8 2.5 miles	5 metres 16ft 5in	OC Dec–Mar. A winding but easy ascent; long level stretch on summit followed by easy descent; good surface; suitable for caravans.
Cayolle 2326 metres (7631ft) France	Barcelonnette 1132 metres (3714ft) Guillaumes 819 metres (2687ft)	30km 1 in 10 19 miles 33km 1 in 10 20.5 miles	4 metres 13ft 1in	UC early Nov–early Jun. Narrow and winding road with hairpin bends; poor surface and broken edges; steep drops. Long stretches of single-track road with passing places.
Costalunga (Karer) 1753 metres (5751ft) Italy	Cardano 282 metres (925ft) Pozza 1290 metres (4232ft)	24km 1 in 6 14.9 miles 11km 1 in 8 7 miles	5 metres 16ft 5in	OC Dec–Apr. A good well-engineered road but mostly winding; caravans prohibited.
Croix 1778 metres (5833ft) Switzerland	Villars-sur-Ollon 1253 metres (4111ft) Les Diablerets 1155 metres (3789ft)	8km 1 in 7.5 5.0 miles 9km 1 in 11 5.6 miles	3.5 metres 11ft 6in	UC Nov–May. A narrow and winding route but extremely picturesque.
Croix-Haute 1179 metres (3868ft) France	Monestier-de-Clermont 832 metres (2730ft) Aspres-sur-Buëch 764 metres (2507ft)	34km 1 in 14 21 miles 29km 1 in 14 18 miles	5.5 metres 18ft	UO Well engineered; several hairpin bends on the north side; suitable for caravans.
Envalira 2407 metres (7897ft) Andorra	Pas de la Casa 2091 metres (6860ft) Andorra 1029 metres (3376ft)	5km 1 in 10 3.1 miles 25km 1 in 8 16 miles	6 metres 19ft 8in	OC Nov–Apr. A good road with wide bends on ascent and descent; fine views; negotiable by caravans (maximum height vehicles 3.5 metres/ 11ft 6in on northern approach near L'Hospitalet).
Falzárego 2117 metres (6945ft) Italy	Cortina d'Ampezzo 1224 metres (4016ft) Andraz 1428 metres (4685ft)	17km 1 in 12 10.6 miles 9km 1 in 12 5.6 miles	5 metres 16ft 5in	OC Dec–Apr. Well engineered bitumen surface; many hairpin bends on both sides; negotiable by caravans.

* Permitted maximum width of vehicles 7ft 6in + Permitted maximum width of vehicles 8ft 2.5in ++ Maximum length of vehicle 30ft

Mountain passes

Pass name, height and country	From and to	Distances from summit and max gradient	Min width of road	Conditions (see page 193 for key to abbreviations)
Faucille 1323 metres (4341ft) France	Gex 628 metres (2060ft) Morez 702 metres (2303ft)	11km 1 in 10 6.8 miles 27km 1 in 12 17miles	5 metres 16ft 5in	UO Fairly wide, winding road across the Jura mountains; negotiable by caravans, but it is probably better to follow La Cure-St-Cergue-Nyon.
Fern 1209 metres (3967ft) Austria	Nassereith 843 metres (2766ft) Lermoos 995 metres (3264ft)	10km 1 in 10 6 miles 10km 1 in 10 6 miles	6 metres 19ft 8in	UO An easy pass, but slippery when wet; heavy traffic at summer weekends; suitable for caravans.
Flexen 1784 metres (5853ft) Austria	Lech 1447 metres (4747ft) Rauzalpe (near Arlberg Pass) 1628 metres (5341ft)	6.5km 1 in 10 4 miles 3.5km 1 in 10 2.2 miles	5.5 metres 18ft	UO The magnificent 'Flexenstrasse', a well-engineered mountain road with tunnels and galleries. The road from Lech to Warth, north of the pass, is usually closed between November and April due to danger of avalanches.
***Flüela** 2383 metres (7818ft) Switzerland	Davos-Dorf 1563 metres (5128ft) Susch 1438 metres (4718ft)	14km 1 in 10 9 miles 14km 1 in 8 9 miles	5 metres 16ft 5in	OC Nov–May. Easy ascent from Davos; some acute hairpin bends on the eastern side; bitumen surface; negotiable by caravans.
+Forclaz 1527 metres (5010ft) Switzerland France	Martigny 476 metres (1562ft) Argentière 1253 metres (4111ft)	13km 1 in 12 8.1 miles 19km 1 in 12 11.8 miles	5 metres 16ft 5in	UO Forclaz; OC Montets Dec–early Apr. A good road over the pass and to the frontier; in France, narrow and rough over Col des Montets (1461 metres/4793ft); negotiable by caravans.
Foscagno 2291 metres (7516ft) Italy	Bormio 1225 metres (4019ft) Livigno 1816 metres (5958ft)	24km 1 in 8 14.9 miles 14km 1 in 8 8.7 miles	3.3 metres 10ft 10in	OC Nov–May. Narrow and winding through lonely mountains, generally poor surface. Long winding ascent with many blind bends; not always well guarded. The descent includes winding rise and fall over the Passo d'Eira (2200 metres/7218ft).
Fugazze 1159 metres (3802ft) Italy	Rovereto 201 metres (660ft) Valli del Pasubio 350 metres (1148ft)	27km 1 in 7 16.4 miles 12km 1 in 7 7.4 miles	3.5 metres 11ft 6in	UO Very winding with some narrow sections, particularly on northern side. The many blind bends and several hairpin bends call for extra care.
***Furka** 2431 metres (7976ft) Switzerland	Gletsch 1757 metres (5764ft) Realp 1538 metres (5046ft)	10km 1 in 9 6.2 miles 13km 1 in 10 8.1 miles	4 metres 13ft 1in	UC Oct–Jun. A well-graded road, with narrow sections and several sharp hairpin bends on both ascent and descent. Fine views of the Rhône glacier. Alternative rail tunnel available.
Galibier 2645 metres (8678ft) France	Lautaret Pass 2058 metres (6752ft) St-Michel-de-Maurienne 712 metres (2336ft)	7km 1 in 9 4.4 miles 34km 1 in 8 21.1 miles	3 metres 9ft 10in	UC Oct–Jun. Mainly wide, well surfaced but unguarded. Ten hairpin bends on descent then 5km (3.1 miles) narrow and rough. Rise over the Col du Télégraphe (1600 metres/5249ft), then 11 more hairpin bends. (The tunnel under the Galibier summit is closed.)
Gardena (Grödner-Joch) 2121 metres (6959ft) Italy	Val Gardena 1862 metres (6109ft) Corvara in Badia 1568 metres (5144ft)	6km 1 in 8 3.7 miles 10km 1 in 8 6.2 miles	5 metres 16ft 5in	OC Dec–Jun. A well-engineered road, very winding on descent.

* Permitted maximum width of vehicles 7ft 6in + Permitted maximum width of vehicles 8ft 2.5in ++ Maximum length of vehicle 30ft

Pass name, height and country	From and to	Distances from summit and max gradient	Min width of road	Conditions (see page 193 for key to abbreviations)
Gavia 2621 metres (8599ft) Italy	Bormio 1225 metres (4019ft) Ponte di Legno 1258 metres (4127ft)	25km 1 in 5.5 15.5 miles 18km 1 in 5.5 11 miles	3 metres 9ft 10in	UC Oct–Jul. Steep and narrow, but with frequent passing bays; many hairpin bends and a gravel surface; not for the faint-hearted; extra care necessary. (Maximum width for vehicles 1.8 metres/5ft 11in.)
Gerlos 1628 metres (5341ft) Austria	Zell am Ziller 575 metres (1886ft) Wald 885 metres (2904ft)	29km 1 in 12 18 miles 15km 1 in 11 9.3 miles	4 metres 13ft 1in	UO Hairpin ascent out of Zell to modern toll road; the old, steep, narrow, and winding route with passing bays and 1-in-7 gradient is not recommended, but is negotiable with care; caravans prohibited.
+Grand St Bernard 2473 metres (8114ft) Switzerland–Italy	Martigny 476 metres (1562ft) Aosta 583 metres (1913ft)	46km 1 in 9 29 miles 34km 1 in 9 21 miles	4 metres 13ft 1in	UC Oct–Jun. Modern road to entrance of road tunnel (usually open; then narrow over summit to frontier; also good surface in Italy; suitable for caravans using tunnel. Pass road closed to vehicles towing trailers.
***Grimsel** 2164 metres (7100ft) Switzerland	Innerkirchen 630 metres (2067ft) Gletsch 1757 metres (5764ft)	26km 1 in 10 16.1 miles 6km 1 in 10 3.7 miles	5 metres 16ft 5in	UC mid-Oct to late Jun. A fairly easy road, but heavy traffic weekends. A long winding ascent, finally hairpin bends; then a terraced descent (six hairpins) into the Rhône valley. Negotiable by caravans.
Grossglockner 2503 metres (8212ft) Austria	Bruck an der Glocknerstrasse 755 metres (2477ft) Heiligenblut 1301 metres (4268ft)	34km 1 in 8 21 miles 15m 1 in 8 9.3 miles	5.5 metres 18ft	UC late Oct–early May. Numerous well-engineered hairpin bends; moderate but very long ascent, toll road; very fine scenery; heavy tourist traffic; negotiable preferably from south to north, by caravans. Road closed 10pm to 5am.
Hochtannberg 1679 metres (5509ft) Austria	Schröcken 1269 metres(4163ft) Warth (near Lech) 1500 metres (4921ft)	5.5km 1 in 7 3.4 miles 4.5km 1 in 11 2.8 miles	4 metres 13ft 1in	OC Jan–Mar. A reconstructed modern road.
Ibañeta (Roncesvalles) 1057 metres (3468ft) France–Spain	St-Jean-Pied-de-Port 163 metres (535ft) Pamplona 415 metres (1362ft)	27km 1 in 10 17 miles 49km 1 in 10 30 miles	4 metres 13ft 1in	UO A slow and winding, scenic route; negotiable by caravans.
Iseran 2770 metres (9088ft) France	Bourg-St-Maurice 840 metres (2756ft) Lanslebourg 1399 metres (4590ft)	47km 1 in 12 29 miles 33km 1 in 9 20.5 miles	4 metres 13ft 1in	UC mid-Oct to late Jun. The second highest pass in the Alps. Well graded with reasonable bends, average surface; several unlit tunnels on northern approach.
Izoard 2360 metres (7743ft) France	Guillestre 1000 metres (3281ft) Briançon 1321 metres (4334ft)	32km 1 in 8 20 miles 22km 1 in 8 14 miles	5 metres 16ft 5in	UC late Oct to mid-Jun. A winding and sometimes narrow road with many hairpin bends. Care is required at several unlit tunnels near Guillestre.

* Permitted maximum width of vehicles 7ft 6in + Permitted maximum width of vehicles 8ft 2.5in ++ Maximum length of vehicle 30ft

Mountain passes

Pass name, height and country	From and to	Distances from summit and max gradient	Min width of road	Conditions (see page 193 for key to abbreviations)
***Jaun** 1509 metres (4951ft) Switzerland	Broc 718 metres (2356ft) Reidenbach 845 metres (2772ft)	25km 1 in 10 15.5 miles 8km 1 in 10 5 miles	4 metres 13ft 1in	UO A modernised but generally narrow road; some poor sections on ascent, and several hairpin bends on descent; negotiable by caravans.
+Julier 2284 metres (7493ft) Switzerland	Tiefencastel 851 metres (2792ft) Silvaplana 1815 metres (5955ft)	35km 1 in 10 22miles 7km 1 in 7.5 4.4 miles	4 metres 13ft 1in	UO Well-engineered road, approached from Chur by Lenzerheide Pass (1549 metres/5082ft); negotiable by caravans, preferably from north to south.
Katschberg 1641 metres (5384ft) Austria	Spittal 554 metres (1818ft) St Michael 1068 metres (3504ft)	37km 1 in 5 23 miles 6km 1 in 6 3.7 miles	6 metres 19ft 8in	UO Steep though not particularly difficult, parallel toll motorway, including tunnel available; negotiable by light caravans, using tunnel via Tauern Autobahn.
***Klausen** 1948 metres (6391ft) Switzerland	Altdorf 458 metres (1503ft) Linthal 662 metres (2172ft)	25km 1 in 10 15.5 miles 23km 1 in 11 14.3 miles	5 metres 16ft 5in	UC Late Oct–early Jun. Narrow and winding in places, but generally easy, in spite of a number of sharp bends; no through route for caravans as they are prohibited from using the road between Unterschächen and Linthal.
Larche (della Maddalena) 1994 metres (6542ft) France–Italy	La Condamine-Châtelard 1308 metres (4291ft) Vinadio 910 metres (2986ft)	19km 1 in 12 11.8 miles 32km 1 in 12 19.8 miles	3.5 metres 11ft 6in	OC Dec–Mar. An easy, well-graded road; narrow ascent, wider on descent; suitable for caravans.
Lautaret 2058 metres (6752ft) France	Le Bourg-d'Oisans 719 metres (2359ft) Briançon 1321 metres (4334ft)	38km 1 in 8 23.6 miles 28km 1 in 10 17.4 miles	4 metres 13ft 1in	OC Dec–Mar. Modern, evenly graded, but winding, and unguarded in places; very fine scenery; suitable for caravans.
Loibl (Ljubelj) 1067 metres (3500ft) Austria–Slovenia	Unterloibl 518 metres (1699ft) Kranj 385 metres (1263ft)	10km 1 in 5.5 6.2 miles 26km 1 in 8 16 miles	6 metres 19ft 8in	UO Steep rise and fall over Little Loibl pass to tunnel (1.6km/1 mile long) under summit. The old road over the summit is closed to through traffic.
***Lukmanier (Lucomagno)** 1916 metres (6286ft) Switzerland	Olivone 893 metres (2930ft) Disentis 1133 metres (3717ft)	20km 1 in 11 12 miles 20km 1 in 11 12 miles	5 metres 16ft 5in	UC early Nov–late May. Rebuilt, modern road; suitable for caravans.
+Maloja 1815 metres (5955ft) Switzerland	Silvaplana 1815 metres (5955ft) Chiavenna 333 metres (1093ft)	11km level 6.8 miles 32km 1 in 11 19.8 miles	4 metres 13ft 1in	UO Escarpment facing south; fairly easy, but many hairpin bends on descent; negotiable by caravans, possibly difficult on ascent.
Mauria 1298 metres (4258ft) Italy	Lozzo Cadore 753 metres (2470ft) Ampezzo 560 metres (1837ft)	13km 1 in 14 8 miles 31km 1 in 14 19.2 miles	5 metres 16ft 5in	UO A well-designed road with easy, winding ascent and descent; suitable for caravans.

* Permitted maximum width of vehicles 7ft 6in + Permitted maximum width of vehicles 8ft 2.5in ++ Maximum length of vehicle 30ft

Pass name, height and country	From and to	Distances from summit and max gradient	Min width of road	Conditions (see page 193 for key to abbreviations)
Mendola 1363 metres (4472ft) Italy	Appiano (Eppan) 411 metres (1348ft) Sarnonico 978 metres (3208ft)	15km 1 in 8 9.3 miles 9km 1 in 10 6 miles	5 metres 16ft 5in	UO A fairly straightforward but winding road, well guarded; suitable for caravans.
Mont Cenis 2083 metres (6834ft) France–Italy	Lanslebourg 1399 metres (4590ft) Susa 503 metres (1650ft)	11km 1 in 10 6.8 miles 28km 1 in 8 17.4 miles	5 metres 16ft 5in	UC Nov–May. Approach by industrial valley. An easy highway, with mostly very good surface; spectacular scenery; suitable for caravans. Alternative Fréjus road tunnel.
Monte Croce di Comélico (Kreuzberg) 1636 metres (5368ft) Italy	San Candido 1174 metres (3852ft) Santo Stefano di Cadore 908 metres (2979ft)	15km 1 in 12 9.3 miles 21km 1 in 12 13 miles	5 metres 16ft 5in	UO A winding road with moderate gradients, beautiful scenery; suitable for caravans.
Montgenèvre 1850m (6070ft) France–Italy	Briançon 1321 metres (4334ft) Cesana Torinese 1344 metres (4409ft)	12km 1 in 14 7.4 miles 8km 1 in 11 5 miles	5 metres 16ft 5in	UO An easy, modern road; suitable for caravans.
Monte Giovo (Jaufen) 2094 metres (6870ft) Italy	Merano 324 metres (1063ft) Vipiteno 948 metres (3110ft)	40km 1 in 8 24.8 miles 19km 1 in 11 11.8 miles	4 metres 13ft 1in	UC Nov–May. Many well engineered hairpin bends; caravans prohibited.
Montets (see Forclaz)				
Morgins 1369 metres (4491ft) France–Switzerland	Abondance 930 metres (3051ft) Monthey 424 metres (1391ft)	14km 1 in 11 8.7 miles 15km 1 in 7 9.3 miles	4 metres 13ft 1in	UO A lesser used route through pleasant, forested countryside crossing the French-Swiss border.
***Mosses** 1445m (4740ft) Switzerland	Aigle 417 metres (1368ft) Château d'Oex 958 metres (3143ft)	16km 1 in 12 10 miles 15km 1 in 12 9.3 miles	4 metres 13ft 1in	UO A modern road; suitable for caravans.
Nassfeld (Pramollo) 1530m (5020ft) Austria–Italy	Tröpolach 601 metres (1972ft) Pontebba 568 metres (1864ft)	10km 1 in 5 6.2 miles 10km 1 in 10 6.2 miles	4 metres 13ft 1in	OC late Nov–Mar. The winding descent in Italy has been improved.
***Nufenen (Novena)** 2478 metres (8130ft) Switzerland	Ulrichen 1346 metres (4416ft) Airolo 1142 metres (3747ft)	13km 1 in 10 8.1 miles 24km 1 in 10 14.9 miles	4.0 metres 13ft 1in	UC mid-Oct to mid-Jun. The approach roads are narrow, with tight bends, but the road over the pass is good; negotiable by caravans.
***Oberalp** 2044 metres (6706ft) Switzerland	Andermatt 1447 metres (4747ft) Disentis 1133 metres (3717ft)	10km 1 in 10 6.2 miles 21km 1 in 10 13 miles	5 metres 16ft 5in	UC Nov–late May. A widened road with a modern surface; many hairpin bends, but long level stretch on summit; negotiable by caravans. Alternative rail tunnel for winter.

* Permitted maximum width of vehicles 7ft 6in + Permitted maximum width of vehicles 8ft 2.5in ++ Maximum length of vehicle 30ft

Mountain passes

Pass name, height and country	From and to	Distances from summit and max gradient	Min width of road	Conditions (see page 193 for key to abbreviations)
***Ofen (Fuorn)** 2149 metres (7051ft) Switzerland	Zernez 1474 metres (4836ft) Santa Maria im Münstertal 1375 metres (4511ft)	22km 1 in 10 13.6 miles 14km 1 in 8 8.7 miles	4 metres 13ft 1in	UO Good, fairly easy road through the Swiss National Park; negotiable by caravans.
Petit St Bernard 2188 metres (7178ft) France–Italy	Bourg-St-Maurice 840 metres (2756ft) Pré St-Didier 1000 metres (3281ft)	30km 1 in 16 19 miles 23km 1 in 12 14.3 miles	5 metres 16ft 5in	UC mid Oct–Jun. Outstanding scenery; a fairly easy approach, but poor surface and unguarded broken edges near the summit; good on the descent in Italy; negotiable by light caravans.
Peyresourde 1563 metres (5128ft) France	Arreau 704 metres (2310ft) Luchon 630 metres (2067ft)	18km 1 in 10 11.2 miles 14km 1 in 10 8.7 miles	4 metres 13ft 1in	UO Somewhat narrow with several hairpin bends, though not difficult.
***Pillon** 1546 metres (5072ft) Switzerland	Le Sépey 974 metres (3196ft) Gsteig 1184 metres (3885ft)	15km 1 in 11 9 miles 7km 1 in 11 4.4 miles	4 metres 13ft 1in	OC Jan–Feb. A comparatively easy modern road; suitable for caravans.
Plöcken (Monte Croce-Carnico) 1362 metres (4468ft) Austria–Italy	Kötschach 706 metres (2316ft) Paluzza 600 metres (1968ft)	16km 1 in 7 10 miles 16km 1 in 14 10 miles	5 metres 16ft 5in	OC Dec–Apr. A modern road with long, reconstructed sections; heavy traffic at summer weekends; delay likely at the frontier; negotiable by caravans, best used only by experienced drivers in cars with ample power.
Pordoi 2239 metres (7346ft) Italy	Arabba 1602 metres (5256ft) Canazei 1465 metres (4806ft)	9km 1 in 10 5.6 miles 12km 1 in 10 7.4 miles	5 metres 16ft 5in	OC Dec–Apr. An excellent modern road with numerous hairpin bends; negotiable by caravans.
Port 1249 metres (4098ft) France	Tarascon 474 metres (1555ft) Massat 650 metres (2133ft)	18km 1 in 10 11.2 miles 12km 1 in 10 7.4 miles	4 metres 13ft 1in	OC Nov–Mar. A fairly easy road, but narrow on some bends; negotiable by caravans.
Portet-d'Aspet 1069 metres (3507ft) France	Audressein 508 metres (1667ft) Fronsac 472 metres (1548ft)	18km 1 in 7 11.2 miles 29km 1 in 7 18 miles	3.5 metres 11ft 6in	UO Approached from the west by the easy Col des Ares (797 metres/2615ft) and Col de Buret (599 metres/1965ft); well-engineered road, but calls for particular care on hairpin bends; rather narrow.
Pötschen 982 metres (3222ft) Austria	Bad Ischl 469 metres (1539ft) Bad Aussee 659 metres (2162ft)	19km 1 in 11 11.8 miles 9km 1 in 11 5.6 miles	7 metres 23ft	UO A modern road; suitable for caravans.
Pourtalet 1792 metres (5879ft) France–Spain	Eaux-Chaudes 656 metres (2152ft) Biescas 860 metres (2822ft)	23km 1 in 10 14.3 miles 32km 1 in 10 20 miles	3.5 metres 11ft 6in	UC late Oct–early Jun. A fairly easy, unguarded road, but narrow in places.
Puymorens 1915 metres (6283ft) France	Ax-les-Thermes 720 metres (2362ft) Bourg-Madame 1130 metres (3707ft)	28km 1 in 10 17.4 miles 27km 1 in 10 16.8 miles	5.5 metres 18ft	OC Nov–Apr. A generally easy, modern tarmac road, but narrow, winding and with a poor surface in places; not suitable for night driving; suitable for caravans (max height vehicles 3.5 metres/11ft 6in). Parallel toll road tunnel available.

* Permitted maximum width of vehicles 7ft 6in + Permitted maximum width of vehicles 8ft 2.5in ++ Maximum length of vehicle 30ft

Pass name, height and country	From and to	Distances from summit and max gradient	Min width of road	Conditions (see page 193 for key to abbreviations)
Quillane 1714 metres (5623ft) France	Quillan 291 metres (955ft) Mont-Louis 1600 metres (5249ft)	63km 1 in 12 39.1 miles 6 km 1 in 12 3.5 miles	5 metres 16ft 5in	OC Nov–Mar. An easy, straightforward ascent and descent; suitable for caravans.
Radstädter-Tauern 1738 metres (5702ft) Austria	Radstadt 862 metres (2828ft) Mauterndorf 1122 metres (3681ft)	21km 1 in 6 13.0 miles 17km 1 in 7 10.6 miles	5 metres 16ft 5in	OC Jan–Mar. Northern ascent steep, but not difficult otherwise; parallel toll motorway including tunnel; negotiable by light caravans, using tunnel.
Résia (Reschen) 1504 metres (4934ft) Italy–Austria	Spondigna 885 metres (2903ft) Pfunds 970 metres (3182ft)	29km 1 in 10 18 miles 21km 1 in 10 13 miles	6 metres 19ft 8in	UO A good, straightforward alternative to the Brenner Pass; suitable for caravans.
Restefond (La Bonette) 2802 metres (9193ft) France	Jausiers (near Barcelonnette) 1220 metres (4003ft) St-Etienne-de-Tinée 1144 metres (3753ft)	23km 1 in 8 14.3 miles 27km 1 in 6 16.8 miles	3 metres 9ft 10in	UC Oct–Jun. The highest pass in the Alps, completed in 1962. Narrow, rough, unguarded ascent with many blind bends, and nine hairpins. Descent easier, winding with 12 hairpin bends. Not for the faint-hearted; extra care required.
Rolle 1970 metres (6463ft) Italy	Predazzo 1018 metres (3340ft) Mezzano 637 metres (2090ft)	21km 1 in 11 13.0 miles 27km 1 in 14 17 miles	5 metres 16ft 5in	OC Dec–Mar. A well-engineered road with many hairpin bends on both sides; very beautiful scenery; good surface; negotiable by caravans.
Rombo (see Timmelsjoch)				
Routes des Crêtes 1283 metres (4210ft) France	St-Dié 343 metres (1125ft) Cernay 296 metres (971ft)	1 in 8 1 in 8	4 metres 13ft 1in	UC Nov–Apr. A renowned scenic route crossing seven ridges, with the highest point at 'Hôtel du Grand Ballon'.
+St Gotthard (San Gottardo) 2108 metres (6916ft) Switzerland	Göschenen 1106 metres (3629ft) Airolo 1142 metres (3747ft)	18km 1 in 10 11 miles 15km 1 in 10 9.3 miles	6 metres 19ft 8in	UC mid-Oct to early Jun. Modern, fairly easy two- to three-lane road. Heavy traffic; negotiable by caravans. Alternative road tunnel.
***San Bernardino** 2066 metres (6778ft) Switzerland	Mesocco 790 metres (2592ft) Hinterrhein 1620 metres (5315ft)	21km 1 in 10 13 miles 9.5km 1 in 10 5.9 miles	4 metres 13ft 1in	UC Oct–late Jun. Easy, modern roads on northern and southern approaches to tunnel. Narrow and winding over summit, via tunnel suitable for caravans.
Schlucht 1139 metres (3737ft) France	Gérardmer 665 metres (2182ft) Munster 381 metres (1250ft)	15km 1 in 14 9.3 miles 18km 1 in 14 11 miles	5 metres 16ft 5in	UO An extremely picturesque route crossing the Vosges mountains, with easy, wide bends on the descent; suitable for caravans.
Seeberg (Jezersko) 1218 metres (3996ft) Austria–Slovenia	Eisenkappel 555 metres (1821ft) Kranj 385 metres (1263ft)	14km 1 in 8 8.7 miles 33km 1 in 10 20.5 miles	5 metres 16ft 5in	UO An alternative to the steeper Loibl and Wurzen passes; moderate climb with winding, hairpin ascent and descent.

* Permitted maximum width of vehicles 7ft 6in + Permitted maximum width of vehicles 8ft 2.5in ++ Maximum length of vehicle 30ft

Mountain passes

Pass name, height and country	From and to	Distances from summit and max gradient	Min width of road	Conditions (see page 193 for key to abbreviations)
Sella 2240 metres (7349ft) Italy	Plan 1606 metres (5269ft) Canazei 1465 metres (4806ft)	9km 1 in 9 5.6 miles 12km 1 in 9 7 miles	5 metres 16ft 5in	OC Dec–Jun. A finely engineered, winding road; exceptional views of the Dolomites.
Semmering 985 metres (3232ft) Austria	Mürzzuschlag im Mürztal 672 metres (2205ft) Gloggnitz 457 metres (1499ft)	14km 1 in 16 8.7 miles 17km 1 in 16 10.6 miles	6 metres 19ft 8in	UO A fine, well-engineered highway; suitable for caravans.
Sestriere 2033 metres (6670ft) Italy	Cesana Torinese 1344 metres (4409ft) Pinerolo 376 metres (1234ft)	12km 1 in 10 7.4 miles 55km 1 in 10 34.2 miles	6 metres 19ft 8in	UO Mostly bitumen surface; negotiable by caravans.
Silvretta (Bielerhöhe) 2032 metres (6666ft) Austria	Partenen 1051 metres (3448ft) Galtür 1584 metres (5197ft)	16km 1 in 9 9.9 miles 10km 1 in 9 6.2 miles	5 metres 16ft 5in	UC late Oct–early Jun. For the most part reconstructed; 32 easy hairpin bends on western ascent; eastern side more straightforward. Toll road; caravans prohibited.
+Simplon 2005 metres (6578ft) Switzerland–Italy	Brig 681 metres (2234ft) Domodóssola 280 metres (919ft)	22km 1 in 9 13.6 miles 41km 1 in 11 25.5 miles	7 metres 23ft	OC Nov–Apr. An easy, reconstructed modern road, but 20.8km/13 miles long, continuous ascent to summit; suitable for caravans.
Somport 1632 metres (5354ft) France–Spain	Bedous 416 metres (1365ft) Jaca 820 metres (2690ft)	31km 1 in 10 19.2 miles 32km 1 in 10 20 miles	3.5 metres 11ft 6in	UO A favoured, old-established route; generally easy, but in parts narrow and unguarded; fairly well-surfaced road; suitable for caravans.
***Splügen** 2113 metres (6932ft) Switzerland–Italy	Splügen 1457 metres (4780ft) Chiavenna 330 metres (1083ft)	9km 1 in 9 5.6 miles 30km 1 in 7.5 18.6 miles	3.5 metres 11ft 6in	UC Nov–Jun. Mostly narrow and winding, with many hairpin bends, and not well guarded; care is also required at many tunnels and galleries (max height vehicles 9ft 2in).
++Stelvio 2757 metres (9045ft) Italy	Bormio 1225 metres (4019ft) Spondigna 885 metres (2903ft)	22km 1 in 8 13.6 miles 28km 1 in 8 12.9 miles	4 metres 13ft 1in	UC Oct–late Jun. The third highest pass in the Alps; the number of acute hairpin bends, all well engineered, is exceptional – from 40 to 50 on either side; the surface is good, the traffic heavy. Hairpin bends are too acute for long vehicles.
+Susten 2224 metres (7297ft) Switzerland	Innertkirchen 630 metres (2067ft) Wassen 916 metres (3005ft)	28km 1 in 11 12.9 miles 19km 1 in 11 11.8 miles	6 metres 19ft 8in	UC Nov–Jun. A very scenic and well-guarded mountain road; easy gradients and turns; heavy traffic at weekends; negotiable by caravans – extra care required. Not for the faint-hearted.
Tenda (Tende) 1321 metres (4334ft) Italy–France	Borgo S Dalmazzo 641 metres (2103ft) La Giandola 308 metres (1010ft)	24km 1 in 11 14.9 miles 29km 1 in 11 18 miles	6 metres 19ft 8in	UO Well-guarded, modern road with several hairpin bends; road tunnel at summit; suitable for caravans, but prohibited during the winter.
+Thurn 1274 metres (4180ft) Austria	Kitzbühel 762 metres (2500ft) Mittersill 789 metres (2588ft)	19km 1 in 12 11.8 miles 10km 1 in 16 6.2 miles	5 metres 16ft 5in	UO A good road with narrow stretches; northern approach rebuilt; suitable for caravans.

* Permitted maximum width of vehicles 7ft 6in + Permitted maximum width of vehicles 8ft 2.5in ++ Maximum length of vehicle 30ft

Pass name, height and country	From and to	Distances from summit and max gradient	Min width of road	Conditions (see page 193 for key to abbreviations)
Timmelsjoch (Rombo) 2509 metres (8232ft) Austria–Italy	Obergurgl 1910 metres (6266ft) Moso 1007 metres (3304ft)	14km 1 in 7 8.7 miles 23km 1 in 8 14 miles	3.5 metres 11ft 6in	UC mid-Oct to late Jun. Pass open to private cars (without trailers) only as some tunnels on the Italian side are too narrow for larger vehicles; toll road. Border closed 8pm to 7am.
Tonale 1883 metres (6178ft) Italy	Edolo 699 metres (2293ft) Dimaro 766 metres (2513ft)	30km 1 in 12 18.6 miles 27km 1 in 10 16.7 miles	5 metres 16ft 5in	UO A relatively easy road; suitable for caravans.
Toses (Tosas) 1800 metres (5906ft) Spain	Puigcerdá 1152 metres (3780ft) Ribes de Freser 920 metres (3018ft)	26km 1 in 10 16 miles 25km 1 in 10 15.5 miles	5 metres 16ft 5in	UO Now a fairly straightforward, but continuously winding, two-lane road with many sharp bends; negotiable by caravans.
Tourmalet 2114 metres (6936ft) France	Luz 711 metres (2333ft) Ste-Marie-de-Campan 857 metres (2812ft)	18km 1 in 8 11 miles 17km 1 in 8 10.6 miles	4 metres 13ft 1in	UC Oct to mid-Jun. The highest of the French Pyrenean routes; the approaches are good, though winding and exacting over summit; sufficiently guarded.
Tre Croci 1809 metres (5935ft) Italy	Cortina d'Ampezzo 1224 metres (4016ft) Auronzo di Cadore 864 metres (2835ft).	7km 1 in 9 4.4 miles 26 km 1 in 9 16 miles	6 metres 19ft 8in	OC Dec–Mar. An easy pass; very fine scenery; suitable for caravans.
Turracher Höhe 1763 metres (5784ft) Austria	Predlitz 922 metres (3024ft) Ebene-Reichenau 1062 metres (3484ft)	20km 1 in 5.5 12.4 miles 8km 1 in 4.5 5 miles	4 metres 13ft 1in	UO Formerly one of the steepest mountain roads in Austria; now much improved. A steep, fairly straightforward ascent is followed by a very steep descent; good surface and mainly two-lane width; fine scenery.
***Umbrail** 2501 metres (8205ft) Switzerland–Italy	Santa Maria im Münstertal 1375 metres (4511ft) Bormio 1225 metres (4019ft)	14km 1 in 11 9 miles 19km 1 in 11 11.8 miles	4.3 metres 14ft 1in	UC early Nov–early Jun. Highest of the Swiss passes; narrow; mostly gravel surfaced with 34 hairpin bends, but not too difficult.
Vars 2109 metres (6919ft) France	St-Paul-sur-Ubaye 1470 metres (4823ft) Guillestre 1000 metres (3281ft)	8km 1 in 10 5 miles 20km 1 in 10 12.4 miles	5 metres 16ft 5in	OC Dec–Mar. Easy winding ascent with seven hairpin bends; gradual winding descent with another seven hairpin bends; good surface; negotiable by caravans.
Wurzen (Koren) 1073 metres (3520ft) Austria–Slovenia	Riegersdorf 541 metres (1775ft) Kranjska Gora 810 metres (2657ft)	7km 1 in 5.5 4.5 miles 6km 1 in 5.5 3.5 miles	4 metres 13ft 1in	UO A steep two-lane road, which otherwise is not particularly difficult; heavy traffic at summer weekends; delay likely at the frontier; caravans prohibited.
Zirler Berg 1009 metres (3310ft) Austria	Seefeld 1180 metres (3871ft) Zirl 622 metres (2041ft)	6km 1 in 7 3.5 miles 5km 1 in 6 3.1 miles	7 metres 23ft	UO An escarpment facing south, part of the route from Garmisch to Innsbruck; a good, modern road, but heavy tourist traffic and a long steep descent, with one hairpin bend, into the Inn Valley. Steepest section from the hairpin bend down to Zirl; caravans prohibited northbound.

* Permitted maximum width of vehicles 7ft 6in + Permitted maximum width of vehicles 8ft 2.5in ++ Maximum length of vehicle 30ft

Port plans

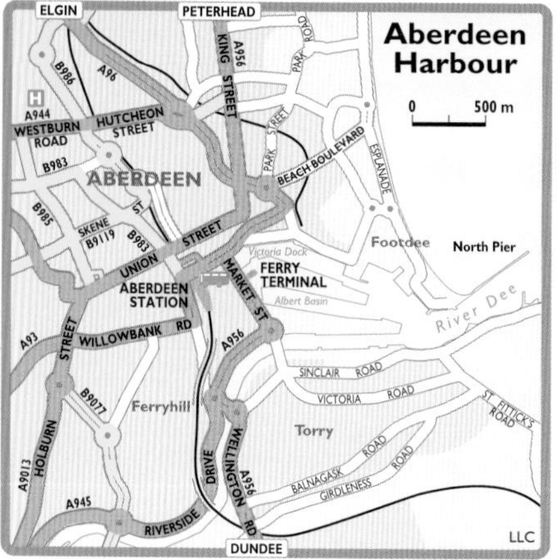

Aberdeen Harbour
0 500 m
ELGIN
PETERHEAD
A96
B986
A944
WESTBURN ROAD
HUTCHEON STREET
KING STREET
A956
PARK ROAD
PARK STREET
B983
ABERDEEN
BEACH BOULEVARD
ESPLANADE
B985
SKENE
B9119
B983
ST
UNION STREET
Victoria Dock
Footdee
North Pier
ABERDEEN STATION
FERRY TERMINAL
MARKET ST
Albert Basin
River Dee
A93
WILLOWBANK RD
STREET
A956
SINCLAIR ROAD
VICTORIA ROAD
ST FITTICK'S ROAD
B9077
Ferryhill
Torry
A9013
HOLBURN
DRIVE
WELLINGTON
A956
BALNAGASK ROAD
GIRDLENESS ROAD
A945
RIVERSIDE
RD
DUNDEE
LLC

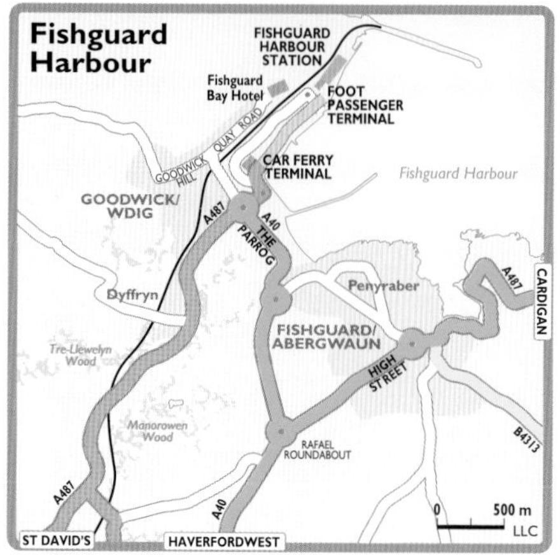

Fishguard Harbour
FISHGUARD HARBOUR STATION
Fishguard Bay Hotel
FOOT PASSENGER TERMINAL
QUAY ROAD
GOODWICK HILL
CAR FERRY TERMINAL
Fishguard Harbour
GOODWICK/ WDIG
A487
A40
THE PARROG
Dyffryn
Penyraber
A487
CARDIGAN
FISHGUARD/ ABERGWAUN
Tre-Llewelyn Wood
HIGH STREET
Manorowen Wood
RAFAEL ROUNDABOUT
B4313
A487
A40
0 500 m
ST DAVID'S
HAVERFORDWEST
LLC

Harwich International Port
PASSENGER & CRUISE TERMINAL
HARWICH INTERNATIONAL STATION
0 400 m
EAST DOCK ROAD
CAR FERRY TERMINAL
A120
CONTAINER TERMINAL
WEST DOCK ROAD
REFINERY ROAD
Parkeston
STATION ROAD
Harwich Industrial Estate
EUROPA WAY
Superstore
A120
HARWICH
PARKESTON ROUNDABOUT
ST NICHOLAS ROUNDABOUT
PARKESTON ROAD
Dovercourt
B1352
CLARKES ROAD
MAIN ROAD
HIGHFIELD AVENUE
IPSWICH, COLCHESTER
A120
MAIN ROAD
Upper Dovercourt
FRONK'S ROAD
B1352
LLC

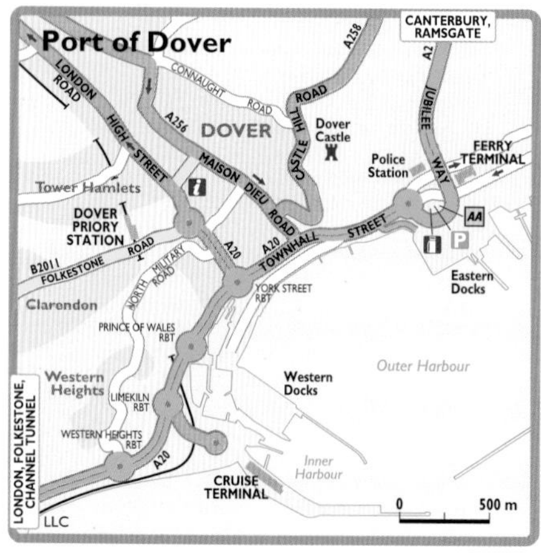

Port of Dover
CANTERBURY, RAMSGATE
A258
A2
LONDON ROAD
CONNAUGHT ROAD
ROAD
HIGH STREET
A256
DOVER
CASTLE HILL
Dover Castle
JUBILEE WAY
FERRY TERMINAL
Police Station
MAISON DIEU ROAD
Tower Hamlets
DOVER PRIORY STATION
A20
TOWNHALL STREET
AA
B2011
FOLKESTONE ROAD
NORTH MILITARY ROAD
Eastern Docks
Clarendon
YORK STREET RBT
PRINCE OF WALES RBT
Outer Harbour
Western Heights
LIMEKILN RBT
Western Docks
WESTERN HEIGHTS RBT
A20
Inner Harbour
CRUISE TERMINAL
0 500 m
LONDON, FOLKESTONE, CHANNEL TUNNEL
LLC

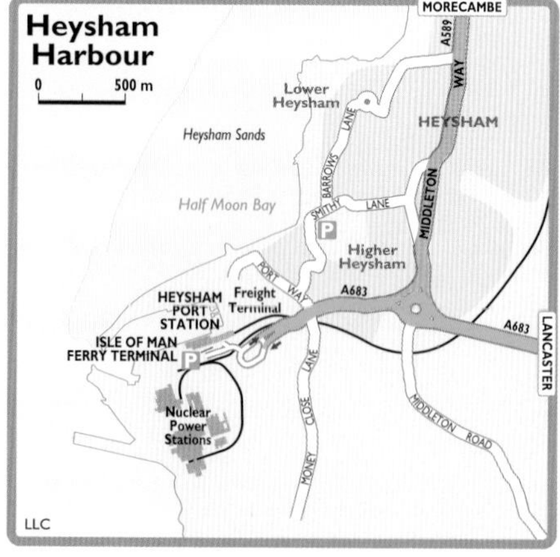

Heysham Harbour
MORECAMBE
0 500 m
A589
WAY
Lower Heysham
Heysham Sands
HEYSHAM
BARROWS LANE
Half Moon Bay
SMITHY LANE
MIDDLETON
Higher Heysham
PORT WAY
A683
HEYSHAM PORT STATION
Freight Terminal
A683
LANCASTER
ISLE OF MAN FERRY TERMINAL
LANE
Nuclear Power Stations
CLOSE
MONEY
MIDDLETON ROAD
LLC

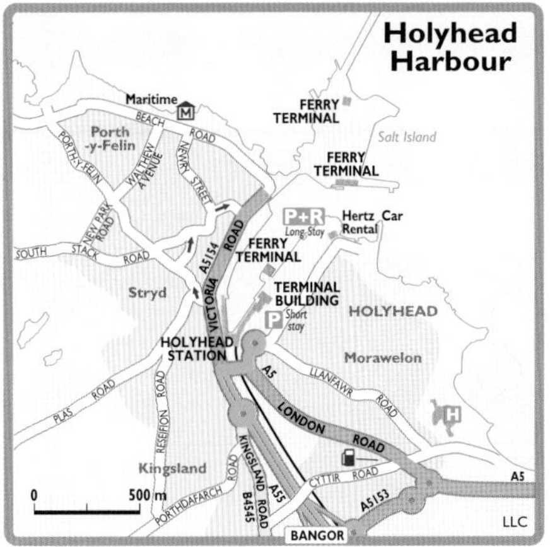
Holyhead Harbour
Maritime
Porth -y-Felin
BEACH ROAD
PORTH-Y-FELIN
WALTHEW AVENUE
NEWRY STREET
NEW PARK ROAD
SOUTH STACK ROAD
FERRY TERMINAL
Salt Island
FERRY TERMINAL
P+R Long Stay
Hertz Car Rental
FERRY TERMINAL
A5154
VICTORIA ROAD
Stryd
TERMINAL BUILDING
P Short stay
HOLYHEAD
HOLYHEAD STATION
Morawelon
LLANFAWR ROAD
A5
LONDON ROAD
PLAS ROAD
RESEIFION ROAD
H
Kingsland
KINGSLAND ROAD
A55
B4545
PORTHDAFARCH ROAD
CYTTIR ROAD
A5153
A5
0 500 m
BANGOR
LLC

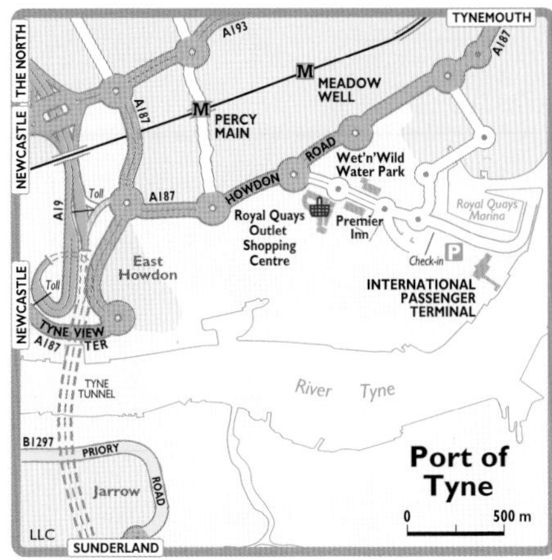
TYNEMOUTH
A193
A187
NEWCASTLE THE NORTH
MEADOW WELL
PERCY MAIN
A187
HOWDON ROAD
Wet'n'Wild Water Park
A19
Toll
A187
Royal Quays Outlet Shopping Centre
Premier Inn
Royal Quays Marina
Check-in
P
East Howdon
INTERNATIONAL PASSENGER TERMINAL
NEWCASTLE
Toll
TYNE VIEW TER
A187
TYNE TUNNEL
River Tyne
B1297
PRIORY ROAD
Jarrow
Port of Tyne
0 500 m
LLC
SUNDERLAND

BRIDLINGTON
A165
GRANGE ROAD
PRESTON ROAD
KINGSTON UPON HULL
SOUTHCOATES LANE
MARFLEET LANE
Marfleet
A63
A1032
M62
Port Office
Gate
Gate
HEDON
King George Dock
FERRY TERMINAL
ROTTERDAM TERMINAL
Q E Dock
KINGSTON TERMINAL
Kingston upon Hull
0 500 m 1km
LLL

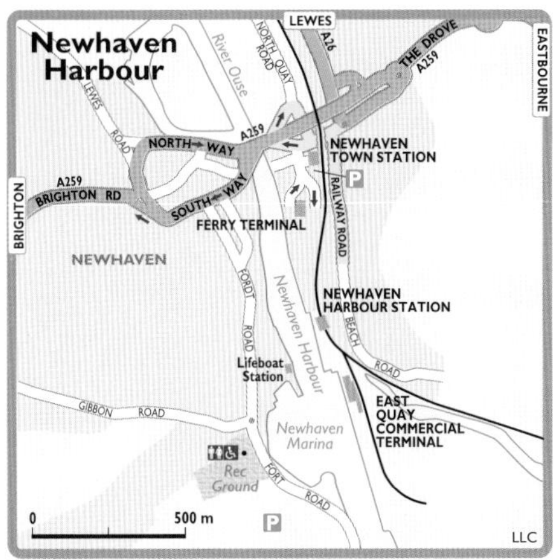
Newhaven Harbour
LEWES
A26
NORTH QUAY ROAD
River Ouse
THE DROVE
A259
EASTBOURNE
LEWES ROAD
NORTH WAY
A259
NEWHAVEN TOWN STATION
P
A259
BRIGHTON RD
SOUTH WAY
RAILWAY ROAD
BRIGHTON
FERRY TERMINAL
NEWHAVEN
FORT ROAD
Newhaven Harbour
NEWHAVEN HARBOUR STATION
BEACH ROAD
Lifeboat Station
GIBBON ROAD
EAST QUAY COMMERCIAL TERMINAL
Newhaven Marina
Rec Ground
FORT ROAD
0 500 m
P
LLC

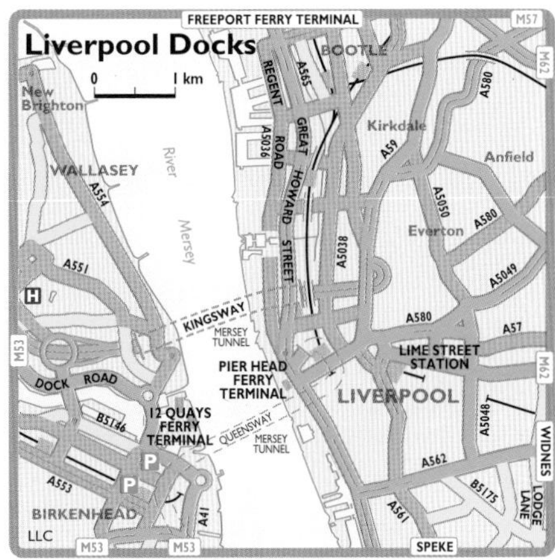
FREEPORT FERRY TERMINAL
M57
Liverpool Docks
BOOTLE
M62
0 1 km
New Brighton
REGENT ROAD
A565
A580
Kirkdale
A5036
GREAT HOWARD STREET
A59
WALLASEY
River Mersey
Anfield
A554
A5050
Everton
A580
A551
A5038
A5049
H
KINGSWAY
MERSEY TUNNEL
A580
A57
M53
LIME STREET STATION
PIER HEAD FERRY TERMINAL
M62
DOCK ROAD
LIVERPOOL
B5146
12 QUAYS FERRY TERMINAL
QUEENSWAY
MERSEY TUNNEL
A5048
P
A562
WIDNES
A553
P
B5175
A561
LODGE LANE
BIRKENHEAD
A41
LLC
M53
M53
SPEKE

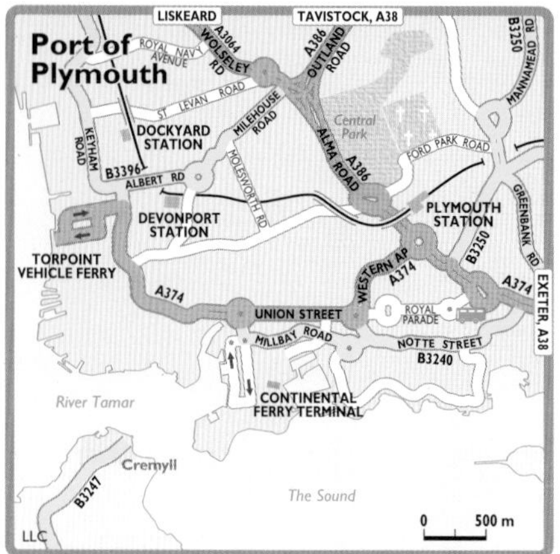
Port of Plymouth
LISKEARD
TAVISTOCK, A38
EXETER, A38
DOCKYARD STATION
DEVONPORT STATION
PLYMOUTH STATION
TORPOINT VEHICLE FERRY
CONTINENTAL FERRY TERMINAL
UNION STREET
River Tamar
Cremyll
The Sound
Central Park
0 500 m
LLC

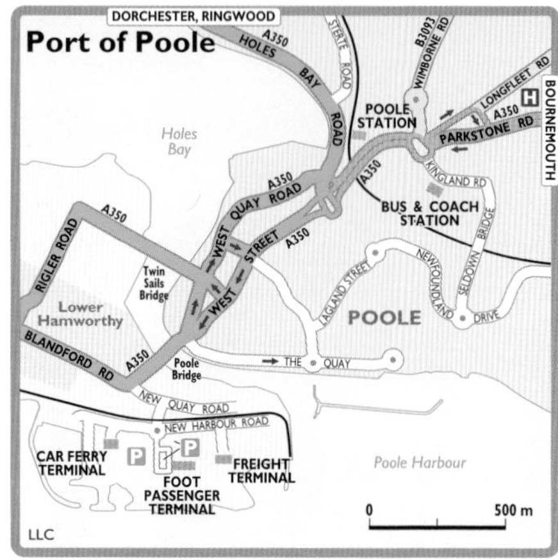
Port of Poole
DORCHESTER, RINGWOOD
BOURNEMOUTH
POOLE STATION
BUS & COACH STATION
Holes Bay
Lower Hamworthy
Twin Sails Bridge
Poole Bridge
POOLE
CAR FERRY TERMINAL
FOOT PASSENGER TERMINAL
FREIGHT TERMINAL
Poole Harbour
0 500 m
LLC

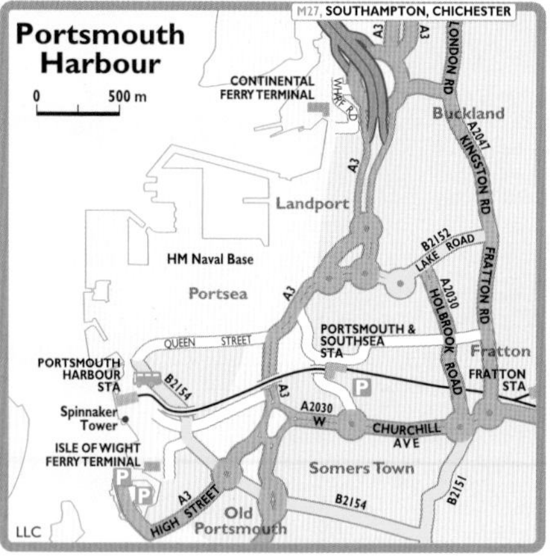
Portsmouth Harbour
M27, SOUTHAMPTON, CHICHESTER
0 500 m
CONTINENTAL FERRY TERMINAL
Buckland
Landport
HM Naval Base
Portsea
PORTSMOUTH & SOUTHSEA STA
Fratton
FRATTON STA
PORTSMOUTH HARBOUR STA
Spinnaker Tower
ISLE OF WIGHT FERRY TERMINAL
Somers Town
Old Portsmouth
LLC

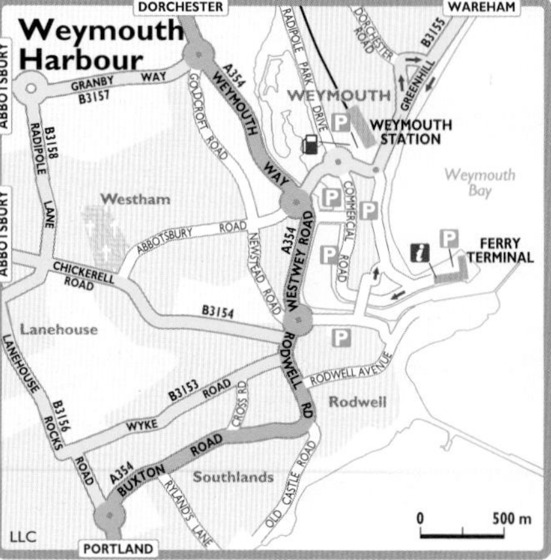
Weymouth Harbour
DORCHESTER
WAREHAM
ABBOTSBURY
WEYMOUTH
WEYMOUTH STATION
Weymouth Bay
Westham
FERRY TERMINAL
Lanehouse
Rodwell
Southlands
PORTLAND
0 500 m
LLC